BIRDS OF BRENT RESERVOIR

The Natural History of the Welsh Harp

Editors:

Leo Batten
Roy Beddard
John Colmans
Andrew Self

Foreword by Bill Oddie

The printing of this book was grant assisted by English Nature

ENGLISH
NATURE

The Welsh Harp Conservation Group
Founded in 1972

Group Objectives and Activities

The WHCG is a small conservation charity based at the Brent Reservoir (or the Welsh Harp) in north-west London. The reservoir was designated a SSSI (Site of Special Scientific Interest) in 1950. The group was formed in October 1972 to organise opposition to a housing development that threatened the key section of the wildlife refuge. Following a campaign led by the group there was a three day public enquiry during which the group was also very active and played a major part. The threat was averted and a suitable compromise was reached. Since then the group has greatly increased its scope and although fighting development threats is still included in the group's brief it is now only part of a wider range of activities. Since the early 1980s the group has been involved in a long-term programme of conservation management. This has greatly increased the effectiveness of the wildfowl refuges and has resulted in a far wider range of habitats for wildlife. Although the main focus of the group's interest is still birds a wide range of other wildlife is also studied and also benefits from the management work. The group has been publishing a regular report on its activities since 1987 and has also constructed two observation hides for group and public use. Many hundreds of school children have taken advantage of these facilities and monthly walks for members of the public are also organised. Group officers work in close co-operation with the two local councils, statutory bodies and the other user organisations at the reservoir and have been recently involved in the planning and implementation of a large Heritage Lottery Fund project.

Group Officers in 2001

President:	Tim Sims JP
Vice-president:	Dr Leo Batten
Chairman:	Roy Beddard
Treasurer:	Patrick Hagglund
Secretary:	Brenda McClane

Published by the Welsh Harp Conservation Group
43 Kenerne Drive, Barnet, Herts EN5 2NW, UK
ISBN: 0–9541862–0–6

Jan 2002

Printed by Crowes of Norwich, Norfolk

Birds of Brent Reservoir

Contents

List of Illustrations

Illustrations
Roy Beddard
p195 Yellow Flag, p200 Smooth Newt, p206 Banded Demoiselle, p208 Essex Skipper

Jan-Paul Charteris
p37 Black-necked Grebe, p163 Snow Bunting, p179 Great White Egret

Dave Darrell-Lambert
p79 Grey Plover, p92 Spotted Redshank, p156 Tree Sparrow

David Russell
p115 Long-eared Owl

Andrew Self
p220 Six-spot Burnet

Jan Wilczur
p6 Reed Bunting, p22 Tufted Ducks, p39 Bittern, p47 Brent Geese,
p53 Blue-winged Teal, p62 Goosander, p67 Osprey, p73 Spotted Crake,
p83 Pectoral Sandpiper, p103 Yellow-legged Gull, p110 White-winged Black Tern, p119 Lesser Spotted Woodpeckers, p122 Richard's Pipit,
p132 Northern Wheatear, p138 Aquatic Warbler, p144 Yellow-browed Warbler,
p147 Bearded Tits, p172 Sparrowhawk, p173 Greenshank, p177 Firecrest,
p178 Great Crested Grebe p184 Cetti's Warbler, p188 Penduline Tits, p190 Serin

Foreword

Bill Oddie

Brent Reservoir just might be the ideal local patch. I know, because it was once mine! It was some time ago, when frankly it probably wasn't quite so well watched as it is nowadays, which is – ironically perhaps – why I've switched to Hampstead Heath. I do rather like having a place almost to myself. Mind you, the Heath has days when not only are there no birders, there are hardly any birds either!

You could never say that about the Brent. One of its joys is that there really is always something to see, even if it might take you a while to find it. But then again, that's another of Brent's attractions. I love the fact that there's quite a big area to explore, with lots of variety, and 'hidden' places that aren't so often or so easily covered (see Andrew Self's account of where and when to look on page 175). It really is possible to lose yourself around Brent. The roar of the North Circular fades as you creep through the reedbeds along the south east shore, or peer through the bulrushes into the 'secret backwaters' of North Marsh. More than once I've found myself fantasising about being in Suffolk or Scilly instead of within a few miles of the middle of London.

And the birds have sometimes added to the illusion. Bearded Tits zinging in the rushes, Short-eared Owls quartering the grassland, even a Serin singing in the allotments. Oh yes, I've seen 'em all. OK, it doesn't happen every time, but hope springs eternal in the local patcher's breast, and it's never totally dull. Common Terns screeching round the rafts, Great Crested Grebes 'penguin dancing', gulls dropping down to roost, all great sights.

Even if the birds aren't performing, there are flowers, butterflies, dragonflies, creepy crawlies, fishy and furry creatures.... Brent really has got the lot. What's more, there are some pretty impressive humans around too. Constructive and imaginative conservation work has long been a feature of the Welsh Harp. It quite simply gets better and better. We know this, because it also has a well documented and fascinating history.

And now it's got its very own book. This is it. Enjoy.

February 2001.

Reed Bunting
(Jan Wilczur)

Chapter 1
A Social History of the Welsh Harp

John Colmans

This book is about the natural history of the Welsh Harp, mostly its birds. Yet it would be an omission to write a book like this without commenting on the reservoir's history from other points of view. This large area of open water, the largest for many miles around, has played a significant part in the social history of London for 160 years and continues to do so. This introduction briefly traces the main elements of that story. Although the reservoir is now known as the Brent Reservoir I have found it convenient, in this historical survey, to refer to it by its best known title, the Welsh Harp (at times it has also been called Kingsbury Lake and Kingsbury Reservoir).

The Welsh Harp was constructed by William Hoof between 1834 and 1835 and was a direct result of the growth of the canal system. It had been coming for a long time, plans having been laid as early as 1803. These initial plans were abandoned because of cost but the seed had been sown: the canal system continued to develop in the early years of the 19th century under the authorisation of various Acts of Parliament. Water shortage, however, remained problematic and by 1820 it was found that there was not enough water to supply both the Grand Junction and the Regent's Canals. So, under powers made available to it by an Act of Parliament in 1819, a decision was made by the Regent's Canal Company to dam the River Brent and create the reservoir.

The reservoir was 69 acres in extent, covering an area between Old Kingsbury Church and the Edgware Road, which consisted of grazing land on either side of the Silk Stream and the River Brent. Hoof, who was awarded the tender for the work, agreed to carry out the construction (which included a bridge) for the sum of £2,740 6s. Detailed planning of the reservoir probably did not begin until around 1833. Work is believed to have begun in late 1834 or early 1835, but was not completed until the November of that year.

The construction was not without its tragedies: in August 1835, only a couple of months before completion, four brothers named Sidebottom were drowned in an accident. This was not the only early misfortune. Further building work to slightly extend the reservoir had been completed in December 1837 but in 1842, following a prolonged spell of cold, wet weather (which culminated in seven days 'non-stop rain'), the reservoir's defences were broken. There was severe flooding, in which several lives, as well as livestock and property were lost. It was after this that a man was employed for the first time at the reservoir as a supervisor, with a cottage built for him near the dam. The Regent's Canal Company made further developments at the reservoir in 1854. As a result of these, the height of the dam was increased and the size of the reservoir enlarged. The company's jurisdiction was also extended to include some of the area covered by the feeder streams.

It was at about this time that the Welsh Harp first attracted the interest of bird-watchers. During the middle years of the century the new habitats created by the construction of the reservoir drew an astonishing succession of rare and uncommon birds. We know about these birds because, in the main, they were shot; indeed, in the days before the high-powered telescope and the fieldguide, there was no other way of satisfactorily identifying an unusual bird. Harting and Walpole-Bond, the latter a distinguished editor of 'The Zoologist' were the leading figures and it was Harting who, in his 'Birds of Middlesex' published in 1866, first collated many of these records into one volume: they are found in the systematic list, which forms the centrepiece of the present book. Nowadays we may deplore the methods of the early 'collectors', but their legacy is beyond price.

Almost simultaneously the Welsh Harp began its period of fame as a feature of London social life. This development was almost entirely due to one man, W P Warner (1832-1899), who in 1858 became landlord of the Old Welsh Harp Tavern. This pub stood on the Edgware Road (along the course of the Roman Watling Street), near to where the road crossed the River Brent. Warner, who had fought with distinction in the Crimean War, created at the Old Welsh Harp what was in effect a version of the great London Pleasure gardens of the eighteenth century (ironically at almost the precise moment when Vauxhall, the most famous of them all, finally closed its doors). For about forty years Warner made the Welsh Harp one of London's most popular places of resort, celebrated in song by the music hall star Annie Adams as 'The Jolliest Place That's Out'.

The amusements were both indoor and outdoor. Outside, Warner operated a racetrack for a number of years until an Act of Parliament made its continuance illegal. In 1876 the reservoir also hosted the first attempt to persuade grey-hounds to chase a mechanical hare. This appears to have been successful, unlike the attempt by Capazza in 1891 to launch his 'Patent Parachute Balloon', a contraption which failed to leave the ground. Contemporary accounts record that there were some 'nasty incidents' among the 5,000 spectators following this non-event and it is perhaps appropriate to say that during this period the reservoir and its activities attracted a mixed clientèle, with crime and violence (often ending in the water) not uncommon. One observer described the races as 'a carnival of vice'. Like Hampstead Heath, not far away, the reservoir was famous for its Bank Holiday fairs and, from 1870 to 1903, the Welsh Harp even had its own station on the Midland Railway, this at a time when Kingsbury had a population of only 662 (in 1876).

The water itself was an important source of recreation. Although angling is no longer permitted, it was very popular in Victorian times, and it was Warner who owned the fishing rights. Angling remained a feature until the arrival of the factories at the end of the century: the pollution they brought with them soon started to have an adverse impact on the fish. In winter the frozen ice proved ideal for skating and national and international ice-skating events were held. In February 1893 a certain Jack Selby became famous for driving a coach and four across the frozen reservoir.

The indoor attractions were equally impressive. Warner built a function room, which held 300 diners and which could seat 500 when turned into a concert hall. The popularity of the Old Welsh Harp coincided with the peak of the music hall and many famous stars appeared there. There were also extensive grounds in which couples could promenade or, if they wanted it (as many no doubt did), find a degree of discreet seclusion. Among other features were a skittle alley and a menagerie from which a large bear once famously escaped, causing much local consternation until its recapture. For the duration of Warner's reign and for some years afterwards the reservoir attained a celebrity it has never reached since, and guidebooks such as Thorne's *Handbook to the Environs of London* (which appeared in 1876) gave detailed accounts of the variety of pleasures that could be had there.

It could not, and did not, last. The semi-rural surroundings of the reservoir began to give way to a more urban environment towards the end of the century. The construction of factories, already mentioned, began in the 1890s with a mineral water bottling plant and others soon followed this. The nature of the area began to change. Roads and houses accompanied industrialisation, and the farmland began to disappear under concrete. The reservoir was gradually reduced in size although there were still occasional problems with flooding (in 1903, for example, after heavy rain). Fewer birdwatchers, too, made visits. The pioneering work of the mid-Victorians was not continued, and although Glegg, Harrison, Kendall and others published books and articles, which incorporated records from the Welsh Harp, the reservoir was under-watched. In the 1930s this began to change, particularly when the London Natural History Society began to publish its annual London Bird Report.

The excitement of the Warner years might have departed but the reservoir still had a part to play. Although it was kept secret at the time the War Office, whose

Mechanical Warfare Department was based in Cricklewood, used the Welsh Harp to carry out the first tests, from 1916 onwards, of a massive new weapon: the tank. Early film of these tests was recently shown on television. The years after the First World War also saw the crucially significant construction of the North Circular Road, as well as the massive development of Wembley for the Empire Exhibition in 1924. The Old Welsh Harp was demolished, although a new building took its place. By the start of the Second World War the reservoir, while it still attracted some activities (including nudism), was little more than a large sheet of water in a largely characterless suburban landscape.

Some might still apply that description, but the half century since the last war's end has seen a growing appreciation of the amenity value of this famous reservoir. Birdwatching in particular saw a massive explosion in popularity after 1945 with the result that the Welsh Harp began to experience a revival of interest. Many distinguished ornithologists (for example Professor E H Warmington and Eric Simms) have had an association with the reservoir, but since the 1950s Dr. Leo Batten has been the prime mover behind most of the developments which have led to the reservoir attaining its present level of wildlife importance. He also produced, in an article in *The London Naturalist* of 1972, the first substantial modern survey of the history of the birds of the reservoir. The opening of the first public hide in February 1991, with its permanent logbook for recording observations, also played a significant part in fostering interest. The result is that the reservoir now has a core of regular and committed observers and is as well watched as it has ever been.

That the growing significance of the reservoir for wildlife has led at times to tensions cannot be disputed. Sailors, walkers, local residents and others all have their corners to defend, as well as naturalists. It was in response to threats of development that the Welsh Harp Conservation Group was formed in 1972 and it has since been the main focus for conservation interests at the reservoir, actively involved in opposing inappropriate development and in making the site more attractive for wildlife. Nor have matters been assisted by the growing number of statutory bodies with a (quite legitimate) involvement in the reservoir and whose interests have not always necessarily coincided. The creation of a Joint Consultative Committee (chaired in alternate years by Barnet and Brent Councils, part of whose boundary bisects the reservoir) to oversee matters at the Welsh Harp has at least ensured that all those interests have a place where their voices can be heard. The Welsh Harp Conservation Group is represented on this Committee.

This body has proved effective as a way of focusing opposition to the many developments over the years which have been seen as a threat to the fragile balance of interests that makes up the reservoir today: a nine-hole golf course plus driving range was among the most recent of these. Hope that this might also prove to be the last, and that the reservoir might gain a degree of security, rose rapidly when it was announced that the National Heritage Memorial Fund had awarded a grant of £420,000 to carry out work at the reservoir for the benefit of all its users. This was very welcome news and the work is now being carried out. And, although the designation of the reservoir as a Site of Special Scientific Interest (SSSI) has helped direct attention towards the conservation interest, anyone with the smallest understanding of the history of the Welsh Harp will see that the reservoir has always been far more than just a resort for naturalists. Diversity, but balanced diversity, must now be the solution.

Everything changes. The Old Welsh Harp was finally demolished in 1971 to make way for the Staples Corner interchange: ironically the Upper Welsh Harp pub (now simply The Harp), on the corner of the Edgware Road and Cool Oak Lane, remains to this day although it was always the poor relation and its own survival has at times been doubtful. And as I write, the twin towers of Wembley Stadium, for so long a familiar sight from so many parts of the Harp, may soon become just another memory. The future of the reservoir remains uncertain, although hopefully less uncertain than it was; that it must have a future is clear. The survival of the Welsh Harp is what counts. And if anyone doubts whether, at least from the point of view of its bird life, the Harp should be preserved then they have only to read this book.

References

A number of general works on London contain information about the history of the reservoir. Particular attention should be drawn, however, to the pamphlet entitled 'The Jolliest Place That's Out' by G. Hewlett, published by the Wembley History Society, which is the best account of these aspects of the reservoir of which I am aware.

A postcard of the Old Welsh Harp Tavern in c1905.

Chapter 2
Habitats and their Management

Leo Batten

At present the Brent Reservoir and its surrounding open space consists of ten broad habitats. These are: open water; swamp; fen and willow carr; rough grasslands; playing fields; allotments; hedgerows; scrub and woodland; suburban gardens; parkland and disused rubbish dump. As a result of man's activities there is surprisingly more diversity of the environment than there was between 1833-1877. Then the main habitats consisted of farmland; homesteads; stony downland; wood and scrub; open water and reed swamp.

Wetland habitats and their management

Swamp, fen, willow carr and open water

Extensive areas of this wetland habitat have developed, the greatest growth being over the last 25 years. Although most of the reservoir is surrounded by a narrow belt of emergent vegetation, with the dominant grass being Reed Canary-grass, the most important areas are situated at the northern and eastern ends where, respectively, the Silk Stream and River Brent enter the reservoir. Here wetland plant communities cover some twelve hectares of silt deposits. There is a gradation from open water sometimes colonised by Amphibious Bistort, to stands of Sea Club-rush, Common Club-rush, Greater and Lesser Reedmace and Common Reed. The reed swamp grades into the more diverse marsh or fen community. Details of the plant species are given in Chapter 5. The vegetation then succeeds to dense willow carr, grading into damp willow woodland further back from the water.

Management

Since the early 1980s the Welsh Harp Conservation Group has been actively involved in the management of the wetland habitat at the northern and eastern ends. The objectives of this management are to increase the carrying capacity of these refuges for waterfowl during sailing activities on the main part of the reservoir, as well as making them more attractive to wildlife generally.

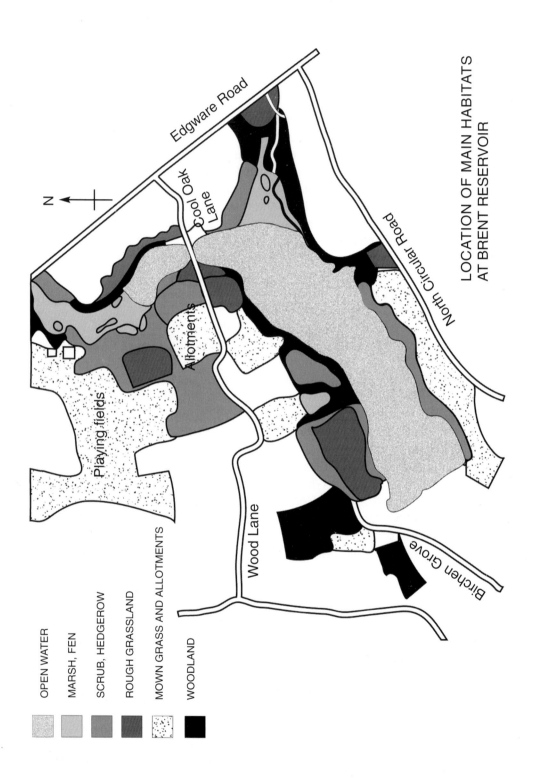

LOCATION OF MAIN HABITATS
AT BRENT RESERVOIR

OPEN WATER

MARSH, FEN

SCRUB, HEDGEROW

ROUGH GRASSLAND

MOWN GRASS AND ALLOTMENTS

WOODLAND

This has been achieved by:
- Maintaining the ecological succession of the wetland to include open water, swamp, fen, willow carr and woodland;
- Increasing the variety of vegetation so as to increase the diversity of animal species, eg removing willows in a monoculture to allow other plants in, or to create wetter muddy areas to provide feeding or nesting places;
- Managing for the benefit of existing wildlife, eg deepening parts of the refuge by dredging, creation of islands, nesting rafts, and removing vegetation from existing islands for feeding or loafing areas for ducks and waders;
- Reducing disturbance from man's activities, eg creating buffer zones and restricting access to sensitive areas;
- Lobbying to improve water quality.

Landscaping the marshes

The Northern and Eastern Marshes have both been extensively reshaped using earth moving tracked hydraulic vehicles. In the early 1980s many tons of soil were moved using these vehicles and an Aquacat, which is a big barge fitted with a bucket and hydraulic arm which can penetrate areas where land based machines would not be supported.

The use of these machines has enabled the creation of islands in both marshes, resulting from the clearance of willows encroaching on to the silt and the cutting of a wide channel in the silt bank to form the island.

The Northern Marsh has also been extended back two hundred metres by the removal of silt and the creation of a channel and two large pools with islands. Several refuge areas have been created by cutting off access to the water's edge through the construction of canals and the resultant creation of islands.

Reed bed extensions have been achieved by transplanting large chunks of reed using the machines mentioned earlier. More recently the willows on the main island in the Eastern Marsh have been removed and eighty tons of shingle brought on by the Environment Agency to create a wader scrape and loafing area for ducks.

In addition to the marsh landscaping a Mudcat suction dredger was used to remove some 12-15 thousand cubic metres of silt to make the refuge deeper in places and create a better balance of open water to marsh. The dredger was able to move tons of silt, sucking it up from the reservoir bed and pumping it through large diameter pipes to be released into settlement lagoons. The earth walls surrounding the lagoon near West Hendon playing Fields, together with the enclosing fence, have also provided an attractive area for migrating birds such as Wheatear and Whinchat.

Nesting raft construction

The original 24 nesting rafts, positioned in the Eastern Marsh to provide a visual screen and safe nesting sites which would rise and fall with the water level, were planned and designed by the WHCG but a lot of the labour was provided by young offenders working off community service sentences. A frame of creosote impregnated railway sleepers was given a floor and buoyancy was provided through large blocks of expanded polystyrene. When completed the rafts weighed over half a ton.They were launched using a specially constructed trolley, and then towed into position and finally secured with steel chain and large concrete blocks. Later three much larger ones were added from an old jetty donated by the sailing association, followed by another six bought from Heritage Lottery Fund money.

A colony of Common Terns has become established on the rafts with over 40 pairs breeding. There has been an additional benefit with the rafts acting like breakwaters and creating a calm area of water away from the prevailing winds; this may have helped the expansion of the Great Crested Grebe colony. The original rafts have been in place since the early eighties, and most survived the hurricane of October 1987.

The rafts do require annual checks and occasional repairs of damage from the winter storms. Those with shingle for nesting terns need some of the shingle which has been washed off during the winter, replaced. Others were covered with soil and planted with a variety of tall marginal plant species and a few willows. These need less attention and provide nest sites for waterfowl.

Water quality and pollution control

The two rivers flowing in to the reservoir are affected by industrial and household effluent which may contain a wide range of pollutants including sewage, heavy metals, detergents and oils. In addition to being toxic and killing off food for birds and other animals, this can cause other problems, for example, detergent can cause loss of waterproofing in the feathers of birds.

In the management of wetlands dealing with pollution is perhaps the most difficult problem of all. The only effective solution is to find the sources of the pollution and stop them. A major source of pollution is connections in houses

Habitats and management
Plate 1

A. Northern Marsh before management work, spring 1984, (Leo Batten)

B. Northern Marsh after management work, spring 1985, (Leo Batten)

C. Northern Marsh after 10 years subsequent growth, winter 1995, (Leo Batten)

Plate 2

A. Hymax creating a canal in the Northern Marsh, March 1984, (Leo Batten)

B. Aquacat digging channels in Typha bed in N.Marsh, April 1984, (Leo Batten)

C. Suction dredger in operation Eastern Marsh, March 1992, (Leo Batten)

D. Maintaining nesting rafts, March 1996, (Leo Batten)

Plate 3

A. View of nesting rafts from main hide, Sept 1993, (Leo Batten)

B. Looking towards dam of drained reservoir in 1974, (Leo Batten)

Plate 4

A. View of north east corner of reservoir from hide, Sept 1993, (Leo Batten)

B. Looking out from Heron hide to island and reedbed, May 1999, (Leo Batten)

Plate 5

A. View of main hide from reedbed, May 1999, (Leo Batten)

B. Wet Willow woodland in Eastern marsh, Sept 1985, (Leo Batten)

Plate 6

A. Ancient hedgerow near northern arm of reservoir, April 2000, (Leo Batten)

B. Scrub near northern arm of reservoir, Sept 2001, (Leo Batten)

involving sewage outflows and the effluent from washing machines, etc, being wrongly connected to the surface water pipes instead of to the sewage pipes. Stopping the sources is however often not practical. Oil has been partly stopped from entering the reservoir by the construction of oil traps.

Vast quantities of rubbish are discarded into the rivers and much of this has been stopped from entering the reservoir by the provision of trash traps on them both. One of these which is on the Silk Stream is automatic and removes rubbish at set intervals of time using a grab, depositing the rubbish into a skip on the river bank. Although these traps do not help significantly with other sources of pollution such as heavy metals, there has been a significant reduction of oil and rubbish entering the reservoir. It is pleasing to report that Kingfishers have returned to breed since these traps have been installed, after an absence of seven decades.

The reservoir is still classified as hyper-eutrophic as the mean orthophosphate concentration of the reservoir is extremely high. This is characterised by heavy growths of blanketweed and cyanobacteria blooms. (Carvalho and Moss 1998).

Much of the management work described in this section was made possible by grants to the Welsh Harp Conservation Group from the then Greater London Council, Barnet Council, Brent Council, English Nature and, more recently, the Heritage Lottery Fund. In addition Greencard provided the money to build two bird-watching hides in the Eastern Marsh. The larger hide, which seats up to 12 adults, provides excellent views over the main reservoir and the tern colony. It has also been used frequently by schools in the past. It is interesting that, since Barnet stopped providing opportunities for schools to use the hide, vandalism has increased with break ins and attempted arson.

Other habitats

Scrub and woodland

The most important area of scrub and woodland at the reservoir, situated on the northern side of the dam by Birchen Grove was at one time destined to become a cemetery. In 1965 Willesden and Wembley were amalgamated to form the London Borough of Brent. There was a large cemetery in Wembley and therefore this area was no longer needed. Before this event was foreseen all the necessary preparations had been completed, including the construction of a chapel which is now used as a field centre for local schools. (Batten 1972).

The dominant species were Oak and Elm but since Dutch Elm disease, the dominant species is Oak. There is also a section dominated by Birch. The bulk of the trees are less than 60 years old at the time of writing. Around the perimeter there are some Oaks of over one hundred years old. These are the remnants of ancient hedgerows, which when no longer managed, expanded to produce the woodland cover which presently exists. In the 1960s and 1970s there was an extensive understorey of Hawthorn and Blackthorn dominant in places and this provided for a large communal roost of Blackbirds and other thrushes, exceeding well in excess of a thousand birds in late autumn and winter. The hawthorn and blackthorn has since been shaded out by the developing Oaks and the roost which drew birds mainly from the adjacent gardens has now dispersed.

Another area of woodland is situated along the boundary between Barnet and Brent on the north bank of the reservoir. This is Oak dominated and developed from trees in a parish boundary hedge which runs down to the waters edge and separates Hendon from Kingsbury. A small area of Oak dominated woodland also exists on the opposite side of Cool Oak Lane to the Barnet Council Plant Nursery.

Quite extensive areas of mature Willow woodland exist at the northern and eastern ends of the reservoir. Much of this woodland dates back to the late 1950s when silt brought down by the River Brent and the Silk Stream had accumulated sufficiently to form banks which laid exposed long enough in the dry summer of 1959 for vegetation to establish itself. Natural succession over the following years resulted in a variety of marshland plants being replaced by the current woodland areas. An example of how rapidly Willow woodland can develop, occurred in 1974 when the reservoir had to be drained: Willows colonised parts of the dry bed of the reservoir and grew up to six feet tall.

Management

In the past management has been confined to thinning out trees to open up the canopy. This helps to maintain an uneven age structure thus increasing structural diversity and allowing a more diverse ground flora to develop. This has also been the practice in eastern and northern ends of the reservoir with the willow woodland. Willows have also been controlled in the reed-bed and along the banks of the reservoir to stop them shading out the fen vegetation.

The disused rubbish dump situated adjacent to the northern arm of the reservoir, was turfed in the autumn of 1970 and has now developed into an area of rough grassland for two thirds of its area and dense scrub for the other. Management work in this latter area consists of cutting rides through the scrub to increase the edge. It supports a rich passerine community.

Hedgerows

The hedgerows of the study area were surveyed in 1986 (Williams 1986, 1987) where full details can be found. About 30 per cent of the 1864 hedgerow length in the London Borough of Brent section is still present, largely accounted for by hedges south of Wood Lane. There are 36 lengths of hedgerows still in existence, totalling approximately six kilometres. There are also a number of remnants which are only recognisable now by a few standard trees, and others have become obscured by scrub spreading outwards.

The dominant species of tree is Oak with about 140 trees, followed by eleven Ash, six Crack Willow, five Common Lime, four Horse Chestnut and two Poplar. Elms were also a dominant tree in the hedgerows before Dutch Elm disease in the 1970s, for example there were 27 standard English Elm trees in the 200 metres of hedge between the field centre grounds and Chilcott Nursery in the 1970s. (Williams 1987). Now Elm survives only as suckers. Altogether 25 species of shrub and tree were recorded in the 1986 hedgerow survey.

Many of the surviving hedgerows can be traced back on old maps to the 1597 All Souls College Hovendon map of Kingsbury, though a number are in a gappy or remnant condition. The presence of species such as Blackthorn, Dogwood, Field Maple, Hazel and Hawthorn suggest that some of these hedges originate from a woodland rather than planted origin. In other words fields have been cut out of the original forest, leaving some woodland and a large number of woodland belts around the fields.

No management of these hedgerows has been carried out for conservation purposes.

Allotments

During and after the second world war a considerable part of the open space was given over to allotments but these have gradually been reduced until at present there are only about 18 hectares left. Those nearest the reservoir are now disused. There are a number of dense Hawthorn thickets and a thick, predominantly Hawthorn, hedge along one side and another which almost bisects the area. The other sides are fenced but have a number of tall trees, mainly Oaks, along the perimeter. No management for conservation purposes has so far been carried out in this habitat.

Playing fields and parklands

A large part of the area is given over to playing fields which provide opportunities for thrushes, starlings and crows to feed, whilst gulls often roost there. The parkland areas are rather poor because they consist merely of a few standards growing in the middle of mown grass fields.

Rough grasslands

Substantial areas of the north bank consist of grasslands which are now only mown once a year. These areas provide a good crop of seeds for passerines in the autumn. They also provide a good habitat for a variety of invertebrates, particularly butterflies and grasshoppers. Recently one area of grassland near the allotments has been planted up with Gorse to provide nesting habitat for birds. Some areas are not being mown and will revert to scrub.

Suburban gardens

Suburban gardens surround the field centre on two sides and provide good feeding areas for thrushes and other passerines. This has enabled unusually high breeding densities of species such as Blackbird, Robin, Dunnock and Song Thrush to be sustained in the field centre woodland. Other suburban gardens form the boundary of sections of West Hendon playing fields, part of the eastern marsh, and a small section of the south west end of Neasden recreation ground. The main benefits are that they have lawns which provide feeding opportunities for some ground feeding passerines in summer. The artificial food put out helps winter survival for a wide range of species such as tits, thrushes and finches.

References

Batten, L. A. 1972. The past and present bird life of the Brent Reservoir and its vicinity. Lond. Nat. 50: 8-62.

Carvalho, C. & Moss, B. 1998. Lake SSSIs subject to eutrophication - an environmental audit. English Nature Freshwater Series. No 3.

Williams, L. R., McLaughlin, J. and Harrison, T. 1986. Hedgerows of the Barnet 'Enclave'. Wembley History Society Journal, 6: 54-9.

Williams, L. R., McLaughlin, J. and Harrison, T. 1987. Hedgerows of Kingsbury South-East. Wembley History Society Journal, 6: 76-80.

Chapter 3
Urbanisation and its Effects

Leo Batten

This chapter presents the results of an investigation into the changing bird-life of the Brent Reservoir recording area during the course of its urbanisation. The area is ideal for a study of this nature because ever since its construction in 1833 there has always been at least one ornithologist working there. An almost complete qualitative history of the bird-life over 165 years is now available in the literature.

At the beginning of the period the natural-banked reservoir was a rural beauty spot surrounded by mixed farmland with scattered copses, overlooked by the wooded height of Barn Hill. Little change in land use occurred until the 1890s when rows of houses were built close to the northern end of the reservoir. By 1913 urbanisation had got underway and 10 per cent of the land area had been built on, mainly towards the north and east of the reservoir. Further developments took place in the 1920s when the North Circular Road was constructed, and by 1930, 30 per cent of the area was built up.

Changes in breeding birds since 1833

In any area of land one must expect changes in the composition of breeding species over as long a period as 165 years. Some of these changes will be due to extrinsic factors such as variations in climate or modifications to the area itself. Other intrinsic differences may be caused by long-term and wide-spread population changes in the birds themselves. It is often difficult to be sure which of these factors is responsible for changes in status of certain species, particularly as there is a possibility that suburban habitats may be second-rate for some species, and occupied only in years of high population level.

Long-term population fluctuations, which might occur nationally or internationally and go unnoticed elsewhere, could be accentuated in this kind of area. Although no quantitative data exist for the first 100 years or so there is evidence based on presence or absence that the Green and Great Spotted Woodpeckers have fluctuated markedly since the reservoir's construction. They were described as common in the early decades of the 19th century, were rare in the latter half, and common again by the 1920s. They declined after the mid-1950s and then increased again in the 1980s and 1990s to become breeding species again. The first oscillation occurred when the area was changing little, in fact the Green Woodpecker was absent as a breeding bird for 30 years and the Great Spotted Woodpecker was absent as a breeding bird 40 years.

During the period under consideration a number of other species have fluctuated in such a way as to show a return to a former status after a period of scarcity or abundance. The most noticeable of these are Coot, Stock Dove, Nuthatch, Goldfinch, Bullfinch, Redpoll, Jay and Magpie. As some of these population changes took place when the area was not being extensively urbanised it seems likely that other factors were responsible for the early fluctuations. Other species such as Grey Wagtail, Reed Warbler, Nightjar, Pheasant, Tree Pipit and Cirl Bunting may have been affected similarly. Red-legged Partridge and Little Owl have also had a period of regular breeding in the area, but these were both species introduced into Britain in the 19th century.

A number of species declined and disappeared as breeding species fairly rapidly by 1910. Although only about 10 per cent of the land was urbanised by then, the surrounding districts nearer London were being developed and with this came the inevitable increase in disturbance from the human population. Some species lost to the area at that time were high forest species which appear not to be able to tolerate human disturbance: Hawfinch, Redstart and Wood Warbler fall into this category. The Kingfisher suffered as a result of the increased pollution of the rivers and tributaries in the area, but amazingly has returned after trash traps and oil booms were constructed on the Dollis Brook and Silk Stream. The Lapwing and Corncrake were also lost and it is likely the former went because of the continual plunder of its eggs. The reasons for the decline of the Corncrake at that time is unclear, although agricultural factors are now known to have caused more recent massive population losses. The loss of Goldcrest and Nightingale seemed premature; the former has recently returned as a breeding species in the Saxon churchyard at Kingsbury.

On the credit side the Great Crested Grebe appeared, presumably helped by the Bird Protection Act of 1880, which banned its slaughter to adorn Victorian ladies' hats. Figure 1 illustrates these changes against a timescale.

Figure 1 - Change in breeding species from 1830 to 2000

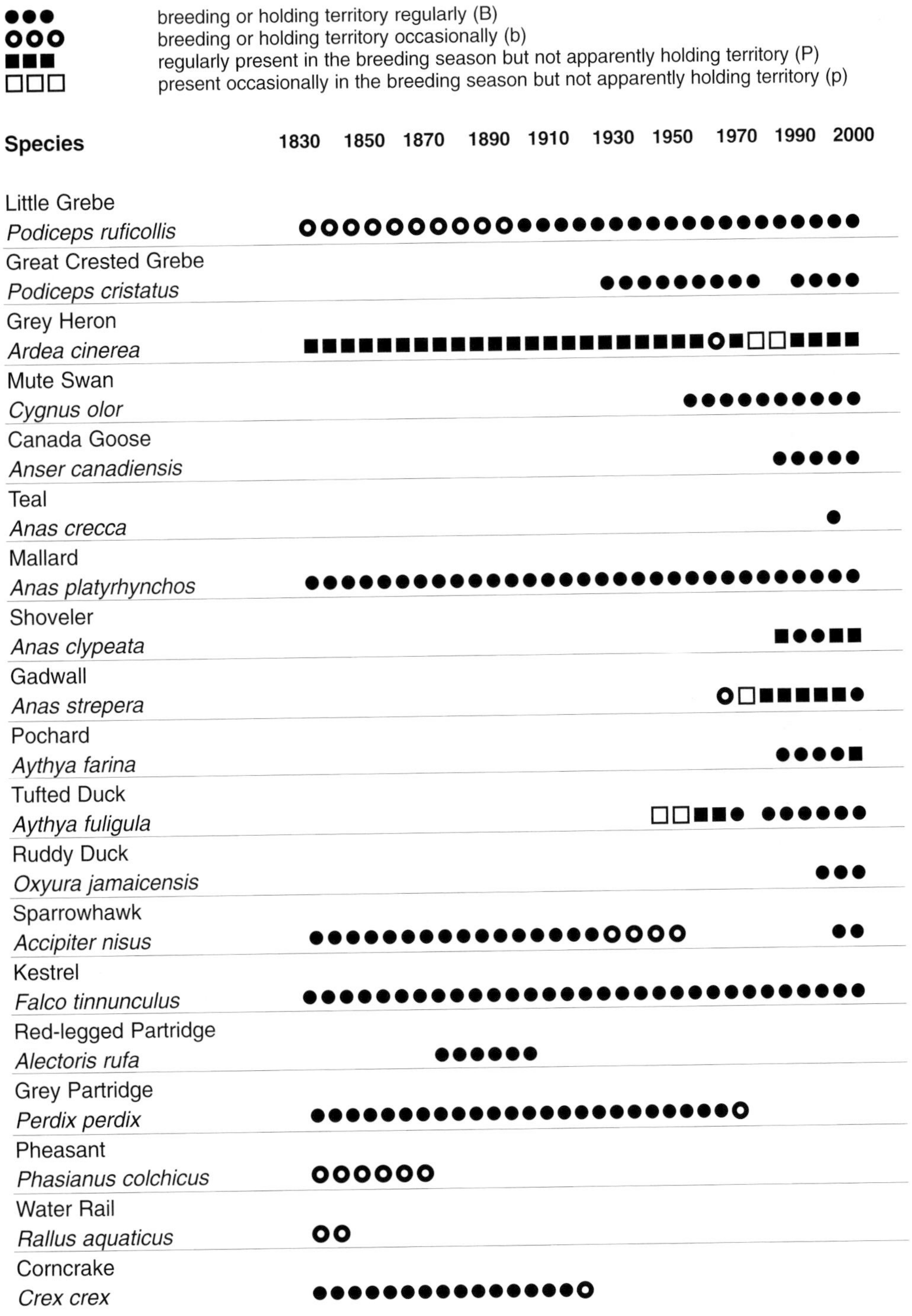

●●●	breeding or holding territory regularly (B)
○○○	breeding or holding territory occasionally (b)
■■■	regularly present in the breeding season but not apparently holding territory (P)
☐☐☐	present occasionally in the breeding season but not apparently holding territory (p)

Species — 1830　1850　1870　1890　1910　1930　1950　1970　1990　2000

Little Grebe
Podiceps ruficollis
○○○○○○○○○○○●●●●●●●●●●●●●●●●●●●

Great Crested Grebe
Podiceps cristatus
●●●●●●●●●　●●●●

Grey Heron
Ardea cinerea
■■■■■■■■■■■■■■■■■■■■■■■■○■☐☐■■■■

Mute Swan
Cygnus olor
●●●●●●●●●●●

Canada Goose
Anser canadiensis
●●●●●

Teal
Anas crecca
●

Mallard
Anas platyrhynchos
●●●●●●●●●●●●●●●●●●●●●●●●●●●●●●●

Shoveler
Anas clypeata
■●●■■

Gadwall
Anas strepera
○☐■■■■■●●

Pochard
Aythya farina
●●●●■

Tufted Duck
Aythya fuligula
☐☐■■●　●●●●●●

Ruddy Duck
Oxyura jamaicensis
●●●

Sparrowhawk
Accipiter nisus
●●●●●●●●●●●●●●●●●●○○○○　●●

Kestrel
Falco tinnunculus
●●●●●●●●●●●●●●●●●●●●●●●●●●●●●●●

Red-legged Partridge
Alectoris rufa
●●●●●●

Grey Partridge
Perdix perdix
●●●●●●●●●●●●●●●●●●●●●●●●●○

Pheasant
Phasianus colchicus
○○○○○○

Water Rail
Rallus aquaticus
○○

Corncrake
Crex crex
●●●●●●●●●●●●●●○

Species	1830	1850	1870	1890	1910	1930	1950	1970	1990	2000

Moorhen
Gallinula chloropus
●●●●●●●●●●●●●●●●●●●●●●●●●●●●●●●●

Coot
Fulica atra
●●●●●●　　　●●●●●●●●●●●●●●●●●●●●

Little Ringed Plover
Charadrius dubius
　　　　　　　　　　　　　　○○□

Lapwing
Vanellus vanellus
●●●●●●●●●●●●●●●

Common Tern
Sterna hirundo
　　　　　　　　　　　　　●●●●●

Feral Pigeon
Columba livia
　　　　　　●●●●●●●●●●●●●●●●●●

Stock Dove
Columba oenas
○○○○○○　　●●●●●●●●●●●●●　　○○

Woodpigeon
Columba palumbus
●●●●●●●●●●●●●●●●●●●●●●●●●●●●●●

Collared Dove
Streptopelia decaocto
　　　　　　　　　　　　　●●●●●

Turtle Dove
Streptopelia turtur
●●●●●●●●●●●●●●●●●●□□□□□□□

Cuckoo
Cuculus canorus
●●●●●●●●●●●●●●●●●●●●●●●○□□□□□□

Barn Owl
Tyto alba
●●●●●●●●●●●●●●●●●●●

Long-eared Owl
Asio otus
●●●●●●●●○○○○○

Little Owl
Anthene noctua
　　　　　○○○○○○●●●●

Tawny Owl
Strix aluco
　　●●●●●●●●●●●●●●●●●●●●●●

Nightjar
Caprimulgus europatus
　　○○○

Swift
Apus apus
○○○○○○○●●●●●●●●●●●●●●●●●●●●●●

Kingfisher
Alcedo atthis
●●●●●●●●●●●●●　　　　■　●●●●●

Wryneck
Jynx torquilla
●●●●●●●●●●●●●●●●●●●

Green Woodpecker
Picus viridis
●●●●●　　○○●●●●●●●●●　　●●●●●●

Great Spotted Woodpecker
Dendrocopos major
●●●●●●　　○○●●●●●●●●●●○□■○●●●

Lesser Spotted Woodpecker
Dendrocopos minor
●●●●●●●●●●●●●●●●●●●　　　○○○

Species	1830	1850	1870	1890	1910	1930	1950	1970	1990	2000

Woodlark
Lullula arborea　●●●●●

Skylark
Alauda arvensis　●●●●●●●●●●●●●●●●●●●●●●●●●●●●●●■□

Swallow
Hirundo rustica　●●●●●●●●●●●●●●●●●●●●●●

House Martin
Delichon urbica　●●●●●●●●●●●●●●●●●●●●●●●●●●●●

Tree Pipit
Anthus trivialis　●●●●●●●●●●●●●●●●●●●●○○

Meadow Pipit
Anthus pratensis　●●●●●●●●●●●●●●●●●●●●　○　　○

Yellow Wagtail
Motacilla flava　●●●●●●●●●●●●●●●●●●●●●●●●●

Grey Wagtail
Motacilla cinerea　　　　　　　○　　　○○○●●●●●

Pied Wagtail
Motacilla alba　●●●●●●●●●●●●●●●●●●●●●●●●●●●●●

Wren
Troglodytes troglodytes　●●●●●●●●●●●●●●●●●●●●●●●●●●●●

Dunnock
Prunella modularis　●●●●●●●●●●●●●●●●●●●●●●●●●●

Robin
Erithacus rubecula　●●●●●●●●●●●●●●●●●●●●●●●●●●●●●

Nightingale
Luscinia megarhynchos　●●●●●●●●●●●●●●●

Redstart
Phoenicurus phoenicurus　●●●●●●●●●●●●●●●

Whinchat
Saxicola rubetra　●●●●●●●●●●●●●●●●●●●●●●　○

Stonechat
Saxicola torquata　●●●●●●●●●●●●●●●●●●●●●●●　○　○

Wheatear
Oenanthe oenanthe　●●●●●●　　　　　　○

Blackbird
Turdus merula　●●●●●●●●●●●●●●●●●●●●●●●●●●●●●

Song Thrush
Turdus philomelos　●●●●●●●●●●●●●●●●●●●●●●●●●●●●●●

Mistle Thrush
Turdus viscivorus　●●●●●●●●●●●●●●●●●●●●●●○○●●●●●

Grasshopper Warbler
Locustella naevia　●●●●●●●●●●●●●●●●●●●○○○○○○○

Sedge Warbler
Acrocephalus schoenobaenus　●●●●●●●●●●●●●●●●●●●●●●●●●●●●●●●

Species	1830	1850	1870	1890	1910	1930	1950	1970	1990	2000

Reed Warbler
Acrocephalus scirpaceus ●●●●●●●●●●●● ●●●●○○●●●●●●●●●●●

Lesser Whitethroat
Sylvia curruca ●●●●●●●●●●●●●●●●●●●●●●●●●●●●●●

Common Whitethroat
Sylvia communis ●●●●●●●●●●●●●●●●●●●●●●●●●●●●●●

Garden Warbler
Sylvia borin ●●●●●●●●●●●●●●●●●●●●●○○○○○○○○●●○

Blackcap
Sylvia atricapilla ●●●●●●●●●●●●●●●●●●●●●●●●●●●●●●

Wood Warbler
Phylloscopus sibilatrix ●●●●●●●●●●●●●

Chiffchaff
Phylloscopus collybita ●●●●●●●●●●●●●●●●●●●●●○○ ○ ●●●●●

Willow Warbler
Phylloscopus trochilus ●●●●●●●●●●●●●●●●●●●●●●●●●●●●●●

Goldcrest
Regulus regulus ●●●●●●●●●●●●●●● ●●●●

Spotted Flycatcher
Muscipapa striata ●●●●●●●●●●●●●●●●●●●●●●●●●

Long-tailed Tit
Aegithalos caudatus ●●●●●●●●●●●●●●●●○○○○ ●●●●●●

Marsh/Willow Tit*
Parus palustris/montanus ●●●●●●●●●●●●●●●●●●●●●○○○○○○○

Coal Tit
Parus ater ●●●●●●●●●●●●●●●●●●●●●●●●●○○●●●●

Blue Tit
Parus caeruleus ●●●●●●●●●●●●●●●●●●●●●●●●●●●●●●

Great Tit
Parus major ●●●●●●●●●●●●●●●●●●●●●●●●●●●●●●

Nuthatch
Sitta europaea ●●● ●●●●●●○○○○○○

Treecreeper
Certhia familiaris ●●●●●●●●●●●●●●●●●●●●●○○ ● □

Red-backed Shrike
Lanius collurio ●●●●●●●●●●●●●●●●●●○○

Jay
Garrulus garrulus ●●●●●● ●●●●●●●●●●●●●●●●●●●●●

Magpie
Pica pica ●●●●●●● ●●●●●●●●●

Jackdaw
Corvus monedula ●●●●●●●●●●●●●●●●●●●●○○●■

Rook
Corvus frugilegus ●●●●●●●●●●●●●●●●●●●●●●●□□

Species	1830	1850	1870	1890	1910	1930	1950	1970	1990	2000

Carrion Crow
Corvus corone
●●●●●●●●●●●●●●●●●●●●●●●●●●●●●●●●●●●●

Starling
Sternus vulgaris
●●●●●●●●●●●●●●●●●●●●●●●●●●●●●●●●●●●

House Sparrow
Passer domesticus
●●●●●●●●●●●●●●●●●●●●●●●●●●●●●●●●●●●

Tree Sparrow
Passer montanus
●●●●●●●●●●●●●●●●●●●●●●●

Chaffinch
Fringilla coelebs
●●●●●●●●●●●●●●●●●●●●●●●●●●●●●○○■■   ○

Greenfinch
Carduelis chloris
●●●●●●●●●●●●●●●●●●●●●●●●●●●●●●●●●●●

Goldfinch
Carduelis carduelis
●●●●●   ○○○○●●●●●●●●

Linnet
Acanthis cannabina
●●●●●●●●●●●●●●●●●●●●●●●●●●●●●●●●●●●●

Redpoll
Acanthis flammea
          ●●●●   ●●○■□□

Bullfinch
Pyrrhula pyrrhula
●●●●●   ●●●●●●●●●●●●●●●○○○○●●●●●●●●

Hawfinch
Coccothraustes coccothraustes ●●●●●●●●●●●●●●●

Yellowhammer
Emberiza citrinella
●●●●●●●●●●●●●●●●●●●●●●●●●   ○

Cirl Bunting
Emberiza cirlus
      ○○○

Reed Bunting
Emberiza schoeniclus
●●●●●●●●●●●●●●●●●●●●●●●●●●●●●●●●●●●●

Corn Bunting
Emberiza calandra
●●●●●●●●●●●●●●●●●●●●●●   □

	1830	1850	1870	1890	1910	1930	1950	1970	1990	2000
Total B**		72	67	68	71	65	56	48	52	
Total B+b		77	72	70	77	69	67	64	63	
Total B+b+p		78	73	71	78	70	68	65	65	
Total B+b+P+p		78	73	71	78	70	69	66	67	
% urbanisation		0	0	0	10	30	50	65	68	

*Willow Tit has been the only one present since 1957. Some earlier records of Marsh Tits may well refer to Willow Tits.

**A species is considered to belong to this category if it bred or held territory in at least ten years of the 20-year period concerned.

Figure 2
The number of species which breed in relation to the increase in urbanisation

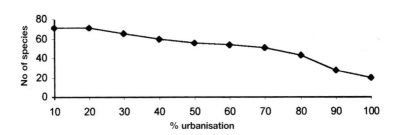

Breeding/Holding Territory regularly (B)

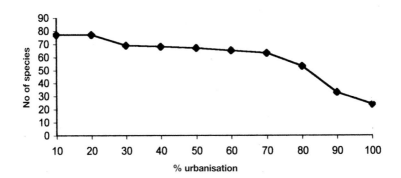

Breeding/Holding Territory regularly + occasionally (B+b)

Of the breeding species which have been lost to the area, at least for the time being, nearly 60 per cent have declined nationally (Parslow 1967) and this has probably contributed to their disappearance. This leaves Turtle Dove, Swallow, Meadow Pipit, Wood Warbler, Nightingale, Nuthatch, Hawfinch and Jackdaw which are presumably victims of the changes inflicted by urbanisation.

It is clear that the number of species present in the breeding season has decreased as the area has become increasingly built up. Figure 2 illustrates this graphically. Although the total number of species regularly breeding has dropped from 72 to 51, only 31 of the species which regularly bred before 1860 still do so. Twelve regular breeding species have been gained: Great Crested

Grebe, Little Grebe, Canada Goose, Mute Swan, Pochard, Tufted Duck, Ruddy Duck, Common Tern, Tawny Owl, Magpie, Swift and Grey Wagtail. In addition to this a further six species are now recorded as occasional breeders but were unknown as such before 1860. These are Shoveler, Teal, Gadwall, Little Ringed Plover, Collared Dove and Redpoll.

Detailed information on species present in many breeding seasons since 1957 is available. During this time the area has been in a state of 60-68 per cent urbanisation. There is considerable variation in the actual species involved each year. For example, out of 75 which bred in at least one of the years, only 32 (43 per cent) bred every year. It would seem therefore that the breeding avifauna of this urbanised area contains a very large proportion of irregular breeders. This principle has also been found to occur in other habitats. For example, on a farm in Suffolk which has been censused for eight years 64 per cent of the species occurring were regular breeders, and another farm in Westmorland censused for 10 years had only 52 per cent of its species in this category (Benson and Williamson, 1972; Robson and Williamson, 1972). In recent years, probably as a result of management work (see Chapter 2), the number of regular breeding species has increased slightly from 48-52.

So far the area has only reached the stage of 68 per cent urbanisation and at the present rate of increase it will be a very long time before total urbanisation occurs, if it ever does. An attempt was made to predict the number of breeding species which would remain when that hypothetical stage was reached, by examining a part of the study area which was already fully developed; 24 species were found breeding at this stage, but only 20 of these were regular. The effect of development could even be beneficial up to the first 10 per cent because new habitat is created, allowing the Swift to become a regular breeding species. Preliminary observations were made on a high density housing estate containing over 370 people to the hectare, with no gardens, merely lawns and a few trees. The breeding avifauna was restricted to seven species; Woodpigeon, Blackbird, Blue Tit, House Sparrow, Starling and Carrion Crow. In addition the Feral Pigeon was also found to be present.

References

Not all these references are mentioned in the text, they are however the main sources of published information for the data presented in the figures.

Batten, L. A. 1972. The past and present bird life of the Brent Reservoir and its vicinity. Lond. Nat. 50:8-62.

Batten, L. A. 1972. Breeding bird species diversity in relation to increasing urbanisation. Bird Study, 19: 157-166.

Benson, G. B. G. & Williamson, K. 1972. Breeding birds of a mixed farm in Suffolk. Bird Study, 19: 34-50.

Bond, F. 1844. Note on the arrival of summer birds at Kingsbury, Middlesex. Zool. for 1844, 650-651.

Dixon, C. 1909. The Bird-life of London, London.

Glegg, W. E. 1935. A History of the Birds of Middlesex. London.

Harting, J. E. 1866. The Birds of Middlesex, London.

Homes, R. C. et al. 1957. The Birds of the London Area since 1900. London.

Kendall, W. B. 1907. The Birds of Willesden (unpublished MS in Willesden Public Library).

London Natural History Society. 1921-1935. Lond. Nat. Nos.1-15

London Natural History Society. 1936 et seq. Lond. Bird Rep. Nos.1-63

Read, R. H. 1896. The birds of the Lower Brent Valley (reprinted from Rep. and Trans. Ealing Nat. Science Soc. for 1896).

Robson, R. W. & Williamson, K. Breeding birds of a Westmorland farm. Bird Study. 19: 202-214

Welsh Harp Conservation Group 1987-2001. Annual / Biennial Reports. Nos.1-10.

Tufted Ducks

Chapter 4
Birds of Brent Reservoir

SYSTEMATIC LIST OF BIRDS

Order and nomenclature
The birds are classified in the manner adopted by K.H.Voous in his *List of Recent Holarctic Bird Species (1977)*. Sequence and nomenclature follow that used in the *London Bird Report* and closely follow the **BirdWatch** publication: *A Checklist to the Birds of the Western Palaearctic (2000)*.

Recording area, current and historic
In its 170-year history the reservoir and the surroundijng area have changed enormously. In the 19th century the area was essentially rural consisting of a mosaic of small fields. The reservoir extended almost to the Hendon Way (A41) in the east and some way up the course of the Silk Stream to Colindeep Lane in the north-east. Since that time it has gradually reduced in size through a combination of infilling, lower water levels and siltation. It is not clear what the northern and southern boundaries were but we believe they were the Kingsbury Road to the north and the position of the North Circular Road to the south. Records are included from the enlarged historic area although the vast majority of today's records come from within the area covered by the reservoir and the adjacent open space. Where possible we have tried to include only those records we are certain have come from within this area; for records where there is some doubt this is mentioned in the text and they are bracketed. The accompanying map shows both historic and modern boundaries.

Inclusion of records
Over such a long period of time there has obviously been some variation in the rigour with which records are assessed. We have included records prior to 1930 when they have been deemed acceptable by the two main authors of that period, namely Harting and Glegg. Subsequently records have generally been included if they meet the criteria of the LNHS vetting process. There are a very few records that have been included which have not been accepted by the LNHS or the British Birds Rarities Committee in the case of rarities. These cases are identified in the text together with the circumstances of the observation.

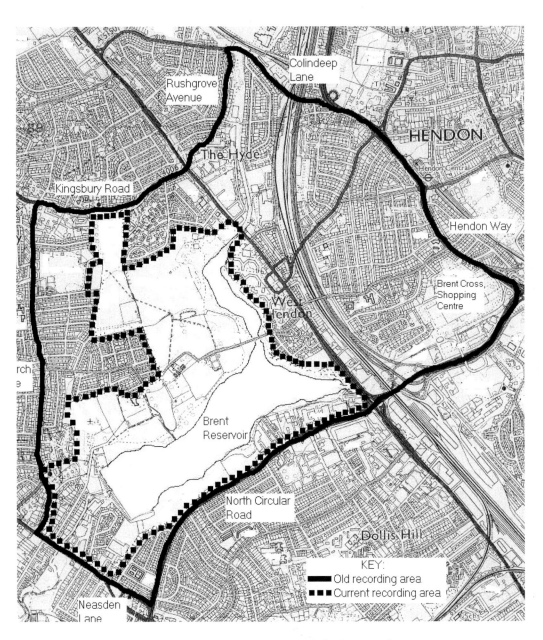

Reproduced by kind permission of Ordnance Survey.
© Crown copyright NC/01/404

Birds and Mammals

Plate 7

A. Great Crested Grebes nesting in eastern marsh, June 1984, (Leo Batten)

B. Pair of Great Crested Grebes nesting at reservoir, (Leo Batten)

C. Black-necked Grebe, a scarce visitor, Sept 1995, (Leo Batten)

Plate 8

A. Cormorants resting on rafts, May 1995, (Leo Batten)

B. Shag, an occasional visitor, on jetty, November 1991, (Bob Watts)

C. Whooper Swans, rare visitors, December 1997, (Leo Batten)

1. RED-THROATED DIVER *Gavia stellata*

Very rare straggler in winter. Harting (1866) stated that this species was occasionally seen or shot during the winter. However, since 1950 there have only been three properly documented records:

  1954 One on Nov 7th.
  1986 One from Mar 1st-2nd.
  1991 One briefly on the morning of Dec 9th was flushed by sailing boats.

The last two birds both arrived following snowstorms in the London area.

2. BLACK-THROATED DIVER *Gavia arctica*

Very rare straggler in winter. There have been just three winter records of this diver, the rarest of the three species in London.

  1843 One young male shot 'in the winter'.
  1893 One immature shot on Jan 15th.
  1962 One on Jan 21st.

The 1843 bird was the only one recorded in Middlesex by Harting (1866) so is presumably a county first. The record from 1962 was not submitted to the LNHS for adjudication but is considered acceptable and so included here.

3. GREAT NORTHERN DIVER *Gavia immer*

Very rare straggler in winter. Four records exist, three of which surprisingly occurred in consecutive years from 1949 to 1951.

  1875 One shot (exact date not recorded).
  1949 An immature from Nov 26th to the year's end.
  1950 The same immature until Jan 3rd, and another on Feb 5th.
  1951 One on Nov 22nd.

The long stay of the 1949-50 bird is unusual for any diver at the reservoir, especially in view of the disturbance by boats, although Great Northern Divers do over-winter in London most years.

4. LITTLE GREBE *Tachybaptus ruficollis*

Breeding resident. Harting (1866) knew this species as an occasional breeder which was more numerous in spring and autumn, when there was apparently a migration in the county, but he does not specifically mention its status at Brent Reservoir. Subsequently it used to be more common during the autumn passage period at the site, as reflected in the highest ever count of 121 on October 11th 1953. These high autumn congregations no longer occur and the highest number recorded in recent years was 42 on September 12th 1999, when there was a very large weed growth that attracted many wildfowl.

Year	1991	1992	1993	1994	1995	1996	1997	1998	1999	2000
Max, mth	21 Feb	14. Jan	9 Sep	33 Dec	18 Sep	22 Dec	16 Sep	17 Oct	42 Sep	41 Sep
Bred	6	7	2	2	2	3	4	4	4	3

From 1920 until 1945, between four to six pairs bred. In 1957 and 1958 three pairs bred, but then only one pair bred irregularly up to 1971. Breeding numbers gradually increased to a peak of 16 pairs in 1977. In the past ten years the species has fluctuated at between two and 7 pairs. It is possible that the low breeding number in recent years is due to fluctuating water level, as with Great Crested Grebes.

5. GREAT CRESTED GREBE *Podiceps cristatus*
Common breeding resident. This species was rare in the 19th century with few records, all of which concerned immatures or non-breeding adults. First recorded nesting in the 1920s, it continued to do so in small numbers until 1962. There then followed a gap until 1969, but the species has bred every year since (see the bar graph below). The presence of nationally important numbers is a relatively recent phenomenon and the reservoir's SSSI designation is partly in recognition of this. Indeed, the reservoir has in the past been second only to Rutland Water, Leicestershire, in hosting the highest nesting counts, but is significantly higher in actual breeding density. The number of pairs peaked at about 50 in 1991 but with poor breeding success. Heavy rain in spring in 1991 and 1992 caused the population to crash when many nests were flooded out. In 1992, for example, only five young were raised. In 1993 numbers were even lower with only 31 birds seen on June 12th and only two broods raised in the whole year. Many birds appeared to have moved elsewhere – for example a record five pairs bred on nearby Hampstead Heath. Numbers are gradually recovering but still remain low, and just five broods were seen in 1995. The majority of birds leave in the autumn with only a few overwintering, although even these depart during severe weather if the reservoir begins to ice over. The graph below shows the number of breeding pairs since 1969:

Great Crested Grebe: Breeding Pairs 1969-2000

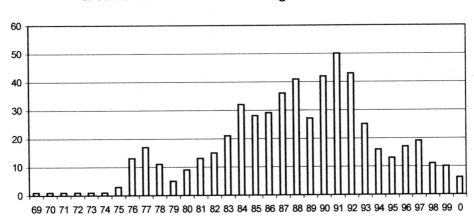

6. RED-NECKED GREBE *Podiceps grisegena*

Rare visitor, mainly in winter. Unknown at Brent Reservoir prior to 1939, there have since been up to four birds per decade. This species is becoming more regular in the London area – for example there were 29 records in 1996 alone – and this is reflected in the recent increase in Brent occurrences. The 15 records probably involve a total of 14 birds:

1939	Two on Mar 18th.
1940	One on Dec 27th.
1953	One on Feb 3rd.
1955	One from Dec 25-26th.
1962	An immature on Feb 28th.
1968	Singles on Jan 16th, 19th and 22nd probably refer to the same individual.
1979	One from Feb 6th-24th, with a second present between Feb 19th-24th.
1983	One in summer plumage on May 23rd.
1991	One on Nov 16th.
1995	One on Mar 11th.
1997	One on Dec 19th.
1998	A juvenile from Aug 28th-Sept 3rd.
2000	First summer bird from Sept 2nd-Sept 7th.

The 1998 and 2000 records, both immatures in early autumn, are noteworthy for southern England.

7. SLAVONIAN GREBE *Podiceps auritus*

Rare visitor, mainly in winter. This species was unknown in Middlesex in the 19th century and was first recorded at Staines Reservoirs in 1924. The history of occurrences at Brent is not dissimilar to that of Red-necked Grebe, with some 15 records (probably involving 16 birds) after the first in 1947. All fall between September and March:

1947	One on Sept 11th.
1950	One on Nov 30th.
1954	One from Feb 27th-Mar 30th.
1958	One on Mar 14th.
1968	One on Dec 12th.
1970	Two from Nov 7-8th.
1979	Singles from Feb 3rd-28th and on Dec 17th.
1985	One from Dec 4th-7th.
1991	One on Jan 19th.
1995	Singles on Jan 8th and Dec 8th.
1996	One from Feb 1st-4th and again on 10th.
1997	One on Dec 19th.

The records from 1996 were part of a record influx into the London area involving 58 birds.

8. BLACK-NECKED GREBE *Podiceps nigricollis*
Irregular visitor, mainly in autumn and spring. 19th century records of this species at Brent Reservoir consist only of two shot in 1841 and another in 1843. In contrast it was virtually annual between 1949 and 1960, when it was mainly recorded in autumn, with one or two reported on 20 occasions. Most birds have remained for only one day, although longer stays are not unknown. Annual occurrences from1995-1998 seemed to indicate a comeback, but there have been no records in 1999 and 2000. All records since 1960 are listed:

1960	One on Aug 12th.
1964	Two on Aug 10th.
1965	One on Nov 3rd.
1969	One on Jan 24th.
1972	One on May 7th.
1973	One on Apr 14th.
1977	Three in summer plumage on May 2nd.
1984	One on Sept 13th.
1990	Two in summer plumage on June 10th.
1995	One from Sept 15th-Oct 8th, with two on Sept 30th.
1996	Two in summer plumage on Apr 29th.

1997   Two on Aug 5th.
1998   Three on May 10th, a juvenile from Aug 14th-Sept 9th joined by
       another on Sept 5th. Further juveniles on Sept 19th and Nov 22nd.

Black-necked Grebes

Black-necked Grebe - Monthly Distribution

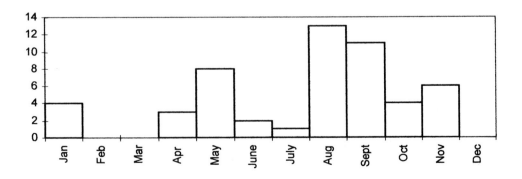

The two in 1990 were presumed to be the pair that arrived the next day at Hilfield Park Reservoir and then remained to breed there. The pair in 1996 were observed displaying, raising hopes that they might one year stay to breed at Brent as well.

[STORM-PETREL *Hydrobatidae sp.*
An individual seen flying over the Field Studies Centre on October 23rd 1966 was not specifically identified but considered by the observer likely to have been a European Storm-petrel. This is supported by the fact that a positively identified individual of this species was seen six miles or so away on the same date in the Lea Valley.]

9. LEACH'S STORM-PETREL *Oceanodroma leucorhoa*
Very rare straggler in autumn and winter. This oceanic species is only likely to occur inland when forced inshore by severe winds and other adverse weather conditions at sea. All five records, each involving short-staying singletons, are given:

    1952   One on Nov 3rd.
    1976   One on Oct 15th.
    1979   One on Dec 15th.
    1989   One on Dec 23rd.
    1998   One on Jan 2nd.

The individuals in 1952 and 1989 both coincided with inland 'wrecks' of the species, while the 1979 record also occurred during strong gale force winds in the South-East of the country.

10. CORMORANT *Phalacrocorax carbo*
Common winter visitor; increasingly reported in summer. The first record for Middlesex was of one shot at Brent Reservoir on Sept 3rd 1887. The species remained almost unknown at the reservoir until the 1930s, but then reports gradually became more frequent, reflecting the general increase in the London area and elsewhere which continues today. The highest recorded count is of 43 on December 29th and 30th 1988. Birds have only recently started occurring during the summer months, coinciding with the rapidly expanding breeding colony at Walthamstow Reservoirs to the east. During the early part of the year 'white-headed' birds are often seen at Brent Reservoir and elsewhere, including in the Walthamstow colony, and it seems likely that at least some, perhaps most, of these birds are of the continental *sinensis* race, which is now known to nest inland in Britain.

11. SHAG *Phalacrocorax aristotelis*

Irregular visitor, recorded almost annually in winter in recent years. First recorded in 1960, there has now been a minimum of 23 individuals. It is interesting to note that birds have been recorded almost annually since 1988, reflecting the increase in records in the London area. The species' status has now changed to the point where it is almost expected to make an appearance every winter. All records are given:

1960	Singles on Jan 24th and Feb 21st.
1961	Two on May 18th, three on Dec 22nd and one on Dec 27th.
1962	An immature found dead on Apr 5th, and four on May 16th.
1972	One on Dec 9th.
1988	One from Sept 11th-17th.
1989	One on Dec 25th.
1990	One from Dec 14-29th.
1991	An immature from Nov 9th-Dec 8th.
1993	An immature from Jan 30th-Feb 3rd.
1994	Records of adults on May 9th,16th,18th and June 8th may all refer to the same individual.
1995	One on Feb 3rd.
1996	One flew over on Nov 2nd.
1997	Two on Jan 26th.

12. BITTERN *Botaurus stellaris*

Very rare winter visitor. At least five birds are believed to have occurred this century, more than 100 years after Bond (1843) documented the collecting of the first at Brent Reservoir. As elsewhere in lowland England, most of the recent records are thought to involve wintering Bitterns from the Continent. It is likely that the increased sightings since 1980 reflect the habitat management work that has increased the size of the reedbed in the Eastern Marsh. All records are given:

1843   One collected prior to this date (Bond 1843).
1959   One on Aug 5th.
1980   One on Dec 26th.
1981   Singles on Jan 12th and Dec 30th.
1982   One on Jan 9th.
1986   One from Jan 31st-Mar 14th.
1987   Singles on Jan 31st and Feb 7th.
1988   Singles on Nov 27th and Dec 15th.
1995   One on Dec 27th.
1996   One on Dec 31st.
1997   One from Jan 1st-Feb 15th.

The August 1959 record is unusually early, but one was also seen on August 1st 1963 just 1km south of the reservoir flying over the Ox and Gate Inn. The winter records between 1980-82 and 1986-88 probably relating to single returning individuals.

13. LITTLE BITTERN   *Ixobrychus minutus*
Vagrant. This species' national status as a rarity is reflected well in the London area, which can claim only 11 records this century (including one just 2kms away at West Heath, Hampstead, on June 18th 1995). There is just one historical record at Brent Reservoir.

1843   A male shot prior to this date (Bond 1843).

14. NIGHT HERON   *Nycticorax nycticorax*
Vagrant. There are four occurrences which relate to this rare heron at Brent Reservoir, though only one has been accepted by the BBRC. The three dated records are all in spring, which is fairly typical for this species.

1843   One prior to this date (Bond 1843).
1951   A heron, believed to have been of this species, on Apr 25th.
1994   A first-summer bird on May 19th.

1996   A bird showing elements of juvenile and first-summer plumage briefly in flight on Apr 5th.

The 1951 bird was not accepted as a confirmed record, with the London Bird Report for that year stating that 'this bird, seen in the late afternoon, was in an unusual plumage phase. From the notes received there seems little doubt of the species, with which the observer is familiar abroad, but as the species was only seen in poor light and not in flight, square brackets are used in agreement with the observer'. The 1994 individual, which was accepted by the BBRC and was the 8th for the London area, was seen by six observers between 19.30-21.30. It originally appeared on the island opposite the small hide (now the wader bank) and preened for about half an hour before it was harassed by crows; it flew off towards the north bank but returned around dusk. About 11 individuals were noted around the country in spring that year. The 1996 individual was seen only briefly, but by two observers very familiar with the species.

15. SQUACCO HERON *Ardeola ralloides*
Vagrant. There are two historical records of this species, the rarest European heron to occur in Britain.

1840   One shot (Harting 1866).
1840-1866   One recorded, date(s) unspecified, during this period (Harting 1866).

This heron was recorded several times in the London area in the 19th century, but just twice since 1900.

16. LITTLE EGRET *Egretta garzetta*
Very rare visitor. A very recent addition to the reservoir's list, this species was long expected as it has undergone a remarkable change in status in Britain. It only ceased to be an official rarity in 1991, by which time records had increased to just over 100 per year nationally. Six years later, however, and some individual roost counts alone were already exceeding 200. The species has also bred in southern England since 1996 and occurs inland in ever-increasing numbers. Of 26 previous records in the London area to the end of 1996, one on July 25th that year was seen flying north-west over Hampstead Heath (3kms away) in the direction of the reservoir, but was not relocated despite searching.

1998   One on Feb 17th spent most of the day feeding and roosting in the Eastern Marsh.

In addition, there is also an unsubstantiated record of one flying over the reservoir recording area on March 29th 1997.

17. GREAT WHITE EGRET   *Egretta alba*
Vagrant. The first (and only) record for the reservoir was also the first for the London area. Records of this species nationally have risen in recent years, reflecting the increasing population in the Low Countries.

>   1997   One on May 13th.

This bird was first seen from the hide when it flew out of a creek in the main reed-bed at 16.30. It flew around the reservoir and landed briefly before flying off towards the Northern Marsh. Despite much searching it was not relocated until it was seen flying over the Eastern Marsh again at 18.05, and it was then positively identified as a Great White Egret. It flew off east and was not seen again. The record has been accepted by the BBRC.

18. GREY HERON   *Ardea cinerea*
Common visitor throughout the year. Grey Herons are present in small numbers throughout the year at Brent Reservoir. There has been one attempt at breeding when a pair built a nest behind the dam in the early 1950s, but the eggs were taken. The nearest breeding site is Regent's Park, where there were 25 pairs nesting in 1998. Another large colony exists at Walthamstow with 126 nesting pairs in 1998, most birds at Brent are likely to be from either of these two sites. Only small numbers were seen in the 1960s and 70s; it was not until the 1980s that counts exceeded 20 for the first time, probably due to the increasing breeding numbers in London. Yearly maximum counts have been between 16 and 26 until 1997 when 28 were recorded in August. This was probably due to the water level which had been kept low during spring and summer due to emergency work further down river. More recently the peak has been from 10-13.

19. PURPLE HERON   *Ardea purpurea*
Very rare visitor. There have been two records of this very rare heron, which was removed from the list of official rarities in 1982 but which remains a very irregular visitor to Britain. Most occur in well-vegetated freshwater habitats in spring and autumn.

>   1972   One on Sept 12th.
>   1999   A sub-adult seen intermittently from May 30th to June 3rd.

The 1972 bird, one of three in London that autumn, was flushed from the edge of reed-grass bordering the Northern Marsh and the allotments. The 1999 individual chose the Eastern Marsh as its preferred site, but frequently remained out of view during its five day stay.

20. WHITE STORK *Ciconia ciconia*
Vagrant. Small numbers of White Storks are recorded in Britain each year, generally in spring and autumn when occasional continental birds turn up on migration. In the London Area the species is an extremely rare visitor, with most of the 13 records to the end of 1997 relating to fly-over migrants in the peak spring period. The Brent record accords well with the regional and national pattern:

> 1999   One flew over on May 3rd.

A previous record at the reservoir, of two birds in 1990, is thought to have involved escapes from captivity (see Escapes page 165 for details).

21. SPOONBILL *Platalea leucorodia*
Very rare visitor. There have been three records of this fine heron, the first of which was the only Middlesex record of this species in the 19th century.

> 1865   Two shot on Oct 23rd.
> 1993   An adult flew east at 19.30 on May 25th.
> 1997   An adult flew over on July 8th at 10.00.

The two in 1865 were dissected and found to be first-year male and female birds. The 1993 record was only the 20th for the London area this century, and may have been the same as the one seen at Cliffe, Kent, on May 26-27th and Pegwell Bay, also Kent, on May 28th (Evans 1997).

22. MUTE SWAN *Cygnus olor*
Common resident. This species was rare in the 19th century when it occurred during hard weather; three were shot in January 1867 and another met the same fate in 1888. Since about 1940 birds have attempted to breed in most years. A decrease was noted from the mid-1960s when peak counts ranged from 2-11 but numbers recovered when fishing with lead weights was banned in the 1980s. There had never been more than one pair attempting to breed until 1998, when there were two pairs and three pairs in 1999 and 2000. The number of birds outside the breeding season increased dramatically in the

early 1990s and now usually peaks around November. The highest count so far has been 49 birds on November 30th 1997.

Recent breeding records and highest counts are shown below:

Year	1991	1992	1993	1994	1995	1996	1997	1998	1999	2000
Max, mth	14 Jun	21 Oct	23 Aug	40 Nov	38 Nov	35 Nov	49 Nov	15 Oct	46 Oct	36 Aug
Bred	None	1pr, 2j	1pr, 6j	1pr, 2j	1pr, 2j	1pr, 2j	1pr, 0j	2pr, 4j	3pr, 5j	3pr, 5j

A male with the 'Darvic' ring code TPT was originally ringed on the River Thames at Hampton, Middlesex, on May 25th 1990 as a second-year bird. This individual bred from 1993 until 1997.

23. BEWICK'S SWAN *Cygnus columbianus*
Rare and irregular winter visitor. Recorded 10 times at the reservoir with a total of 45 birds seen. The majority of records fell in the 20-year period from 1947-66, with a 30-year gap before the next sighting. This is surprising given that this species is now annual in the London area, although three records in the last two years suggests that they may possibly have passed through unobserved.

> 1947   Two on Dec 20th.
> 1955   An immature on Mar 18th.
> 1956   An immature from Feb 25th-Apr 30th.
> 1962   A flock of 19 on Jan 5th.
> 1963   Four from Dec 20th-22nd.
> 1965   Seven on Jan 20th.
> 1966   An immature on Jan 16th.
> 1996   Five (three adults and two immatures) on Dec 6th, and two on Dec 31st which probably roosted overnight.
> 1997   Two flew off N at dawn on Jan 1st, and three adults all day on Oct 22nd.

The sight of 19 standing on the ice in 1962 must have been wonderful for the lucky observers, earlier on the same day a flock of 54 Pink-footed Geese had flown south-east. Additionally, six unidentified swans seen flying over on December 27th 1970 were also believed to be this species.

24. WHOOPER SWAN *Cygnus cygnus*
Rare and irregular winter visitor. Slightly rarer than Bewick's Swan, with nine records involving 31 birds, all of which are listed below:

1843   Included on F. Bond's 1843 list of birds occurring at the reservoir.

1846   A flock of five during the winter, one wounded by F. Bond and captured.

1871   Three seen on Jan 28th.

1955   A flock of 10 on an unknown date.

1956   Two on Feb 27th, one on Mar 6th and two immatures on Nov 27th.

1965   One on Nov 7th.

1990   Two on Nov 4th.

1997   Three adults on Dec 12th, and five adults for one hour on Dec 29th.

The two birds in February 1956 arrived just two days after an immature Bewick's Swan, during a particularly cold winter which brought an influx of both wild swans to the London area. The flock of 10 in 1955 was not reported to the LNHS. This species is recorded much less frequently in London than Bewick's Swan, so it is surprising that the records of both species at Brent are so similar.

25. PINK-FOOTED GOOSE   *Anser brachyrhynchus*

Extremely rare straggler. This species rarely occurs in south-east England in a wild state, despite the fact that many thousands winter on the north-west Norfolk coast. It is therefore perhaps unsurprising that there has been just one record at Brent Reservoir.

1962   A flock of 54 flew south-east at 08.25 on Jan 5th.

This record, which is typical of those for the London area, certainly involves wild birds, but escaped or feral individuals have also been seen (see Escapes page 166).

26. WHITE-FRONTED GOOSE   *Anser albifrons*

Rare and irregular winter visitor. White-fronted Goose is the most regularly occurring wild grey goose in London and the South-East, although it is by no means numerous in the region. There are five acceptable records for the reservoir, all in the first part of the year and three of them involving flocks flying over in January.

1957   23 flew north-west on Jan 13th.

1962   An immature remained for a few hours on Mar 5th.

1966   A large flock was heard calling after dark on Jan 17th.

1969   A flock of 45-50 flew east, calling, after dark on Jan 8th. The skein could be seen as it passed white clouds.

1996   Two flew low over the Eastern Marsh at 07.25 on Apr 1st.
2000   A flock of 110 flew through on Jan 16th.

These records are not a clear indicator of the number of times that this species must have passed over undetected on its way to and from its wintering grounds. The 1957 flock was also seen flying west over Ruislip. The two in 1996 also flew over Hampstead Heath and were aged as an adult and an immature (HHOR, 1997). A flock of 35 grey geese reported flying north-west on December 30th 1968 probably also referred to this species. The flock of 110 on January 16th 2000 is the largest known flock seen at the reservoir.

27. GREYLAG GOOSE   *Anser anser*
Visitor in small numbers annually. This species was rare in Middlesex in the 19th century, when wild birds were occasionally observed at the reservoir. In the winter of 1860-61, for example, two were shot out of a flock of 30 birds (Harting 1866). Feral birds are now recorded in most years in small numbers mainly in late winter and spring. The majority perhaps originating from the Royal Parks elsewhere in London or from the Lea Valley to the north-east.

28. CANADA GOOSE   *Anser canadiensis*
Common resident. During the 19th century this species was very rare. Five were seen in the winter of 1840, two of which were shot. Numbers have increased dramatically since then, to the point that this introduced species now occurs in large numbers in many parts of London and elsewhere. At Brent Reservoir counts of over 150 birds are now recorded most years, maximum counts are usually in June or July and the highest to date was 238 recorded in July 1999. Canada Geese were recorded nesting for the first time in 1983. Breeding numbers (where known) and peak counts since 1987 are given below:

Year	1991	1992	1993	1994	1995	1996	1997	1998	1999	2000
Max, mth	82 Jun	135 Jul	110 Sept	160 Jun	233 Jun	210 Jun	197 Jun	173 Jul	238 Jul	169 Jul

During the late 1980s between ten and fifteen broods were seen each year but more recently there are some indications that breeding success has diminished in part due to aggression from Common Terns reclaiming the nesting rafts each spring. Canada Geese regularly attempt to nest on the rafts on the main reservoir, but rarely raise more than a few young as the returning Common Terns evict sitting Canada Geese before the eggs have hatched. More recently there have only been 4-6 successful broods per year. This decline coincides with the growth in size of the tern colony.

29. BRENT GOOSE *Branta bernicla*

Rare and irregular winter visitor. The increase in the number of wintering birds within the country is reflected by the recent rise in records at Brent. There have been 11 records involving 124 birds of this mainly coastal species:

1843	One record prior to this date (F. Bond 1843).
1964	Two on Jan 10th.
1979	Four on Feb 19th and one on Oct 27th.
1982	Ten on Nov 2nd and nine on Dec 4th.
1989	One on Nov 17th.
1991	A flock of 22 on Dec 2nd.
1992	13 on Feb 8th.
1993	19 on Feb 13th.
1994	42 flew west on Nov 5th.

The records in four consecutive years in the 1990s are notable; those for 1992 and 1993 both occurred during foggy overnight conditions, with birds leaving soon after the fog had cleared. The 1994 record was part of a notable influx into London involving 171 birds at six sites, all on November 5th.

30. EGYPTIAN GOOSE *Alopochen aegypticus*
Rare but increasing. This introduced species has become well established in East Anglia and parts of south-eastern England in recent times, and seems

likely to become a more frequent visitor to the reservoir. Within the period there are five records involving seven birds:

1888   One shot in Jan.
1984   One on July 7th.
1991   Three on Apr 21st.
1992   One on Jan 22nd.
1994   One flew N on Nov 26th.

The 1888 bird was one of just two records in Middlesex in the 19th century. The next Brent record was almost 100 years later, since when it has become more regular – reflecting both the spread of the East Anglian population and the introduction of a pair in the Lea Valley, where breeding occurs sporadically.

31. SHELDUCK *Tadorna tadorna*

Scarce but increasingly frequent visitor throughout the year. Prior to 1940 this was a very rare bird, with two seen in 1875, one in 1929 and one on Nov 4th 1938. In the 1940s seven records of one or two birds marked a change in status. In the 1950s there were nine records of one or two birds, with a flock of seven on March 30th 1959, and in the 1960s 12 records included flocks of 13 on April 24th 1962, 29 flying north-east on February 27th 1965 and 18 on September 3rd 1969. Observer coverage was less in the 1970s, when only six records of between one and four birds were noted. Since 1983, however, Shelduck have been recorded annually, and all records from that date are shown below in a monthly distribution:

Shelduck - Monthly Distribution

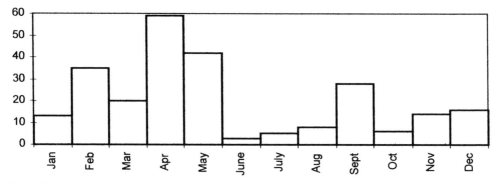

Monthly records are spread throughout the year with a pronounced spring peak in April and May probably relating to prospective breeders looking for suitable sites, a pair on Apr 14th 1999 inspected the artificial nest site on the island in the Eastern Marsh. Records for the past five years are:

1996   Seven records of one-two birds from Jan 26th-May 25th, one on Sept 5th and Dec 22nd.
1997   Nine records of up to five birds between Jan 4th and May 17th followed by two in July, three in Sept and one on Dec 17th.
1998   One on Feb 22nd, Apr 18th and Dec 1st, two on May 2nd.
1999   One on Jan 10-11th, a pair on Apr 14th. One on Apr 25th and two on Oct 20th.
2000   One on Apr 12th, five on Apr 30th and two on May 7th.

32. MANDARIN DUCK *Aix galericulata*

Rare and irregular visitor. There have only been seven records of this introduced species, but it has been seen more regularly in recent years, reflecting the increasing breeding numbers in London (28 pairs or broods in 1997). Nevertheless, it is surprising that Mandarins do not occur more often at Brent, as the species is now recorded annually on Hampstead Heath (HHOR 1997). There are also regular roost counts of up to 60 birds in the autumn at Grovelands Park, Southgate, which is approximately only 7 miles away.

1964   One on Jan 23rd.
1972   A female on Jan 17th.
1989   A male on July 7th, and a female from July 8th-12th.
1990   Four on Dec 27th.
1994   A male on Mar 6th.
1995   A pair on Aug 7th.

In addition to these records, a bird was released at the reservoir on Nov 16th 1993 by the RSPCA after being treated for a broken wing; it was not seen the following day.

33. WIGEON *Anas penelope*

Visitor in small numbers outside the breeding season, usually in autumn. In the 19th century this species was a regular winter visitor with parties of 20-30 birds, and was often recorded as the commonest duck. However, numbers had declined to below five by the 1920s but again increased in the mid 1940s with up to 30 regularly present in winter. This was short-lived however and by the late 1950s numbers had returned to the previous level (<5) with only occasional flocks of larger size. In recent years the bias seems to have changed towards autumn migrants rather than wintering birds; for example, in 1988 numbers rose to a peak for that year of 17 on Sept 15th. In 1989 four were present on Sept 9th, and one from 23rd-24th. By 1997, this level of occurrence had risen to 22 records of up to 13 birds in September and October, with a further seven records for the rest of the year. A typical pattern of records would now involve a small number arriving in late August or early September, growing to perhaps 5-10 individuals, and then dispersing by late October; winter and spring records are more unusual. This follows the pattern shown by other ducks where the large late summer weed growth is an obvious attraction. It is possible that increased sailing activity may be a reason for the lack of the large winter concentrations that once occurred.

34. GADWALL *Anas strepera*

Common winter visitor, now also present in summer and occasionally breeding. This was a rare bird in 19th century London, with one obtained at Brent Reservoir in the winter of 1842-43 being the only Middlesex record (Harting 1866). There were no further records at Brent until a drake on Dec 9th 1933, followed by another single bird in 1944. The species remained scarce until 1960, with birds occurring during the summer of each year. It then became a regular autumn visitor and numbers reached 36 in September 1969. The species is now present throughout the year, with numbers regularly exceeding 100 in the peak season of early winter. A pair attempted to breed in 1957, but the nest and eggs were flooded. In the 1990s Gadwall have stayed throughout the summer months. Breeding was attempted again in 1991 in the Eastern Marsh, but following a rapid increase in water levels it was unsuccessful. In 1993 up to five birds were present during June, and although they showed all the signs of breeding no broods were seen – again probably due to the high increase in water levels. The first successful breeding took place in 1996, when two broods were seen: there were three young in the Eastern Marsh and four young in the Northern Marsh.

Year	1991	1992	1993	1994	1995	1996	1997	1998	1999	2000
Max, mth	44 Nov	40 Nov	64 Dec	64 Oct	143 Dec	94 Oct	111 Nov	115 Oct	180 Oct	306 Oct
Bred	–	–	–	–	–	2br	–	–	1br	3br

The highest ever count recorded at the reservoir is of 306 birds on Oct 22nd 2000. Recent yearly maximum counts show how numbers have continued to increase with birds arriving in August to moult and to feed on the large growths of aquatic weed that have occurred in the past few years, maximum counts are now always in the last three months of the year.

35. TEAL *Anas crecca*

Common visitor outside the summer months; has bred. Historically, this species was an annual visitor in small flocks and mainly in winter. Its status remained largely unchanged, but during the 1950s-70s it was only an autumn visitor with up to 10 birds recorded each year. As with many dabbling ducks, numbers have increased dramatically in the last few decades. Now it is a common autumn and winter visitor, though it remains scarce during the summer months. In 1991 a pair bred for the first time, hatching a brood of eight young on August 10th at the back of the Northern Marsh. This represented the only definite successful breeding record in the London area in that year. A pair also summered in 1992, but no evidence of breeding was observed. In 1993 only a female was seen during the breeding season.

Year	1991	1992	1993	1994	1995	1996	1997	1998	1999	2000
Max,	120	60	76	60	100	66	67	60	140	83
mth	Oct	Nov	Sept	Dec	Dec	Dec	Feb	Nov	Oct	Oct

The recent yearly maximum counts show a consistent 60-80 maximum each year with occasional peaks of up to 140.

36. MALLARD *Anas platyrhynchos*

Common resident and winter visitor. In the 19th century this now-familiar species was mainly a winter visitor, with only a few birds remaining to breed in the summer months. A flock of 12 observed in the autumn of 1892 (Read 1896) gives an indication of its status at the time. It is now a common resident, although numbers vary considerably throughout the year; for example, during the 1995 Wetland Bird Survey there was a minimum of 10 on Feb 19th and a maximum of 79 on Dec 16th. There also seems to be a movement of birds between Brent and the local parks, which may explain the fluctuation in numbers. About 10-15 broods are seen each year at the reservoir. Many of the birds are tame and are fed by visitors. Yearly maximum counts since 1991 are as follows:

Year	1991	1992	1993	1994	1995	1996	1997	1998	1999	2000
Max,	155	100	90	126	79	123	122	136	171	104
mth	Jul	Jun	Aug	Dec	Dec	Aug	Aug	Jul	Jul	Sept

In the past few years Mallards have also taken advantage of the large weed growth at the reservoir each autumn resulting in consistently high maximum counts, the highest counts are usually immediately after the breeding season in late July, August or September. The highest number recorded at the reservoir was 300 on Nov 17th 1984.

37. PINTAIL *Anas acuta*

Scarce and irregular visitor. This species was first noted by Bond (1843) when he included it in his list of the birds of the reservoir. Harting (1866) described it as 'an uncertain visitor'. It remains a scarce and irregular species at Brent, with records having declined in recent years until a slight upsurge in the Nineties. The largest party was of five birds on Dec 20th 1996.

All known records for the 20th century have been included in this monthly distribution:

Mnth	Jan	Feb	Mar	Apr	May	Jun	Jul	Aug	Sep	Oct	Nov	Dec
No.of brds	13	7	3	4	1	5	–	3	7	1	3	9

Birds have been recorded in all months except July with a pronounced peak in the four main winter months of November through to February that is probably due to cold weather movements. 32 birds out of a total of 52 included in the distribution have been seen in these months. There were several summer records between 1989 and 1991 that may possibly relate to escaped birds. Also noteworthy is that none were recorded between 1961 and 1977, a gap of 16 years during a period when the reservoir was being regularly covered by birders. Records for the 1990s are as follows:

1990   Two males and a female on June 8th, a pair on June 23rd, one from June 27th-July 10th.
1991   A male irregularly from June 6th-Sept 7th.
1992   One on Apr 12th.
1996   Two males on Jan 3rd, two females and a male on Mar 2nd, and five on Dec 20th.
1998   One on Oct 4th.
1999   A female on Nov 7th and 14th.
2000   A female on Sept 9th.

38. GARGANEY *Anas querquedula*

Scarce visitor, now recorded almost annually. Now a spring and autumn migrant in small numbers through the London area, it is difficult to conceive that Garganey was not recorded in the capital until 1927 (LNHS 1964) and at the reservoir the first record was not until 1947. Since then it has become almost annual in occurrence at Brent with a total of about 77 birds having been recorded. Numbers are generally low; up to 11 in the autumn of 1959 was an exceptional count as were the five seen during August in 1961 and 1977. A summering male in 1990 went into eclipse plumage and represents the reservoir's only summering record, raising hopes for the possibility of a breeding attempt which so far has not been realised. The over-wintering bird in 1995-96 was very unusual, but not unknown for this species in Britain; more exceptional was the fact that it could be seen alongside both Teal and Blue-winged Teal during its stay.

Mnth	Jan	Feb	Mar	Apr	May	Jun	Jul	Aug	Sep	Oct	Nov	Dec
No.of brds	1	–	–	3	5	1	6	33	23	1	2	1

The monthly totals show a pronounced peak in autumn (August and September) with a much less pronounced secondary peak in spring (April and May), in all records at the reservoir. Records for the past ten years are as follows:

1992 One from Sept 19-20th.
1993 Two males on May 23rd.
1995 A male from May 16-19th, another male on Aug 9th and a juvenile female from Sept 2nd-Dec 31st.
1996 The same bird again on Jan 6th.
1998 A female and an immature bird were present on Aug 19th, single birds were seen on six further dates up to Sept 5th.

39. BLUE-WINGED TEAL *Anas discors*

Vagrant. The first record for Middlesex and the third for the London area was a female discovered at Brent during a large cold-weather influx of Teal in December 1995. It disappeared when the cold spell ended, but was subsequently rediscovered in the small tree-lined pools at the back of the Northern Marsh, where it was often to be found during the remainder of its stay.

1995 A female from Dec 9th-12th, and again from Dec 28th-31st.
1996 The same bird from Jan 6th-30th.

There was an influx of this vagrant North American duck into the country during the autumn of 1995, and it seems likely that it was one of these birds that chose Brent Reservoir at which to spend part of the winter. The other London records were in February 1981, April 1984 and August 1998; nationally, most occurrences are in spring and autumn.

40. SHOVELER   *Anas clypeata*

Common visitor outside the summer months; has bred. This species was a scarce winter visitor in the 19th century, with seldom more than five or six birds at one time; occasionally a pair would remain until spring. Between 1925-30 the only record was of one on Jan 17th 1926 (Harrison 1929). Numbers of this distinctive duck have increased in recent years. As well as being a regular winter visitor, birds now congregate during the autumn with numbers building up in August and peaking in September and October. During this period flocks of over 100 are regularly seen, with the highest count being 241 on October 10th 1999. Breeding was recorded for the first time in 1979 and has occurred sporadically since then with single pairs in 1985, 1988, 1990, 1992, 1999 and 2000. Despite frequent over-summering the species has not become established as a successful annual nester. Annual maximum counts and breeding records for the past ten years are as follows:

Year	1991	1992	1993	1994	1995	1996	1997	1998	1999	2000
Max, mth	134 Aug	70 Sep	89 Sep	85 Sep	130 Oct	109 Sep	93 Sep	185 Oct	241 Oct	184 Sep
Bred	–	1 br.	–	–	–	–	–	–	1 br.	1 br.

The very high maximum counts in recent years correspond to very extensive growths of aquatic weed in late summer and autumn that have the effect of attracting large numbers of dabbling ducks.

41. RED-CRESTED POCHARD   *Netta rufina*

Rare visitor of uncertain origin. The status of this bird, both locally and nationally, is clouded by escapes from captivity and feral birds. However, it seems possible that some records, particularly those in autumn, do relate to occurrences of wild birds. First recorded in 1966, at least 19 birds have been seen:

    1966   Two males and a female on Sept 18th.
    1972   One on Aug 12th, and one on Sept 17th and 19th.
    1973   Present from Oct 14th until the year's end, with a maximum of
           four on Dec 16th.
    1974   A female on unspecified date in Jan.
    1975   A female from Mar 23rd-30th and again on Apr 12th.

1980   A male on May 23rd.
1983   A female on July 20th.
1986   An immature male on Nov 8th.
1990   A female on Nov 11th.
1991   A female from Mar 9th-10th, feeding with Mallards close to
        Cool Oak Lane Bridge.
1995   A male from June 13th-14th.
1995   A male from May 23rd-30th.

The individual in 1991 is probably best treated as an escape due to its very confiding behaviour.

42. POCHARD *Aythya ferina*

Common winter visitor; formerly bred in small numbers. In the 19th century Pochard was described as 'an uncertain visitor' to the Reservoir (Harting), but by the late 1920s it had become a regular winter visitor from late October to March. A peak count of 170 was made on Dec 23rd 1929. At that time numbers in January and February rarely exceeded 50, although 150 were seen on Feb 11th 1926. In March there was a regular passage, with flocks of 150 being frequent although numbers varied daily. Between 1947 and 1950 up to 500 were sometimes present in winter, but since then between 100-250 seem to be the highest flocks recorded, with an exceptional count of 500-600 birds in February 1979 during very cold weather. In winter Pochard seem to be especially prone to disturbance by boating activity, and they are often the first birds to leave as soon as the boats appear; it is thought that they fly to nearby Hilfield Park Reservoir and return again at night. Breeding first took place in 1976, and from 1979 until 1993 one to four pairs were present each summer, with an average of one brood raised each year. No breeding has taken place since 1993 and the numbers wintering have also declined. Annual maximum counts and breeding records since 1991 are given:

Year	1991	1992	1993	1994	1995	1996	1997	1998	1999	2000
Max, mth	100 Nov	157 Sep	61 Jan	40 Feb	118 Sep	75 Dec	112 Dec	134 Nov	58 Jan	17 Oct
Bred	1 br.	1 br.	1 br.	–	–	–	–	–	–	–

The maximum counts have never returned to the higher numbers (100-250) recorded prior to 1980. Breeding appears to have ceased at the reservoir although summering birds are present in small numbers most years.

43. FERRUGINOUS DUCK *Aythya nyroca*

Vagrant. Reflecting its status as a national rarity, this species is a rare visitor to the London area. A bird at Brent Reservoir in 1863 was the only Middlesex record in the 19th century; the next county record came from Staines in 1928, after which the species was considered fairly scarce in London until 1950, when it was increasingly reported. Reflecting its decline within its European range, Ferruginous Duck has become rarer again both locally and nationally since the late 1980s. There are five records from Brent Reservoir:

       1863   A female shot on Dec 24th.
       1960   A male from Sept 8th-11th, and a female on Sept 24th.
       1965   A male on Nov 5th.
       1973   A male on Dec 26th.

Unlike most Ferruginous Ducks recorded in Britain that tend to spend the winter at one site, the birds recorded at Brent have all moved on fairly quickly.

44. TUFTED DUCK *Aythya fuligula*

Common resident. In the 19th century, Harting recorded this species as a regular winter visitor of usually 10-12 birds, with up to 30 during hard weather. It was first recorded breeding in 1967, and now about 10-20 pairs summer each year. As with Pochard, since 1985 the average annual highest count seems to be 150-250 birds, with 261 birds in December 1993. However more recently higher numbers have been recorded and late in 1995, following the draining of the reservoir the previous winter, numbers built up to an exceptional 580 on November 19th, coinciding with high counts of Coot, Teal and Gadwall. Maximum yearly counts and breeding records since 1991 are given:

Year	1991	1992	1993	1994	1995	1996	1997	1998	1999	2000
Max, mth	186 Jan	214 Dec	261 Dec	250 Nov	580 Nov	215 Nov	242 Dec	200 Feb	200 Dec	214 Jan
Bred	3 br.	9 br.	6 br.	8 br.	5 br.	4 br.	4 br.	7 br.	10 br.	6 br.

The maximum count is always obtained in one of the winter months, between November and February.

45. SCAUP *Aythya marila*

Scarce and irregular winter visitor. Harting was only aware of two Middlesex records at the time of writing his book. Glegg writing in 1933 only reported two more 19th century records. In the first half of the 20th century there were only seven more birds recorded. Since then birds have been reported more frequently and in all a total of 71 birds has been recorded, with occurrences in every month except July and the vast majority between November and February. Most records are of one or two birds, but there was a flock of six in January 1996. In 1971 a pair occupied a nesting raft between April 12th and May 17th. The species is now a scarce and irregular winter visitor. All records are listed before 1950 and for the 1990s:

1843   Two prior to this date (Harting 1866).
1867   One on Nov 2nd (Glegg 1933).
1892   One on an unspecified date (Glegg 1933).
1924   One on Dec 2nd (Glegg 1933).
1930   One on Apr 7th (Glegg 1933).
1939   Males on Feb 4th and 12th.
1946   Singles on Jan 9th and 12th, and one on Nov 30th.
1990   One on Oct 21st.
1991   One seen intermittently from Mar 9th to 30th.
1993   Singles from Jan 9th-10th, on Aug 22nd, from Sept 5-6th and on Sept 26th.
1994   One on Feb 16th.
1996   Six on Jan 2nd, with two females staying to Jan 6th, and singles from Jan 27th-Feb 6th, on Mar 9th and 14th.
1997   Two males on June 28th, one from Dec 19th-20th and a different bird from Dec 21st-31st.
1998   An immature female remained from 1997 until Jan 4th, a female seen on Dec 9th.
2000   A female on Nov 4th.

The distribution by month of all birds recorded at the reservoir is as follows:

Scaup - Monthly Distribution

There is a clear peak in the winter months but birds have been recorded in all but one month of the year, December through to February are the best months.

46. EIDER *Somateria mollissima*
Very rare straggler in winter. This is the rarest seaduck in London, with only 40 records up to 1997 (LBR 1997). Most were single birds remaining for one day only, so two birds at Brent for 11 days during the exceptionally cold winter of 1961-62 was noteworthy.

    1961   Two immature males from Dec 17th-27th.

47. LONG-TAILED DUCK *Clangula hyemalis*
Very rare straggler in winter. A scarce visitor to the London reservoirs, with a few seen each winter. The first Middlesex record was not until 1932. There have been just two Brent records.

    1951   A female/juvenile from Nov 18th-Dec 31st.
    1952   The same bird from Jan 1st-Feb 16th.
    1973   One from Dec 9th-29th.

The 1973 bird was present among a gathering of 520 diving duck which included a Ferruginous Duck, a Red-crested Pochard, six Smew and a Goldeneye – an amazing flock for the reservoir!

48. COMMON SCOTER *Melanitta nigra*
Irregular visitor. Although primarily a seaduck, movements of this species over-land are a long-recorded phenomenon. Harting (1866) quotes the local keeper who, in an apparent reference to this species, reported that 'a few black ducks generally made their appearance every winter'. Apart from these unspecified numbers, there have been 21 records involving 39 individuals. All are listed:

    1866   Two shot prior to this date in severe weather.
    1890   One shot in Dec.
    1944   A male on Apr 16th.
    1945   A female on Nov 9th.
    1946   A female on Apr 29th, and three females on Nov 9th.
    1949   A male on Nov 28th.
    1957   Two on July 31st, and one on Sept 6th.
    1958   Three on Apr 6th.

1959   Three on Apr 3rd, a female on Nov 25th.
1962   Two females on Aug 7th.
1963   A male on Jan 10th, and two immature males on Apr 26th.
1966   Two males and a female on Apr 6th.
1973   Four males and two females on Apr 14th.
1979   One male on June 9th.
1991   Two immature males on May 7th.
1995   A female in early Dec.
1998   A male from Apr 4th-8th.

April is clearly the main month for passage, although the species may occur at any time of the year. It is interesting to note that, except for the most recent record, no bird stayed longer than one day. Common Scoter turn up in London regularly, sometimes in small parties, so it is surprising that there are so few records at the reservoir.

49. VELVET SCOTER   *Melanitta fusca*

Very rare straggler. A rare visitor to London, this species was not recorded in Middlesex until 1927. There are just five records involving nine birds at Brent Reservoir:

1947   One in Jan and Feb.
1948   A male and two immature females on Oct 30th, and a male found dead on Nov 27th.
1956   An immature male from Feb 28th-Mar 7th, when it was found dead.
1966   A male and three females on Mar 14th.

The record in 1948 coincided with a major influx of Velvet Scoter in the London area that day. Up to 20 were seen at Staines, along with single birds at Walton and Walthamstow Reservoirs, and five or six Common Scoter were on the Thames (LBR 1948).

50. GOLDENEYE   *Bucephala clangula*

Scarce winter visitor. During the 19th century small parties of 10-12 Goldeneye were not infrequent in winter. Harting wrote that he shot three birds in the winter of 1863-64, and he also observed two very shy drakes on March 25th 1865 which were still present on April 2nd. Today the species is a scarce visitor, with up to three recorded most years, usually between October-February. Goldeneyes prefer to keep out in the open water during the day. All birds since 1980 are included in the monthly distribution:

Mnth	Jan	Feb	Mar	Apr	May	Jun	Jul	Aug	Sep	Oct	Nov	Dec
No.of brds	6	9	3	–	–	–	–	1	–	5	11	11

The table shows the expected winter biased distribution with all records bar one being in the period from October through to March.

51. SMEW *Mergus albellus*

Scarce winter visitor. There were only three records of this species at Brent Reservoir in the 19th century, with one shot prior to 1843, three shot in January 1849 and one shot in the winter of 1860-61, but there were no further records until 1925. In 1942 eight were seen on Mar 19th, but in the following year there was a dramatic increase with 70-80 birds noted on Feb 28th. This was the start of a 40-year period in which Smew wintered annually. Numbers varied considerably (see chart below), but the first flock of over 100 occurred in February 1951 and in 1956 an incredible flock of 144 birds was recorded on Feb 28th – the largest flock ever in the London area, and probably also in Britain. At this time Brent Reservoir was the place to see Smew in Britain, and groups of visiting birdwatchers were almost as common as the large numbers of Smew that they had come to see. Since then numbers have decreased, and although flocks of up to 10 were still common as recently as 1979, it is now scarce at the reservoir. It is not known why Smew has declined so dramatically, but it is probably due to a combination of factors such as increased sailing, milder winters and the increased numbers wintering in the Baltic and the Ijsselmeer in the Netherlands.

All records since 1971 are included in the following table which shows months of occurrence:

Smew - Peak Counts 1041/99

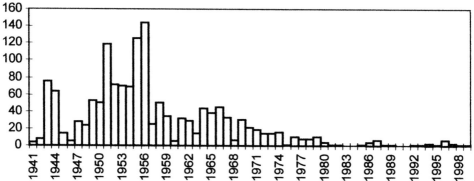

The records for the 90s are as follows:

1992   One from Nov 28-Dec 3rd and again on Dec 10th.
1993   One from Oct 23-24th.
1994   Three from Feb 15-19th.
1995   A male on an unspecified date in Feb.
1996   One from Jan 29th-Mar 10th and one on Dec 21st, rising to six on Dec 31st.
1997   One or two birds present on most dates between Jan 1st and Feb 27th.
1998   A female flew over on Jan 11th.
1999   A female flew north from Eastern Marsh on Nov 21st.
2000   A drake briefly on the main reservoir on Nov 21st.

All birds were recorded between late October and mid-April. The 1993 bird on Oct 23rd is the earliest arrival in the London area.

52. RED-BREASTED MERGANSER *Mergus serrator*
Irregular winter visitor. There are two or three records of birds shot in the winter during the 19th century, then no further records until 1947. This is another seaduck which is regular but scarce in the London area. All 20th century records are listed:

1947   A female on Nov 29th.
1954   One from Jan 31st-Feb 4th.
1956   One on Feb 22nd, four on the 25th and three on the 26th.
1961   A female on Dec 27th.
1963   Two females on Jan 2nd and a male from Mar 16th-Apr 30th.
1968   A female on Mar 14th and 17th.
1970   A female on Apr 6th-7th.
1973   Two on Oct 6th-7th.
1989   A female/immature on Oct 2nd.
1991   A male on Mar 26th.
1995   A pair on Dec 27th.
1996   A female on Mar 31st.
2000   A pair flew in at 08.30 hrs on Apr 2nd.

February 1956 produced a major influx of Red-breasted Mergansers into the London area, with up to 70 birds present in the Lea Valley and 24 at Walton Reservoir.

53. GOOSANDER *Mergus merganser*

Very scarce winter visitor. During the 19th century Goosander appeared to be very rare and there were only two Middlesex records, one of which was a drake shot at the reservoir (Harting 1866). By 1930 the species had become an annual winter resident at Staines Reservoir and other localities (Glegg). Today there are a few reports most years, but numbers are small. In 1962 two flocks totalling 65 birds flew south on December 30th, and 18 were reported flying south on January 5th 1963, but these numbers are exceptional. More recently a flock of seven flying over on Jan 12th 1997 has been the highest. All records for the past ten years are included in this table of winter occurrence:

Mnth	Oct	Nov	Dec	Jan	Feb	Mar
No. birds	1	3	20	30	17	2

There is a clear concentration in the hardest winter months, the only record outside this period is of one seen on June 10th 1997, a very unusual date.

54. RUDDY DUCK *Oxyura jamaicensis*

Common resident. Ruddy Ducks were released from Slimbridge, Gloucestershire, during the 1960s, with the first individual arriving in London in 1965. It then took a further 16 years before birds were recorded at Brent Reservoir, when a male was seen on September 9th 1981. In 1983 two males were present from April 22nd-23rd, then later that year a female was seen on September 3rd. Numbers continued to increase and in 1987 nesting was recorded for the first time. Since then breeding has taken place each year, with a maximum of six broods totalling 36 young noted in 1994. Ruddy Ducks have a late breeding season at Brent, with broods often seen in September and October, exceptionally, in 1992 a duckling only a few weeks old was recorded on November 18th. Maximum counts are invariably in the autumn and to date the highest count has been of 62 birds in October 2000. Birds are usually absent in winter, with most departing in November and returning in February, with a notable passage in April.

55. HONEY BUZZARD *Pernis apivorus*

Very rare visitor. This species is a rare summer visitor and passage migrant to Britain, and although it has increased in numbers in recent years its occurrences in the London area remain very infrequent. There are six records at the reservoir:

1994	One circled overhead and then drifted low to the north on July 31st at 10.50 hrs.
1995	One flew south-east on Aug 12th at 09.50 hrs.
2000	One flew south-west on Sept 23rd, three individuals flew south-west in the morning and early afternoon of Sept 24th.

Birders on Hampstead Heath were alerted by mobile phone about the 1995 bird as soon as it flew over Brent, and they were able to watch it drift past the Heath at some range and continue over central London. The 1994 and 1995 records were only the 25th and 26th in the London area. Considering the relative scarcity of the species the occurrence of records in consecutive years was remarkable, although 1995 was a record year for this species in London with four other birds also seen. However four birds seen on 23rd and 24th September that were part of a massive influx of Honey Buzzards into the UK in late September 2000 eclipsed these earlier records. Many hundreds of birds were seen throughout the country, from Shetland to Scilly.

56. RED KITE *Milvus milvus*

Very rare visitor. Although this species bred in London several centuries ago, in recent times the indigenous population has declined dramatically and during the 20th century became confined to central Wales. However, a reintroduction programme saw birds released at several sites in England and Scotland during the 1990s, and the species is now breeding successfully in the wild again in these parts of the UK. In addition, there is a very small but discernible passage of continental birds in Britain, mainly in early spring and in eastern counties. There are four records of this fine raptor at the reservoir.

    1850 One on Apr 3rd.
    1995 One flew north at 09.10 hrs on Feb 26th.
    1996 One flew over on an unspecified date in Aug.
    1999 One flew south on May 17th.
    2000 One seen flying north on Apr 23rd.

The first recorded sighting was in 1850 and was seen by Frederick Bond when it flew within 20 yards of him. He also saw another bird in 1855 in the parish of Kingsbury, about a mile north-west of the reservoir. The 1995 bird coincided with a small influx on the east coast of England, and it is presumed to be of continental origin. The individual in 1996 was seen flying over the observer's garden in the north-eastern part of our area; although no wing-tags were observed, the time of year suggests it probably came from the southernmost reintroduced population, just 30 miles to the west of London. It seems likely there will be more Red Kites at Brent following the breeding successes of this scheme, as records are now increasing in the London area.

57. MARSH HARRIER *Circus aeruginous*

Very rare visitor. During the years 1900-60 there were just four records of Marsh Harriers in the London area, so the absence of the species at the reservoir during this time is unsurprising. Subsequently the species has increased in numbers, and sightings in London now reflect the general rise in the numbers breeding in England. There have been five records, four of which were in the 1990s:

    1964 One on Apr 26th.
    1994 A male flew south-east on Apr 30th at 07.45 hrs.
    1995 An immature flew north on Aug 5th at 10.35 hrs.
    1997 A male passed through on May 11th at 12.40 hrs.
    1998 A female flew east on May 2nd.

The 1964 bird was not accepted by the LNHS and although birds were very rare nationally at the time a reliable observer saw it. Spring 1994 produced many records in London, and a total of 20 birds were recorded in the London area that year and in 1995. There is another unconfirmed report at the reservoir, from Sept 10th 1978, of a Buzzard-sized raptor with long narrow wings being mobbed by crows; it was considered by the observer to be probably of this species.

58. HEN HARRIER *Circus cyaneus*

Very rare visitor. This was a very rare species in Middlesex in the 19th century, with only one other record in the county in addition to the reservoir's first occurrence. It was observed more frequently in London in the 20th century, with most records from the marshes adjoining the Lower Thames. However in the 1990s it ceased over-wintering there and has once again become a very rare visitor to the London area (for example, there were just two records in 1995).

1869   One on Jan 12th.
1996   One flew over high heading south-west at 15.00 hrs on Dec 22nd.
1999   A ring-tail flew low over the reed-bed in the Northern Marsh on Nov 25th.

The 1996 record was accepted by the LNHS only as a harrier species, although the observer believed it to be a Hen Harrier.

59. GOSHAWK *Accipiter gentilis*

Very rare visitor. Goshawks have been increasing in Britain, especially in the 1990s, and are colonising new areas so it is perhaps not unsurprising that this raptor has now been added to the Brent list. There is one recent report of this species at the reservoir:

1997   A male circled over the Northern Marsh before flying north-west at 07.00 hrs on Mar 23rd.

This is the 15th record for the London Area. A full account and description appears on page 181.

60. SPARROWHAWK *Accipiter nisus*

Common resident. This species was a scarce breeder until the beginning of the 1900s. Glegg (1930) recorded that it was 'a decreased species' in Middlesex. Following the Second World War, it became a very rare bird throughout eastern Britain and was only recorded occasionally at the reservoir between 1940-80; in 1962, for example, it was only seen twice (January 8th and July 22nd) and in 1983 there was only one record (September 27th). This was part of the nation-wide decline in populations of birds of prey due to the use of organo-chloride pesticides and their adverse impact on breeding. Following the banning of these chemicals and the species' increase throughout the country during the last decade, birds are now resident. Having returned to Brent in the late 1980s, Sparrowhawks were proved to breed again in 1990. They were able to recolonise the area successfully and now up to three pairs breed each year.

61. COMMON BUZZARD *Buteo buteo*
Scarce visitor. Until recently this species was regarded as a bird of northern and western Britain, but Buzzards have spread successfully into parts of south-eastern England and now breed in very small numbers on the fringe of the London Area. However, most birds occurring in the capital are thought to be passage migrants. There have been 16 records at Brent Reservoir, of which just three were in the spring; all the others occurred between July and November. The species is now recorded almost annually at Brent. All records are given:

1929	One on Apr 18th.
1931	One on May 19th.
1949	One on Sept 21st.
1952	One on Aug 4th.
1953	One on Aug 3rd.
1956	One in Sept (undated).
1958	Two on Sept 15th.
1965	One on Sept 2nd.
1991	One on Sept 10th flew south in the evening.
1993	One on Nov 15th flew north-east at 10.40 hrs.
1994	One on Oct 23rd flew south at 09.40 hrs.
1995	One on Sept 18th flew south over Cool Oak Lane at 11.15 hrs.
1996	One on July 16th flew west at 12.30 hrs.
1997	One heard on July 20th at 13.00 hrs over North Bank.
1999	Singles on June 1st and Sept 26th.

The 1993 record was not submitted to the LNHS.

62. OSPREY *Pandion haliaetus*
Rare visitor. The Scottish breeding population continues to increase, and consequently more passage birds are seen in London. There have been eight records of this raptor at the reservoir, five of which were in the last five years.

At the time of the 1961 bird this species was not even recorded annually in London, whereas in 1996 there was a total of 16 records for the LNHS recording area. All Brent occurrences are listed below:

1961 One on Nov 9th.
1982 One on Mar 28th.
1994 One flew north on May 1st at 19.30 hrs.
1996 One on May 5th at 06.15 hrs.
1997 One on Apr 12th flew north at 09.00, one flew south-west on Aug 23rd at 07.20 hrs.
1998 One flew west on Sept 4th at 17.00 hrs.
2000 One seen on Apr 24th.

The 1961 bird was watched fishing amongst 65 sailing boats, but was perhaps more notable for the particularly late date. The 1982 individual was the second earliest spring date for the London area. The 1994 record was not submitted to the LNHS. On September 25th 2000 an Osprey was seen soaring over Wembley Stadium which is only a mile from the south-west end of the reservoir.

63. KESTREL *Falco tinnunculus*
Common resident. This species was noted as breeding at Brent by Read (1896) and has always been the most common raptor at the reservoir. Harting (1866) referred to this species being particularly common in the autumn and partially migratory. It bred occasionally between 1925 and 1945 and then bred more regularly with up to three pairs most years, although in a few years it did not even hold territory. Today two or three pairs breed each year around the reservoir, mainly taking Short-tailed Voles that abound in rough grassland in the area. On November 9th 1957 a Kestrel was seen to swoop down to the water and catch a small fish in its bill (Batten 1959).

64. MERLIN *Falco columbarius*
Rare visitor. The Merlin remains as it was in Harting's day – a rare winter visitor to the London area. By the time his book was published in 1866 he was only aware of two records in the area, neither of which was at the reservoir. Since then more records have come to light, but there are still only six records at

Brent, including two seen by Power in the 1860s. The 1997 record was the first for over 35 years. All records are listed:

1864   One on an unspecified date.
1866   One on an unspecified date.
1932   A male on Feb 23rd.
1958   One on Apr 4th.
1961   One on Dec 17th.
1997   One seen flying over rooftops on Jan 5th then flew north-east over the Dam at 07.50 hrs.
2000   One seen over the Eastern Marsh on Jan 1st.

65. HOBBY *Falco subuteo*

Increasingly regular summer visitor. At one time this species was a very rare visitor, and the only published Brent record in the 19th century was on April 24th 1863, involving a bird shot by Bond (Harting 1866). Prior to 1935 it was recorded in Middlesex only 15 times in the period since the reservoir was built (Glegg 1935). This level of occurrence only slightly increased in the middle of the last century, and between 1950 and 1970 just six were recorded at the reservoir. As recently as the late 1980s birds were still only being recorded in the area once or twice a year as passage migrants. A dramatic increase took place in the Nineties, and in 1991 and 1992 birds began nesting less than five miles away and have since used the reservoir regularly as a hunting ground during the spring, summer and early autumn. This is part of a national increase in the population. In the very recent past birds have taken to staying at the reservoir during September to feed on dragonflies. There is usually a large hatch of Migrant Hawker *Aeshna mixta* at the reservoir in late August /September each year. In September 2000 up to three birds were present at this time. Now the first bird is usually seen before the end of April, and three individuals have been recorded on the same day on several occasions. Hobby was also recorded nearby by Eric Simms from his home on Dollis Hill in both 1958 and 1973. All 20th century occurrences are detailed or summarised below:

1949   One on Apr 25th.
1952   A pair on May 1st.
1959   Singles on Aug 4th and Sept 20th.
1960   One on June 26th.
1964   One on Apr 24th.
1987   One in July.
1988   One took a House Martin on an unspecified date in Sept.
1990   Several records July 6-10th.

Year	1991	1992	1993	1994	1995	1996	1997	1998	1999	2000
Recs.	5	18	21	17	17	6	13	9	14	20

66. PEREGRINE *Falco peregrinus*

Scarce visitor. Harting (1866) stated that Peregrine was 'formerly not uncommon in winter and early spring, when gunners were not so numerous'. By 1896 when Read wrote The Birds of the Lower Brent Valley it was far more scarce in the area, and he only makes mention of a pair shot in Harrow in 1888 and of a bird seen in 1893 in Hillingdon. Writing in 1935, Glegg described Peregrine as an occasional winter visitor with a total of 20 Middlesex records. In comparison and more recently, at the Brent Reservoir there have been 13 records involving 14 birds, representing something of an increase. Apart from the most recent records, all other reservoir records fall between 1951 and 1970, which is surprising as the species had declined dramatically nationally at this time due to insecticide poisoning. Eric Simms recorded the species on several occasions in the 1950s, 1960s and 1970s at nearby Dollis Hill. Reservoir records since 1950 are listed below:

1951   One on Jan 20th.
1954   Two flew north-west on Mar 20th.
1958   A male flew south-east on Jan 7th.
1961   One south-east Jan 29th, further singles on July 25th, Aug 9th and Sept 24th.
1962   One on Jan 26th.
1963   One on Apr 20th.
1965   One circled over the reservoir on Oct 9th and drifted south-west.
1970   One on Nov 22nd.
1995   A male on Oct 28th.
1997   A male on 11 occasions between May 17th and July 19th, another on Oct 21st.
1998   A male on four occasions between Mar 8th and May 10th, a female on Apr 4th.
2000   One seen Apr 5th.

The summer bird of 1961 is not included in the London Bird Report of that year as it was presumed to relate to an escape from captivity. The 1995 record coincides with the residency of a pair of birds during autumn 1995 on Bankside Power Station in Southwark, central London, and the general increase in sightings that resulted throughout north London. In the past two winters there have been several suspicious raptor kills of Woodpigeons and Black-headed Gulls found on the ground in open areas, possibly suggesting more frequent visits. In summer 1997 the male which was present for nine weeks was believed to be roosting on Wembley Stadium; on four occasions it was seen stooping on or chasing flocks of pigeons.

67. RED-LEGGED PARTRIDGE *Alectoris rufa*

Rare visitor. Having been first introduced into this country in Suffolk in 1770, it was not until 1865 that the first Middlesex records were reported. Harting regarded its occurrence in Middlesex as accidental and due to stragglers from Hertfordshire. In 1935 Glegg described the species as 'an unusual resident in suitable localities; it is scarce compared to the "Common" Partridge'. He detailed a small number of late 19th century records involving birds either breeding or collected nearby, including Hampstead (July 1871), Mill Hill (October 1889) and Willesden (Apr 1891). At Brent Reservoir it remains rare, with only five 20th century records involving six birds, and curiously all in spring:

```
1944    One on May 7th.
1946    Two on May 14th.
1960    One on Apr 10th.
1976    One on May 20th.
1985    One on Apr 6th.
```

In recent years the nearest regularly recorded birds have been on farmland in Enfield, Middlesex, and at Tyttenhanger, Hertfordshire.

68. GREY PARTRIDGE *Perdix perdix*

Former breeder, now rare visitor. Harting and Glegg noted that Grey Partridge was still relatively common where suitable habitat existed, especially in the north of the county. The species was still killed in numbers by shoots on large estates just prior to the publication of Glegg's book in 1935: at East Lodge Estate (500 acres), 165 were killed in 1929-30, 310 in 1930-31 and 278 in 1931-32, although these were likely to have been bred in captivity. Birds bred at the reservoir until 1961 and were still occasionally seen during the breeding season until 1963. A major reason for this species' decline locally was probably loss of habitat. This was mainly due to the conversion of allotments to playing fields and the loss of un-mown grassland to a rubbish tip. However, the decline also reflected the national situation. All records after 1963 are listed:

```
1967    One on Apr 12th.
1970    One on Mar 1st.
1974    One from July 14-Aug 24th.
1975    One on Feb 7th.
1977    One on Apr 23rd.
```

1984   One on Feb 18th.
1993   One on Apr 10th.
1995   One on May 8th.

As with Red-legged Partridge, the nearest regularly breeding birds are at Tyttenhanger, Hertfordshire.

69. QUAIL   *Coturnix coturnix*
Very rare visitor. Harting (1866) described this species as being 'of rare occurrence', and to Glegg some 70 years later it was a 'rare straggler to the county', although it had occurred more frequently in the past and had bred on several occasions in the north of Middlesex. This status remains unchanged today, and only one historic record exists from the area:

1882   One heard near Kingsbury in May.

In addition, a bird was present and calling from uncultivated fields at nearby Barn Hill on June 5-6th 1983. In the same year there was an unconfirmed report of a Quail at the reservoir in early September which was mentioned in the LNHS bulletin.

70. PHEASANT   *Phasianus colchicus*
Rare visitor. In the middle of the 19th century in Middlesex this species was described as 'nowhere plentiful, even where strictly preserved', with 'a few stragglers occasionally found in thick hedgerows and bean-fields' (Harting 1866). Pheasants have always been scarce at the reservoir but today they are very rare, although the species has bred recently as close as Hampstead Heath. All known 20th century records are listed:

1968   One on Apr 6th.
1970   A male held territory near the reservoir.
1972   A male was present for a week in mid-May.
1990   A male from Mar 6th was present until the end of the month.
1991   A male on Apr 13th.
1993   A male on several occasions during Apr.
1995   A female on July 14th and a male on Sept 14th.

71. WATER RAIL   *Rallus aquaticus*
Winter visitor and passage migrant. As it was in Harting's day, the Water Rail remains a passage migrant and winter visitor, with little evidence of breeding

activity. The only local breeding record dates back to before 1866, when Harting reported that Frederick Bond's dog caught several young birds at a small pond near Kingsbury. In the winter there are often 10 or more birds present, mainly in the wet areas around the Northern and Eastern Marshes, but also in rank waterside vegetation all around the reservoir. It is probably more common than in the past due to an increase in the area of undisturbed marshland, and is regularly heard but less frequently seen between September and April. In 1994 an early returning bird was recorded on August 23rd, and late birds have been recorded in May. Some recent large counts include:

     1987   Nine on Jan 17th.
     1989   Nine on Nov 5th.
     1994   10 on Dec 17th.
     1995   Eight on Jan 10th.
     1999   A total of 13 counted with the aid of a tape lure on Dec 28th.
     2000   A total of 22 counted with the aid of a tape lure on Jan 16th.

Previously larger counts were made in very cold weather when the birds were forced out to feed along the edge of the frozen marsh. The January 1995 count relates to the draining of the reservoir during that month, when eight rails were in view simultaneously in front of the main reed-bed. These counts clearly underestimate the number of birds present and a clearer picture is obtained with the assistance of a tape recording.

72. SPOTTED CRAKE   *Porzana porzana*

Extremely rare visitor. The first record at Brent Reservoir comes from Bond's list of 1843 published in The Zoologist, while Harting (1866) mentioned a second caught by a retriever some years prior to 1857. Glegg (1935) added no further records, so there were no more documented records for over 100 years. However, regular walks through the reedbeds in the period 1957-59 produced one record in each year! All records are listed:

     1843   One obtained prior to this date.
     1850s One caught in the early part of the decade at Hyde Bridge.
     1957   One on Sept 4th.
     1958   One on Sept 20th.
     1959   One on Aug 23rd.
     1972   One on Aug 15th.
     1975   One on Nov 8th.

Spotted Crakes are secretive birds. The reedbeds can now be viewed in part from the hides, so apart from winter working parties this prime habitat is now left largely undisturbed: this may explain the lack of records since 1975. The 1957 and 1958 records were not accepted by the LNHS. The 1975 record was reported by a visiting evening class, and involved a bird seen swimming in open water several yards from the bank of the Eastern Marsh!

73. CORNCRAKE *Crex crex*

Bred in 19th century; no recent records. At the time of Harting's 1866 publication the Corncrake was a regular breeding bird in Middlesex, described as a 'common summer visitant'. The number of birds present at the reservoir was clearly variable, Harting reporting that it was 'by no means numerous at Kingsbury in 1861, yet in 1862 it appeared in great numbers and [I] could have had any amount of birds and eggs'. Glegg (1935) commented that a decline was already being reported by 1877 throughout the county, and this continued until the early part of the present century when breeding ceased in the area. Harrison, writing in the London Naturalist for 1930, reported the last local breeding in Mill Hill in 1928. Now, as with most parts of the British Isles, Corncrakes are unknown in the area.

74. MOORHEN *Gallinula chloropus*

Common resident. This species is a familiar bird at the reservoir, although it is often under-recorded. There has been no apparent change in status since Harting's day, when he described the bagging of three or four brace during an autumn Moorhen hunt! Glegg wrote in 1935 of a count of at least 40 birds at the reservoir on November 13th 1932 made by L Parmenter. Data from the two marshland census areas show that between 30-40 pairs breed each year. Highest recent counts include, 56 on 16th November 1996, 70 on November 16th 1997, 148 on December 28th 1999 and 84 on November 19th 2000. The highest counts are usually obtained when either the margins are frozen or the water level is low.

75. COOT *Fulica atra*

Common resident. Harting (1866) wrote that 'the greatest number of Coots reckoned in one "cover" was forty-one'. Glegg (1935) believed that (for Middlesex) 'as a result of the creation of the large reservoirs it is probably a much increased species during the winter'. Today it is the most common water-fowl species at the reservoir, with a breeding population usually numbering between 50-70 pairs. Data from the two marshland census areas in the late 1980s and early 1990s showed that between 42-63 pairs bred there each year, with others elsewhere on the reservoir. There are regular autumn and winter peak counts of over 500 birds. The largest counts to date are of 644 on November 12th 1995, 703 on November 17th 1996, 700 on Oct 19th 1997, 924 on Oct 10th 1999 and 873 on October 22nd 2000.

76. OYSTERCATCHER *Haemotopus ostralegus*

Scarce passage and winter visitor. There were four records at the reservoir in the 19th century, the first being a mention in Bond's list of 1843 which was the first record for the county. By 1935, when Glegg's book was published, Oystercatcher was still a fairly rare bird in Middlesex and he reported only 11 records in total from the whole of the county. These days Oystercatcher is regularly seen away from the Thames, and there have been 18 records at the reservoir since 1947. All records are listed prior to 1950:

      1843   One prior to June.
      1859   One shot in July.
      1866   Three on Apr 12th.
      1886   One shot on an unspecified date during the year.
      1947   Singles on Apr 30th and Aug 3rd.

Since the 1950s annual occurrence per decade has been as follows:

Decade	1950s	1960s	1970s	1980s	1990s
Years	4	6	2	4	3

Monthly occurrence for all records is as follows:

Oystercatcher - Monthly Distribution

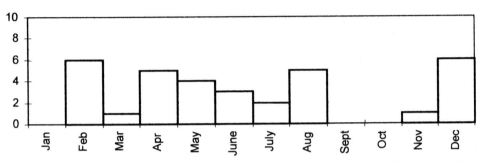

Oystercatcher is a scarce visitor with records in eight months of the year, but with the majority (over 60 per cent) in the period April-August and the remainder in the winter period December-February. The first group clearly are passage birds while the second group relate to winter cold weather movements.

77. BLACK-WINGED STILT *Himantopus himantopus*
Vagrant. Black-winged Stilt is an annual vagrant to Britain and a major rarity in London. The first record for the city was in 1918, of two birds seen at close range on the muddy foreshore of the reservoir, referred to by J C M Nichols in his book Shooting Ways and Shooting Days (1941). The reservoir was empty at that time except for the main channel, and had attracted many waders.

1918   Two on an unspecified date in Sept.

This remains the only record for Brent Reservoir, and there have been just four further records in London since then.

78. AVOCET *Recurvirostra avosetta*
Very rare straggler; no recent records. Today a relatively familiar British bird, the Avocet has undergone a remarkable change in fortunes over the years. Formerly it was known only as a scarce migrant in East Anglia and the South-East and was rare almost everywhere else, with the first breeding for almost a century taking place as recently as 1941. The population has grown rapidly in

size and Avocets have since spread out widely from their Suffolk base, with nesting even taking place in London in 1996. It is therefore all the more surprising that the only two Brent records date back to the 19th century, when the species was at a particularly low ebb:

1854   One in May.
1897   Two shot on Aug 30th.

Neither of these records features in The Birds of the London Area (1964) which details five occurrences between 1909 and 1954. Nowadays, with the huge increase in the UK breeding and wintering population, Avocets occur annually in London in small numbers.

79. STONE CURLEW   *Burhinus oedicnemus*

Very rare straggler. This species is a rare migrant throughout the London area and has only been recorded on one occasion at Brent Reservoir. Glegg reported just seven reliable records for the whole county of Middlesex by 1935 and the LNHS (1964) mentioned a total of only 17 for the London Area in the 20th century. Of these, 12 were in spring, one in July and four in autumn. The species is possibly under-recorded due to its nocturnal habits, although in the past experienced birders in the London Area have identified night migrants by call on eight occasions during March and April (LNHS 1964).

1969   One on Apr 15th, flushed from the north bank.

This is a typical date for a spring migrant of this species, which is still of less than annual occurrence in the London area. This record was not accepted by the LNHS, although it was seen by an observer familiar with the species.

80. LITTLE RINGED PLOVER   *Charadrius dubius*

Passage migrant. Three were shot or seen at the Welsh Harp in the 1860s when this species was a very rare migrant in Britain. These three birds constituted the only London records until 1944, when the species bred at Ashford, Middlesex, and occurred again at the Brent. This followed the first British breeding pair at Tring, Hertfordshire, in 1938. The species has since successfully colonised southern England and elsewhere and is more widespread on migration; at Brent Reservoir since 1991 it has been an annual visitor. The increase in records mirrors the expansion of sympathetically landscaped disused gravel workings in the Lea and Colne Valleys, and the numbers of breeding birds now established in those areas. All records up to 1991 are listed:

1864   An immature shot on Aug 20th, and another shot on Aug 30th.
1865   One seen on Apr 29th.
1944   One on Aug 3rd and 6th.
1945   One on Aug 19th and 23rd-27th.
1955   Juveniles on Aug 21st and Sept 4th.
1960   Singles on May 6th, Apr 26th and 30th, and Sept 9th.
1972   One on June 22nd.
1974   One on June 2nd, and a nest found on 30th; birds still present in July.
1984   Singles on July 25th and 28-29th, Aug 17th, 20th and 22-23rd, and Sept 8th.
1988   Up to three birds from June 5th-July 15th, including two mating on June 18th.
1989   One on Apr 15th and 23rd, and two-three between May 9th July 12th probably bred nearby.

The following table shows the monthly distribution of all records since 1991:

Mnth	Mar	Apr	May	Jun	Jul	Aug
No. birds	2	13	19	7	6	2

The nest found in 1974 is the only proof that Little Ringed Plovers have bred at the reservoir. It contained two eggs but no young were seen. In 1988 mating was observed and in 1989 a pair found suitable habitat very close to the North Circular flyover. In that year, and also in 1993, mating and displaying were observed, but again no young were seen. Predation from crows was probably to blame but the site is also subject to disturbance. The normal arrival period is late April/early May, with two early dates of March 28th.

81. RINGED PLOVER *Charadrius hiaticula*

Occasional passage migrant. This species was listed by Bond (1843) as occurring at Brent Reservoir, and Harting (1866) reported that flocks of between six and 20 were frequent on migration. In the period 1837-1866 small groups of birds were recorded nearly every year, mostly during the spring and autumn passage. Today the species retains its status as an occasional passage migrant, although there has been some evidence of a reduction in passage numbers since Harting's day and Ringed Plovers are not recorded annually. However, when water levels are low, especially in the autumn, there can still be a number of birds present. Records for this century are summarised up to 1989 and all listed subsequently:

1935-39 Present from Aug 19th-Sept 5th 1937, max. six. Five on Mar 12th 1938 and one on Apr 10th 1938.

1940-44 Nine records of 11 birds, max. four on May 2nd 1944.

1945-49 A maximum of five between Aug 19th-Sept 1st 1945, a total of 18 birds.

1950-54 Four records of single birds.

1955-59 16 records of a total of 15 birds, max. five.

1960-64 18 records of a total of 24 birds.

1965-69 Three records of a total of four birds.

1970-74 Two records of a total of two birds.

1975-79 Two records of a total of two birds.

1980-84 Four records of a total of four birds apart from 1984 when reservoir was drained and there were up to seven birds on many dates in Aug and Sept.

1985-89 Two records of one bird.

1993 One on May 12th.

1996 Singles on Mar 30th and Aug 3rd.

1997 One on ice on Jan 5th, one in the Northern Marsh on May 11th and one flew over on Sept 9th.

1998 One on Mar 8th.

The series of records in August-September 1984 relate to a period when the reservoir's water capacity was reduced by 50% for repair work on the dam wall, and many waders were present. The graph below shows a clear autumn passage peak in the second half of August and early September, with a smaller spring peak in early May.

Ringed Plover - Half-monthly Distribtion

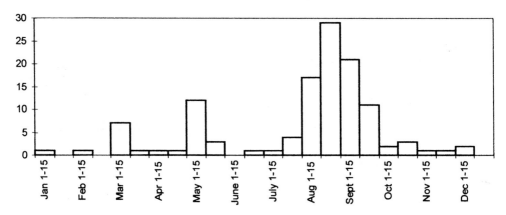

82. GOLDEN PLOVER *Pluvialis apricaria*

Irregular visitor. Harting (1866) reported that Golden Plover was a regular visitor in the late autumn, peaking at the end of November with flocks, sometimes in hundreds, on 'fallows between Kingsbury and Stanmore'. By the time of Harrison (1930) and Glegg (1935), increasing urbanisation had driven it to the outer fringes of London and the species had become an irregular winter visitor. More recently birds are occasionally seen flying over, usually in association with large cold-weather movements of Lapwings. All published records are listed:

1843   Listed by Bond (number not specified).
1929   A juvenile on Aug 18th.
1961   Two on Nov 18th.
1962   One on Mar 12th and two flew north on Aug 15th.
1967   Six flew west on Jan 8th.
1971   One on Oct 9th.
1991   Eight flew south-west on Dec 16th.
1993   Flocks of 26 and 12 individuals flew over on Feb 7th, and a singleton on Mar 16th.
1996   A flock of 14 flew over on Dec 28th at 09.30 hrs.
1997   A flock of 20 flew in from the south then headed north-west on Nov 30th at 11.30 hrs.
2000   One flew south-west on Dec 25th.

Additionally, a flock of 360 flew over Hampstead Heath in the direction of Brent Reservoir on December 26th 1995, a day of considerable Lapwing passage.

83. GREY PLOVER *Pluvialis squatarola*

Irregular visitor. This species is a passage migrant in variable numbers and a scarce winter visitor in the London Area (LBR 1997). No records at all were given by Harting (1866) for Brent Reservoir, and Glegg (1935) mentioned only six satisfactory records for the county of Middlesex, including one of six birds at Staines in 1922. There were over 40 London Area records from 1930-61 (LNHS 1964), and in recent times that number of passage records can occur in London annually, with a small wintering flock of variable size regularly present on the

Lower Thames. The first authenticated Brent record was in 1946 and there have been 10 records since, over half of which have occurred since 1993:

1946	One on Apr 19th.
1950	Singles on Sept 5th and 23rd.
1954	One on Jan 31st.
1961	One on Aug 5th.
1993	One on May 8th flew low over the main reservoir.
1994	One on May 3rd and another on May 10th.
1995	One Dec 6th.
1997	One heard flying over on Jan 3rd.
1998	One on May 30th.
2000	One flew over calling at 06.25 hrs on Apr 29th, another was seen on Dec 23rd.

84. DOTTEREL *Charadrius morinellus*

Very rare straggler; no recent records. This scarce British breeding wader remains one of the rarest to occur in London, with very irregular reports of individuals and small 'trips' occurring on passage. At Brent Reservoir there has been just one record, with another nearby, and both were prior to 1900. In Glegg (1935) these two records still constituted the only occurrences for Middlesex. In total there have been seven records in London in the 20th century, the most recent being of an exceptional flock of 16 birds at London Colney on May 7th 1994.

> 1856   One shot at Fox Mead Farm, Kingsbury, in Sept.

Additionally, one was shot from a small 'trip' in April 1858 at Burnt Oak Farm, Kingsbury, just outside the reservoir recording area.

85. LAPWING *Vanellus vanellus*

Passage migrant and winter visitor; formerly bred. In Harting's time this species was fairly common, breeding where suitable habitat was available. He stated that 'at one time these birds used to breed in a large rushy field near Kingsbury Reservoir, but, finding their nests continually plundered … [they] moved to a less frequented spot about two miles distant'. Clearly, by the time Harting's book was published in 1866, this was already an infrequent breeder at the reservoir because of disturbance and egg-taking. Breeding continued intermittently until the start of the present century. These days birds are seen in small numbers mainly on spring and autumn passage and also during winter cold-weather movements, when they may sometimes occur in large numbers.

A notable winter record was the presence of over 1,000 birds for a few days during the severe weather of February 1956. The majority of birds are recorded between October-March, although as elsewhere in London a small post-breeding dispersal is noted in June and July each year. Recent high counts include:

1972	400 over on Jan 30th.
1984	500 south-west in two hours on Jan 23rd.
1991	200 south-west on Dec 16th.
1993	233 west on Jan 3rd.
1995	161 on Dec 6th.
1997	143 flew over in various directions on Nov 30th.

86. SANDERLING   *Calidris alba*

Irregular passage migrant. In the London Area Sanderling is a double passage migrant in small numbers, an apparent improvement on its former status when it occurred less frequently due to the smaller number of wetland sites. Glegg reported a total of only seven reliable Middlesex records by 1935. It is a very rare bird at the reservoir, with only 15 records in total and none at all between 1973 and 1998. Only two have occurred in spring and one in winter, the rest being in autumn. All records are listed:

1844	One shot prior to this year.
1856	Two shot on an unknown date around this time.
1928	One on Sept 12th.
1946	One on Apr 29th.
1949	Singles on Sept 25th and Oct 9th.
1950	One on Sept 22nd.
1957	One on July 31st.
1958	One on Oct 23rd.
1959	Singles on Sept 6th and 14-17th.
1961	One on May 6th and five on 21st.
1973	One on Jan 7th.
1998	One on May 25th.

87. LITTLE STINT   *Calidris minuta*

Irregular passage migrant. At one time this species was a regular visitor to the reservoir in both spring and autumn. There were at least 17 records involving 34 individuals up to the end of the 19th century, but surprisingly there were only four 20th century records until 1996, when two or three individuals were seen during a major influx into the UK. All records are given:

1843   One shot prior to this date.
1844   One shot in spring 1844.
1862   Five shot in Aug.
1863   Two seen in May, one shot out of two on Oct 29th.
1864   Four shot in autumn.
1865   One shot out of four on June 10th.
1867   Two shot out of three on Sept 4th.
1868   One shot on June 11th.
1870   Singles shot on May 20th and Aug 13th.
1871   Two shot on June 12th, one shot on Aug 7th and another shot out of two on Sept 16th.
1881   Three on Sept 3rd.
1897   One on Sept 4th.
1929   One from Sept 27th-Oct 2nd.
1945   One on Sept 16th.
1951   One on Sept 9th.
1955   One in Sept.
1996   Two on Sept 15th, one remaining until 17th, and another or one of the same from Sept 21st-24th.

All London records prior to 1900 were from the Brent Reservoir. Of these 32 19th century individuals, 22 were shot! Some of the skins are still retained in the British Museum collection.

88. TEMMINCK'S STINT   *Calidris temminckii*

Very rare straggler; no recent records. Glegg (1935) described Temminck's Stint as 'a rare visitor during the spring and autumn migrations'. Prior to this time, there were eight reliable county records, all from the reservoir. In the 19th century this species was seen or shot at Brent Reservoir on nine occasions (including the unsubstantiated 1863 record), in parties of up to five or more birds in autumn and one or two in spring. Since then there were a further five London Area records elsewhere prior to 1957 (LNHS 1964), after which the species appeared with a little more regularity. Autumn records predominate at the reservoir, with a Brent total of at least 14 in autumn compared to three in spring. The last bird recorded at the Brent occurred almost 130 years ago. All records are listed:

1839   One of two shot in spring, and five shot and a few other juveniles seen in autumn.
1859   One killed in May.
1861   One shot on Aug 31st.

1863   Several reported on Aug 4th, included but their identity was
        not confirmed by Harting (1866).
1866   Four shot on Sept 15th.
1869   One shot on Sept 4th.
1871   Two on Oct 4th.
1872   One shot on Aug 29th.

Temminck's Stints visiting the reservoir in the 19th century met a similar fate to Little Stints, and from nine records a total of up to 15 individuals were shot, several of them now residing in the British Museum collections.

89. KNOT *Calidris canutus*

Rare visitor, mainly in autumn. The only records of this species at the reservoir in the 19th century involved the 'summer birds' detailed by Bond (1843), and a small winter flock on February 23rd 1870. Knot is still a very scarce, largely autumn passage migrant and winter visitor in very small numbers; seven out of the 12 records have occurred in September. There have been no records since the reservoir was last drained in 1984. All records are listed:

1844   Unspecified number of 'summer birds' on June 11th.
1870   A small flock on Feb 23rd.
1949   Singles on Sept 25th and Oct 19th.
1960   Singles on Mar 25th and Sept 21st.
1964   Two on Jan 15th.
1957   One on Sept 2nd.
1979   One on Feb 18th.
1982   One on Sept 4th and 10th.
1984   Singles on Sept 8th and 28th.

This pattern of occurrence is similar to that for London as a whole, where Knot are recorded annually in small numbers on passage and in slightly higher numbers in winter.

90. PECTORAL SANDPIPER *Calidris melanotos*

Vagrant. According to Glegg (1935), Harting had been informed in March 1891 by a J H Gurney that 'he had seen a Pectoral Sandpiper, sold with the Rev H T Frere's Norfolk birds, the case bearing the inscription... "shot by Mr Goodhall at Kingston Reser-

voir near Kilbourn" in 1846'. Glegg clearly believed this to be a misspelling and had published the details, but in square brackets.

1846   One shot on an unspecified date.

There have been 55 records of this wader in the London area this century up to 1999, more than the total for all waders of Nearctic origin combined.

91. WHITE-RUMPED SANDPIPER *Calidris fuscicollis*
Vagrant. The details of this record were given by Harting (1866) and Glegg (1935), the latter of whom wrote that 'H E Dresser had in his collection a mounted specimen, stated on the label at the back of the case to have been shot at Kingsbury Reservoir by Mr Goodair'. This bird was said by Harting to be the fifth British record at the time: he only obtained details in December 1865, just prior to publication, and these were included in a special appendix.

1856   One shot on an unspecified date.

There has been only one further record in the London Area, at Perry Oaks, Middlesex, in 1984.

92. CURLEW SANDPIPER *Calidris ferruginea*
Rare passage migrant. This species is an annual autumn passage migrant in London, though somewhat scarcer in the spring. At the reservoir Curlew Sandpipers are rare visitors on passage, with just seven records in the 19th century and eight in the 20th century. All are given here:

1844   Two on Sept 2nd.
late 1840s One shot on an unspecified date.
1864   One on Sept 17th.
1865   Two on Sept 2nd.
1870   Singles on Aug 27th and Sept 10th.
1871   One shot in May.
1873   One on Sept 11th.
1928   Two from Sept 12-17th.
1945   One on Aug 24th.
1959   Two on July 27th and six on Aug 31st.
1960   A flock of 36 on Sept 28th.
1961   Two on May 6th and one on Sept 4th.
1981   One on Oct 4th.

The exceptional record of 36 birds in 1960 remains the largest flock ever recorded in the London Area. In seasonal terms the Brent pattern follows that for London, with 11 of the 15 records being in late August and September.

93. DUNLIN *Calidris alpina*
Passage migrant and winter visitor. Harting described it as 'a regular passage visitant' and today it is still an annual passage migrant in both autumn and spring and also a winter visitor, albeit scarce in all seasons. In a London context The Birds of the London Area (1964) describes Dunlin as 'probably the commonest and most widespread of all shore birds which visit the Area'. Records from 1955-2000 are summarised:

1956-60	16 seen.
1961-65	30 seen.
1966-70	15 seen.
1971-75	Nine seen.
1976-80	12 seen.
1981-85	15+ seen (many dates in '84).
1986-90	Five seen.
1991-95	20 seen.
1996-2000	21 seen.

At least 29 of the records since 1980 have been in autumn, with seven in spring and 13 in winter. When water levels are low and there are large mud-banks exposed during autumn passage, such as in 1984, then Dunlin are often present.

94. RUFF *Philomacus pugnax*
Rare passage migrant, mainly in autumn. In the 19th century Harting (1866) described the Ruff as 'an uncertain visitant appearing occasionally during the vernal and autumn migrations in May and August'. He added that since the construction of the reservoir about a dozen examples had been killed there. In London the species is a double passage migrant and a winter visitor. All records are listed:

1843	Included in Bond's list for this year or earlier.
1845	Two males in breeding plumage shot on an unspecified date.
1864	One shot from a party of three on Aug 25th.
1866	One shot from a party of five on May 21st, and another shot on Sept 13th.
1871	One shot on Sept 16th.
1937	One from Sept 29th-Oct 29th.

1944   A female on Sept 12th.
1945   A female on Aug 12th and further singles on Sept 17th and 21st.
1949   Two on Sept 4th.
1953   One on Sept 12th and 19th.
1959   Singles on Feb 14th and Aug 25th, and two on Sept 5th.
1961   Singles on Feb 19th, Mar 18th and Mar 30th.
1963   One on Sept 9th.
1964   One on Aug 9th.
1966   One on Aug 23rd.
1984   One from Aug 11-31st.
1991   One flew from the Dam on Sept 28th.
1997   Seven flew north on Apr 11th.
1998   One on Sept 13th.
1999   One on Aug 13th.

As with most waders, August and September are the best months for encountering this species, and there are 18 autumn records for the reservoir compared to five in spring and two in February. The largest number recorded was the flock of seven on April 11th 1997.

95. JACK SNIPE *Lymnocryptes minimus*

Very scarce but near-annual visitor, mainly between November-March. This species was a regularly recorded winter visitor in Harting's day, arriving in October and occasionally remaining as late as April. The Birds of the London Area (1964) described Jack Snipe as a winter visitor to sewage farms, reservoirs and marshy ground from mid-October to late March, adding that 'numbers are usually small but frequently increase in severe weather'. At Brent Reservoir nowadays one or two birds are recorded almost annually in winter, mostly around the Northern Marsh. All records since 1980 are given below:

1981   One on Feb 14th, four on Dec 19th, two on Dec 24th and five on Dec 27th.
1983   Three on Feb 11th.
1984   Two on Mar 17th and one on Apr 7th.
1985   One on Jan 12th.
1991   Two from Jan 16th-Mar 2nd, with three on Jan 27th and Feb 2nd, and one from Nov 30th to year's end.
1992   One from Jan 18-21st and another on Oct 29th.
1994   Singles on Mar 12th and Nov 26th.
1995   One on Nov 6th.
1996   One on Dec 24th.
1997   One on Mar 15th.

1999   One on Nov 11th.

The highest count is of five flushed along the north bank in very cold weather on December 27th 1981. The latest departing bird was on April 20th 1967 and the earliest arrival was on October 5th 1959.

96. SNIPE   *Gallinago gallinago*

Passage migrant and winter visitor; formerly bred. Harting (1866) reported the Common Snipe as a resident species at the reservoir, but said it was far more frequent as a winter visitor. More recently, the status was similarly described for the London Area (LNHS 1964), with frequent flocks of 100 or more and exceptionally of 400-500 in the right conditions. At Brent it is now a passage migrant and winter visitor, with the earliest returning birds occasionally seen in August and the last departing individuals leaving in April. In winter the highest concentrations seemed to be on the Northern Marsh, although birds could be flushed and seen anywhere in the right habitat along the edges of the reservoir. Yearly maximum counts for the last 10 years are listed below:

    1991   40 on Mar 2nd.
    1992   30 on Mar 7th.
    1993   30 on Dec 11th.
    1994   27 on Oct 9th and Nov 12th.
    1995   24 on Jan 1st.
    1996   12 on Jan 14th and Feb 24th.
    1997   Seven on Jan 5th.
    1998   Two on Jan 10th.
    1999   Two on Jan 16th.
    2000   Three on Dec 29th.

The highest counts have never exceeded 50 birds, a total attained in both 1970 and 1985. Since 1991 the peak winter counts have fallen steadily, even when there have been large expanses of mud exposed. Since 1995 numbers have declined dramatically and it is now a very scarce bird at the reservoir, this mirrors a national decline.

97. GREAT SNIPE   *Gallinago media*

Vagrant. Though never a common migrant in Britain, Great Snipe used to occur much more regularly in the 19th century than it does today. The first mention of the species at Brent came from Bond, who included what was then the second Middlesex record in his list published in 1843. Two more were taken at Brent in the 1850s, but there were no more occurrences at the reservoir by the time that Glegg (1935) documented seven records in total for Middlesex. Subsequently, there were two further records at the reservoir in 1959, probably involving one individual. All records are listed below:

1842   One shot and mentioned subsequently in Bond's 1843 list.
1851   One in Nov, 'killed in Hendon Fields'.
1856   One shot in autumn by William Sawyer, the keeper of the reservoir at the time.
1959   Singles on July 22nd and Aug 8th.

The two most recent records from 1959 were not accepted by the BBRC, although interestingly they occurred in the same autumn as the first non-Middlesex record for the London Area, at Ponders End Sewage Farm, Enfield, in September. This species is still a great regional rarity, with three out of the total of 12 accepted records for the London Area being at the reservoir; the most recent occurrence was at Rye Meads, Hertfordshire, in September 1996.

98. WOODCOCK   *Scolopax rusticola*
Scarce and irregular winter visitor. In the 19th century this species was described by Harting (1866) as 'formerly not uncommon in winter but now scarce'. This status has not changed, and at Brent Reservoir it is now a bird of less than annual occurrence. The majority of records are from the wooded fringes of the reservoir or in the area around the Field Studies Centre. Amazingly at the latter site, a bird was observed roding one evening in June 1979 during a breeding census visit, and it was flushed on another occasion in the same month. One other summer record exists, from July 25th 1949. All records since 1980 are detailed below:

1981   One on Dec 19th.
1982   One on Jan 10th at North Brook.
1985   One on Jan 12th in the Northern Marsh.
1987   Recorded on two dates in Jan.
1989   One on Feb 11th in the Eastern Marsh.
1991   Singles seen on Feb 9th, 10th and 16th in the Eastern Marsh.
1992   One on Jan 28th in the Woodfield Nursery.
1995   One on Dec 30th.
1996   Singles on Mar 17th, Dec 7th and 30th.
1997   Singles on Jan 2nd, Feb 1st and 18th, with two on Jan 5th and 11-12th.
1998   Two on Nov 15th.

99. BLACK-TAILED GODWIT *Limosa limosa*

Rare and irregular passage migrant, mainly in autumn. Both godwit species are annual passage migrants in variable numbers in the London Area, though they are commoner today than they used to be. Glegg described Black-tailed Godwit as very rare, listing only five records for Middlesex up to 1935. By the early 1960s birds were being seen more regularly in London, with Black-tailed Godwit described as scarce and Bar-tailed Godwit as rare (LNHS 1964). More recently there has been a further increase in the number of London birds reported, and in 1994 there was a double-figure flock at partially-drained Staines Reservoirs on 10 dates during the year. At Brent, Black-tailed Godwit has been recorded on only 12 occasions, additionally Eric Simms reported seeing two flying from Dollis Hill towards the reservoir in 1976. All records are listed below:

1843	Listed by Bond as seen prior to 1843, and by Yarrell in the same year as having occurred three times in spring at the reservoir (this total including Bond's record).
1937	One on Sept 18th and 20th.
1959	One on July 22nd.
1964	Eight on Aug 12th.
1983	One flew south-east over Cool Oak Lane Bridge on May 10th.
1985	36 flew north on Apr 29th.
1994	Two flew over on July 28th.
1997	Two juveniles from Sept 13th-Oct 12th.
1999	One on Aug 22nd and four on Sept 8th.

The 1985 record of 36 is the largest flock seen in London away from the River Thames. In the past two years (1999 & 2000) large concentrations have been seen on the Thames Estuary.

100. BAR-TAILED GODWIT *Limosa lapponica*

Very rare straggler, mainly in spring. This species was recorded only seven times in Middlesex prior to Glegg (1935), with six of these being at Brent Reservoir. The pattern of London occurrences is similar to that for Black-tailed Godwit, with an increase in records during the 20th century: there had been 19 records up to 1964 (LNHS 1964). In 1994, the record year for Black-tailed Godwit in London, Bar-tailed Godwit was recorded at least 25 times in the London Area, with a peak of 26 at Staines Reservoirs on May 7th. At Brent Reservoir this species has been recorded 15 times, the largest flock being seven on April 29th 2000. There have only been nine records this century, all records are given:

1843	One prior to this year in Bond's list.
1851	An adult in summer plumage shot in May.
1863	Four on Apr 29th.
1864	Six on Apr 29th.
1866	One in May.
1872	One in May.
1946	Two on Apr 29th and one from May 9-11th.
1952	One on Sept 10th.
1961	One on Sept 17th.
1965	One on May 1st.
1989	One on May 13th.
2000	Flocks of six then seven on Apr 29th, two on May 1st.

Unlike Black-tailed Godwit, this more coastal species tends to occur at the reservoir in spring, when considerable numbers are often recorded moving up the English Channel. The absence of suitable habitat at the Brent at this time of year means that recent records have usually been of birds flying over. However several of the 2000 spring birds stayed a few hours to roost on the rafts.

101. WHIMBREL *Numenius phaeopus*
Very irregular passage migrant. The three 19th century records from Brent Reservoir were also the first Middlesex records. Glegg (1935) reported a further six county records by 1929, and described the species as an irregular double passage migrant. By 1964, there had been about 100 20th century occurrences in the London Area. Records of the species have continued to increase, and in 1994 about 155 birds were reported on spring migration in the capital (LBR 1994). At Brent, however, the species remains a very scarce passage migrant, with a total of only 19 records of 23 birds, and only five years in the last 34 in which the species has been recorded. All records are listed:

1850	One shot in spring.
1859	One shot in autumn.
1866	One shot on May 10th.
1946	One on May 4th.
1948	One on July 16th.
1951	One on Sept 2nd.
1953	One flew over Colindale on Aug 6th.
1961	One flew south on July 25th.
1963	One flew north-east on May 2nd.
1966	One flew S on Aug 28th.
1973	Two on Aug 6th.
1990	Three flew over on May 3rd.

1996   One on May 10th.
1997   One landed on the rafts on May 1st, one flew from in front of
        hide on July 13th, one heard on Sept 12th.
2000   One on May 1st, another on May 2nd and two on May 4th.

There is a significant concentration of records in the first half of May. As with both godwit species, however, the lack of extensive mud in spring means that many records at this time of year relate to birds passing over.

102. CURLEW *Numenius arquata*

Scarce and irregular visitor on passage and in winter. Harting (1866) wrote that 'the Curlew is occasionally observed during the periods of migration in spring and autumn'. Glegg (1935) described more frequent sightings, saying that 'a number of observers have reported flights, sometimes said to be large, during the spring and autumn migrations'. The species was subsequently described as a frequent passage migrant and local winter visitor (LNHS 1964), a status which it more or less maintains in the London Area today. At Brent the Curlew is chiefly a passage migrant, mainly recorded flying over the reservoir, but winter records are not unknown. All occurrences from the late 1950s onwards are given:

1959   Four on July 2nd, three on July 3rd, two on July 30th, six on
        Aug 28th, eight on Aug 31st and singles on Sept 2nd and 5th.
        The majority of these individuals were observed flying over.
1960   Three on Mar 18th, two on July 2nd and 10 on July 30th.
1961   One on May 7th, two on Aug 8th and three on Sept 17th.
1962   Three on July 22nd.
1965   Two on Sept 2nd.
1966   Two on Sept 18th.
1967   One on Apr 16th.
1969   Three on Aug 30th and two on Oct 17th.
1978   Three on Apr 18th.
1979   Five flew south on Aug 21st.
1984   One on July 25th.
1992   One on Feb 27th.
1994   One on July 28th.
1996   One on Jan 3rd, two on Mar 2nd and one on Dec 31st.
1997   One on Jan 1st, four on Mar 8th and three on Apr 27th.
1998   One flew north on June 27th.

103. SPOTTED REDSHANK *Tringa erythropus*

Very rare visitor. In historical times this species was an uncommon passage migrant at the reservoir, being recorded only five or six times in the 40-year period 1841-81. After the last 19th century record there was a gap of 57 years until the next occurrence in 1938, but despite a flurry of records in the mid-1960s there were just two Brent records in the last 32 years of the 20th century. Although numerous at some favoured sites in coastal south-east England, Spotted Redshanks are far less frequent inland, and in the London Area records are often limited to single figures annually – the London Bird Report for 1997, for example, details only four records of six birds, and describes the species as a scarce passage migrant. Brent records broadly reflect those regionally, with the great majority being in autumn. All records are listed:

1841	One in summer plumage shot in June.
1848	One in winter plumage, shot on an unspecified date.
1859	One shot in Aug.
1865	Two shot on May 25th.
1881	One shot in Aug.
1938	Two on Sept 11th.
1959	One on Aug 15th, two on Aug 16th and one on Sept 12th.
1961	Three on Sept 17th.
1963	Two on Aug 7th.
1964	One from Aug 7-21st.
1967	Two on Sept 12th.
1982	One on Sept 21st.
1984	One on Aug 12th, 13th and 17th.

It is interesting to note that all but two records at the reservoir have been in August or September.

104. REDSHANK *Tringa totanus*

Passage migrant and occasional winter visitor. In the mid-19th century this was an irregular species on passage at the reservoir, and was described by Harting (1866) as 'appearing occasionally at the periodical migrations in spring and autumn'. By the time of Glegg (1935) Redshank had increased in frequency of records, but although it was reported as sometimes breeding in Middlesex, including the Brent Valley, it was stated that 'it is at no time numerous'. There are no breeding records at the reservoir in modern times, and indeed occurrences have decreased in recent years. It is still recorded annually, usually involving single birds at passage times, and occasionally in winter. Recently late May and June have been the favoured months. All records from the mid-1950s are summarised and all records for the past ten years are given:

1956-60	30 seen.
1961-65	13 seen.
1966-70	Six seen.
1971-75	Five seen.
1976-80	Two seen.
1981-85	11 seen.
1986-90	Seven seen.
1991	Two on May 30th and one on June 28th.
1992	Singles on May 19th and June 20th.
1993	Two on June 1st.
1994	One found dead on Apr 10th, and singles on Aug 2nd and Aug 13th.
1995	Singles on July 1st and 31st.
1996	One on Mar 27th, two on June 5th, and singles on June 20th, Aug 15th and from Dec 27th into 1997.
1997	Four flew north-west on Jan 1st, three or four on June 22nd, two from Jan 1st until March 9th, two also on June 8th, July 8th and July 21st and, one was heard on July 2nd, another seen July 19th.
1998	Singles on Mar 29th and May 24th, with three on July 2nd and two on Aug 29th.
1999	Singles on Mar 17th, May 31st and Aug 31st.
2000	One on Apr 22nd, May 14th, July 7th and Sept 2nd.

The graph overleaf shows a clear autumn passage peak of Redshanks in July, with a less distinct spring maximum in March. There is also evidence of a small mid-winter movement, probably due to hard weather. The three month gap in the autumn is surprising and reasons for it are not clear.

Redshank: Monthly Occurrence

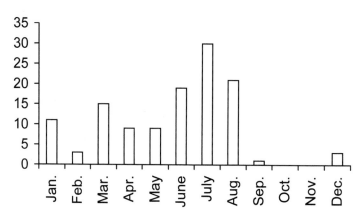

105. GREENSHANK *Tringa nebularia*

Scarce passage migrant. Harting (1866) described Greenshank as 'a rare and uncertain visitant in spring and autumn', and only detailed four Brent records. Glegg (1935) reported it as very scarce on spring passage and less than annual in autumn. The species is now a regular but scarce passage migrant at the reservoir, and since 1988 – partly through increased observer coverage – it is now known to be annual. While most records have been of single birds flying through or alighting only briefly, a few have lingered, especially when the reservoir was drained (for example in 1984), and there are several records of small flocks. Records since the mid-1950s are summarised and all records for the past ten years are given:

1956-60	Ten seen.
1961-65	21 seen.
1966-70	30 seen.
1971-75	Two seen.
1976-80	Four seen.
1981-85	At least 20 seen.
1986-90	Nine seen.
1991	One on Apr 27th and one from Sept 7-12th.
1992	One on June 13-14th and two on Aug 22nd.
1993	Two from May 8th-10th, one on May 24th and one on Aug 21st.
1994	Singles on Apr 30th and Sept 11th.
1995	One on June 24th, July 1st and July 11th.
1996	One on Apr 26th and 27th.
1997	Singles on Apr 18-19th and July 12-14th, three on Aug 12th, one from Aug 29-Sept 1st with three east on 30th, and another single from Sept 4-7th.

1998	Singles on May 17th and from Aug 24th-Sept 16th, with two on Sept 13th.
1999	One on Aug 28-29th, two on 30th and one on Sept 11-12th.
2000	Two on May 7th and one on Sept 2nd.

The highest day count of 26 in August 1967 is noteworthy, as was a long-staying summer bird of 1963 and a December individual in 1984. As might be expected, the majority of birds are seen during spring and autumn passage, with autumn records dominating. The graph shows a distinct passage peak in August.

Greenshank - Monthly Distribution

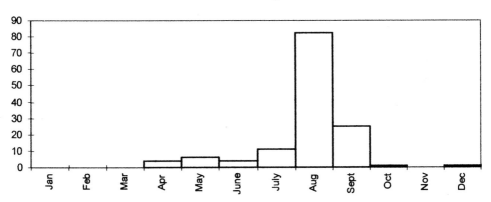

106. GREEN SANDPIPER *Tringa ochropus*

Passage migrant, mainly in autumn. Harting (1866) reported Green Sandpipers to be regular double passage migrants, arriving at the reservoir towards the end of April and occurring until the third week of May, and then returning again in mid-July. The species often occurred in parties of five or six until November, with occasional records in December and January. Nowadays Green Sandpiper is an annual passage migrant at the Brent, mainly in the early autumn period but with a few in spring and summer; there is just one recent winter record. Records since the mid-1950s are summarised and all records for the past ten years are given:

1956-60	Eight seen.
1961-65	Seven seen.
1966-70	Two seen.
1971-75	None seen.
1976-80	Three seen.
1981-85	11 seen.
1986-90	Two seen.
1991	Singles from Aug 19-26th and Dec 28th, two on Dec 19th.

1992	Singles on Apr 24th and Aug 13th.
1993	One on June 13th.
1994	One on July 24th.
1995	Singles on Apr 16th and Aug 19th.
1996	Singles on May 8th, July 16th and 18th and Aug 14-15th.
1997	One behind the dam on Feb 6th, another from Feb 16th until possibly Mar 16th, further singles on Apr 1st and 22nd, May 15th, July 12-13th and 21st, Sept 1st and 25th, with two on March 2nd and July 15th.
1998	Singles on June 6th and 14th and Sept 5th.
1999	Singles on June 13th, July 25th and Aug 5-6th, two on Aug 7th and further singles on 14-15th and 18th.

The distribution shows a large August passage peak, with signs of a very small spring passage in April/May and occasional winter records in December.

Green Sandpiper - Monthly Distribution

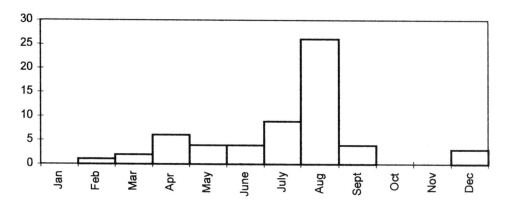

107. WOOD SANDPIPER *Tringa glareola*

Rare passage migrant. Wood Sandpiper is an uncommon passage migrant in the London area, though it is recorded annually (in 1994 there were around 30 records in both spring and autumn). The species is generally much scarcer than Green Sandpiper, and has had a very irregular pattern of occurrence at the reservoir. Batten (1972) stated that in the reservoir's first 50 or so years until 1885 there were 17 records, and then only one in the next 74 years until 1959. Between that date and 1966 the species was recorded almost annually, but since then there were no others until 1997. As with many other wader species until the time of Glegg's book in 1935, Brent records dominated the county totals for Middlesex, with only four birds reported elsewhere. All records are given:

1843	Included by Bond, who had five specimens in his collection.
1863	One shot on Aug 4th.
1864	Two shot on an unspecified date.

Plate 9

A. Tufted Duck and Pochard in Northern Marsh, November 1995, (Leo Batten)

B. Two drake Garganey, scarce visitors May 1993, (Leo Batten)

C. Ruddy Duck drake, a recent breeding colonist, (Leo Batten)

Plate 10

A. Kestrel, a regular breeder, (Leo Batten)

B. Common Sandpiper, a regular double passage migrant, (Brad Charteris)

C. Common Snipe, a wader in serious decline, (Brad Charteris)

1865   One shot on May 25th.
1866   One shot on Aug 30th.
1869   One shot on May 21st.
1870   One shot on May 20th, a further two shot in July and Aug.
1871   Two shot on July 3rd and 31st.
1878   One shot on Aug 2nd.
1884   One undated record..
1959   Two from July 12th to 23rd, one on Aug 4th, and one/two from Aug 7th to Sept 4th.
1960   One on July 29th, three on Aug 3rd and one on 6th.
1961   One on Aug 7th.
1963   One on Aug 30th.
1964   One on Sept 3rd and 30th.
1966   One on July 28th.
1997   One flew north over the Eastern Marsh, calling, on Apr 26th.
1999   One on Aug 7th almost landed on a raft before flying off west, and another flew south on Sept 11th.

108. SPOTTED SANDPIPER *Actitis macularia*

Vagrant. A bird of this American species was purchased in a collection by F Bond in April 1852, and said to have been obtained at the reservoir. Bond traced the story and verified it to his satisfaction. However, Glegg included it in his list of 1929, but only in square brackets as he did not think that the specimen had been critically examined. However, this does not appear logical given that the bird is included in the British Museum catalogue, and the record is treated as confirmed here. There have been three 20th century London Area records: at Hilfield Park Reservoir, Herts, in 1956; at Barn Elms, Surrey, in 1988; and at King George V Reservoir, Essex, in 1989.

109. COMMON SANDPIPER *Actitis hypoleucos*

Common passage migrant. In Harting's time in the mid-19th century this species was described as the commonest sandpiper visiting the reservoir. Glegg (1935) described it as a 'not uncommon double passage migrant', much more numerous in autumn than spring. At the reservoir today it is the most common passage wader, seen each spring and autumn, and sometimes in sizeable flocks; the largest numbers on record include 37 on August 2nd 1970, 41 on August 14th 1984 and 40-50 on July 21st 1987. In spring 1997 birds were present on 19 dates from April 26th until June 6th, with a peak of seven on May 26th. In autumn that year the first bird was seen on June 20th and the species was recorded on 49 other dates until October 20th, with a maximum of 21 on July 19th.

110. TURNSTONE *Arenaria interpres*

Rare straggler on passage. Harting (1866) listed only two occurrences of this species, but a third dated 1866 was included in Glegg (1935), this bird originally reported by R H Read. The next Middlesex record, also reported by Glegg, was not until 1931 at Queen Mary Reservoir. Today, Turnstone is a regular double passage migrant and a localised winter visitor in London, but it remains a rare wader at Brent, with a total of only 13 or 14 records involving up to 16 birds. Since 1940 it has been mainly a spring migrant at the reservoir, with most recent records occurring in May. All records are given:

1865	Several years prior to this date the lock-keeper shot two in autumn.
1865	One on Aug 24th.
1866	An immature on Sept 15th.
1937	Two on Aug 8th and one on Sept 4th.
1944	One on May 11th.
1945	One on Dec 9th.
1946	One on May 14th.
1960	One on May 1-2nd and 9th.
1961	One from May 27-29th.
1963	One on Mar 3rd.
1989	One on May 21st.
1993	One on Apr 28th.
1997	One flew over Cool Oak Lane on Aug 17th.

111. GREY PHALAROPE *Phalaropus fulicarius*

Very rare straggler. Nationally this is a scarce species inland, usually recorded after westerly storms in the autumn. Nothing is known about the weather conditions for the records at the reservoir in the 19th century, but the record from 1950 coincided with a considerable influx across the country after severe storms. All records are listed:

1841	A pair shot, the female on Sept 28th and the male on Sept 30th.
1850	Two birds shot in the autumn.
1870	One shot on Oct 13th.
1892	One shot in Oct.
1950	Two from Sept 8-14th.

A photograph of the two birds in 1950 appeared in the London Bird Report for that year. Frustratingly incomplete descriptions of two seen the day after the famous storm of October 1987 probably also relate to this species.

112. POMARINE SKUA *Stercorarius pomarinus*

Very rare straggler; no recent records. Glegg (1935) reported that there were just four Middlesex records of this species, although in a comprehensive review of London's birds almost 20 years later (LNHS 1964) just one record was detailed for the whole LNHS recording area, from Banbury Reservoir in the Lea Valley in 1954. To the end of 1997 there was a total of 21 Pomarine Skua records in the London Area, nearly 50 per cent of them between 1985-87 (LBR 61: 1996). The only record of this species at the reservoir is of an immature bird reported by Bond in The Zoologist in 1843, though the exact date of the occurrence is unknown. Harting reported another young bird found dead close by at Wembley Park, also on an unknown date but later than 1841.

113. ARCTIC SKUA *Stercorarius parasiticus*

Very rare straggler. In Glegg's day this species was as rare as Pomarine Skua in Middlesex, with just four records by 1935, one of which was from Brent Reservoir. Subsequently it has been observed more frequently in the county, and is now regarded as a regular, but scarce, autumn migrant in the London Area. The first Brent record of this species was mentioned in Yarrell's British Birds (1843) and relates to four immature birds shot at the reservoir in the autumn of 1842. Yarrell commented: 'Two of these specimens were more uniformly dark brown than the other two from having lost many more of the light brown margins of the first set of feathers.' It is not clear whether these four birds were shot together or on different occasions. There are only two other records:

1842   Four juveniles shot in the autumn.
1970   An immature on Sept 11th.
2000   A group of five adults flew through on Sept 16th at 11.45 hrs.

The five seen in September 2000 were part of a small influx into the London area with 21 being seen at the QE II Reservoir on the same date.

[GREAT SKUA *Stercorarius skua*

Very rare straggler; no recent records. This species is of similar rarity status to Pomarine Skua in the London Area, with a total of 23 records to the end of 1997 and an increase in occurrences in recent years. There is only one record of Great Skua near the reservoir, and that concerns an individual flying over Kingsbury on January 15th 1942. The species is regarded as a rare autumn and winter visitor in the capital, and this record is one of the scarcer mid-winter occurrences. The details available about this record do not prove that the bird was seen in the recording area and so it is included in square brackets.]

114. MEDITERRANEAN GULL *Larus melanocephalus*

Very rare visitor. The first two records of Mediterranean Gull in the London Area, in 1866 and 1957, were separated by over 90 years. Yet in 1991, when Brent Reservoir recorded its first individual, there were at least 30 records in London in that year alone. Brent's second record, two years later, was a juvenile, a less frequently recorded age with just nine London records up to 1991. This particular bird appeared on a day when there was an influx of juvenile Black-headed Gulls, and perhaps originated from the small but increasing British breeding population. None of the Brent birds have been long-staying individuals, but it is expected that this species will be encountered more frequently given the huge increase in national and regional sightings. All records are listed:

1991   A first-winter on the morning of Nov 30th for one and a half hours at the Northern Marsh.
1993   A juvenile on Aug 15th for 10 minutes on the dam wall.
1995   A first-winter on Mar 12th.
1998   Two adults on Aug 17th and a first-winter on Sept 3rd and 5th.
2000   One on Aug 26th and another on Oct 8th.

115. LITTLE GULL *Larus minutus*

Rare visitor. Harting (1866) mentioned only two occurrences of this diminutive gull for Middlesex, both shot over the Thames, while Glegg (1935) reported a total of just 11 records for the county. This must represent either a significant under-recording or more likely a change in status, as in recent years up to 150 or more individuals have been recorded in London annually (London Bird Report for 1997). Little Gulls have been recorded in all months in the London Area, with the autumn peak in September much higher than the spring peak in April. Surprisingly, it is a rare gull at the reservoir, with most records in autumn and two in winter. First recorded in 1871, there have been occurrences in just 11 subsequent years:

1871   Two shot in Aug. (Glegg 1933).
1932   An adult on Dec 16th.
1952   One on Oct 7th.
1958   An adult on Sept 8th.
1967   An immature from Sept 5-6th.
1972   Recorded between Aug 28th and Sept 5th, with a maximum of four on Sept 1st.
1980   Two juveniles on Aug 24th.
1984   An immature from Aug 12-21st.
1994   An adult on Oct 15th.
1996   An adult and a first-winter on Dec 20th.

1998   Two on Apr 4th.
2000   One adult on Apr 13th.

116. BLACK-HEADED GULL   *Larus ridibundus*

Very common visitor. In the 19th century Black-headed Gull was described as a spring and autumn migrant (Harting 1866). By Glegg's day (1935) it had become a common winter resident, and was very numerous at this time. Today Black-headed Gull is the commonest gull species at the reservoir, and is seen throughout the year. It is scarcest during May and June, while peak numbers occur in autumn when a sizeable roost is formed; the maximum numbers recorded then are c 6,000 on September 12th 1988 and 4,500 on August 18th 1998. The roost declines in late autumn and very few birds roost on the reservoir during the winter months, although there are usually several hundred birds around during the day. An interesting ringing recovery is that of a corpse found in 1990, originally ringed in Finland in June 1985.

117. RING-BILLED GULL   *Larus delawarensis*

Vagrant. The first British record of this Nearctic Gull came as recently as 1973, and although in a national context there have been many hundreds of other sightings since it remains a rare vagrant in south-east England. In London there had been 15 records to the end of 1997, and the species has been recorded annually since 1991. However, with the exception of a regularly returning wintering bird in west London, most individuals have been short-stayers. The Brent record is as follows:

1996   A first-summer on Mar 23rd.

118. COMMON GULL   *Larus canus*

Common visitor. Harting (1866) reported that this species was an 'accidental visitant' with just three records to 1866; it had previously been mentioned in Bond's list (1843). Glegg (1935) recorded the species as 'a common winter resident in increasing numbers, and occasional birds are seen through the nesting season'. Numbers have continued to rise in winter, and today this gull is fairly common except in May and June, when it is rarely recorded. Numbers regularly exceed 100 throughout the winter period, peaking in December-March when over 200 can be seen around the reservoir. One passage record of note was on March 16th 1991, when 230 were reported flying north in just three hours. A record count of over 350 was made on Dec 31st 1997.

119. LESSER BLACK-BACKED GULL   *Larus fuscus*

Common visitor and local colonist. This was a rare species in Harting's time, recorded at Brent only in severe weather or after a prevalence of easterly winds, and he mentioned only two occurrences in his 1866 book. By Glegg's time (1935) Lesser Black-backed Gull had become an autumn passage migrant in considerable numbers. Counts peaked during the 1960s when the rubbish dump was in operation, and included 450 on September 29th 1962 and c 500 on March 30th 1966. In recent times the winter peak count usually numbers less than 25, although c 40 were seen flying north on May 26th 1991, there were c 60 on Oct 2nd 1994, 51 were counted in the roost on September 27th, and there were 75 on Nov 28th 1999. Its present-day status in the London Area is regarded as common, most regular in autumn and winter with small numbers breeding in central and east London. At Brent Reservoir it is seen increasingly frequently during the summer months. In 1985 a pair held territory on a raft from April 28th to May 3rd, and were often observed displaying and calling to each other. In 1999 a number of pairs bred on nearby warehouse roofs, and 30 juveniles were counted on the reservoir on July 31st. They probably also bred the previous year, as 14 juveniles were seen on July 25th 1998. Birds showing the blackish mantle and wings of the continental race *intermedius* are occasionally reported; there are several records from the 1940s, with a maximum of six on October 1st 1944. The most recent records are of singles seen on February 14th and September 30th 1993 and December 21st 1997. This race is probably under-recorded, as most reports of Lesser Black-backed Gull are not assigned to a specific race.

120. HERRING GULL   *Larus argentatus*

Common visitor and local colonist. Harting (1866) described the Herring Gull as an 'accidental visitant', with no regular migration taking place. However, Glegg (1935) regarded it as a common and increasing winter resident. In London today it is common, most regular in winter when large gatherings are reported at rubbish dumps and roosts, but also with small numbers breeding in central London. At the reservoir in the 1960s this species was attracted to the rubbish dump in large numbers – for example up to 600 were present during the winter months of 1962. It is now recorded irregularly throughout the year, either singly or in small numbers, and in the summer months there are often six-eight birds present which are presumably visitors from one of the breeding colonies in the city. In 1999 at least one pair bred on nearby ware-house roofs; two juveniles were seen on July 24th. Occasionally winter passage is recorded, with 75 east on December 25th 1996 being notable. Since the winter of 1994-95 a Herring Gull has returned to the reservoir in company with a Yellow-legged Gull, with which it is apparently paired.

121. YELLOW-LEGGED GULL   *Larus cachinans michahellis*

Scarce visitor. This larid, formerly considered to be a race of Herring Gull, has in recent years been widely treated as a full species in its own right. Although still not formally recognised as such by the British Ornithologists' Union Records Committee, it seems likely that Britain will follow suit in the near future. Yellow-legged Gulls of the Mediterranean form *michahellis* are being reported in ever greater numbers nationally, with peak numbers sometimes well in excess of 100 on the Lower Thames in autumn. Many of the Brent occurrences relate to an individual which is apparently paired with a Herring Gull. In winter there has been an increase in records, with several occurrences of two or three birds and at least six different individuals in 1997. Recent records are listed below:

1991	Singles on Mar 25th and Dec 15th.
1994	One on Dec 3-4th and four other dates in Dec.
1995	One from Jan 28th-Apr 29th and from Aug 27th-Dec 31st.
1996	One from Jan 1st almost throughout the year, with three on Dec 26th (two adults and a third-winter) and 30th (an adult, a second-winter and a third-winter).
1997	An adult was present from Jan 1st in most months except July September. Additionally, there were two adults on Jan 5th; a third-winter on Jan 18th and Feb 2nd; a third-summer on May 20th; a first-winter on Sept 19th; a second-winter on Oct 17th; and a third-winter on Dec 20th.

1998   An adult on many dates during the year except May-Aug.

1999   Single adults on 10 occasions between Jan 5-Apr 5th and on June 20th, and further singles on Nov 11th and 21st and Dec 15th.

2000   Single birds on seven occasions between Jan 1st and Apr 30th and one on Sept 2nd.

• **Caspian Gull** *Larus cachinans cachinans*

In recent years there has been much ornithological debate on the taxonomy of large gulls and Caspian Gull has figured in these debates. Although currently linked sub-specifically with Yellow-legged Gull it is likely to be split as a separate species in the future. Yellow-legged Gull itself is in the process of being split from Herring Gull. The first example of Caspian Gull to be identified at the reservoir was seen on April 15th 2000.

122. ICELAND GULL *Larus glaucoides*

Very rare straggler. Iceland Gull was first specifically identified in London as recently as spring 1939, though since that time its occurrences have become more frequent. Today it is regarded as a scarce late winter/early spring visitor, and is recorded annually in London in very small numbers. It is a rare gull at the reservoir, with just five confirmed records spanning 50 years. In spite of its annual occurrences in the capital in recent times, the most recent record in 1993 was the first for the Brent in over 30 years, and coincided with a major influx into Britain. All records are given:

1943   One on Dec 18th.

1961   A first-winter on Feb 1st.

1962   A second-winter on Mar 17-18th, and a separate individual from Apr 16-18th.

1993   A first-winter on Feb 8th.

The dates of the Brent individuals conform with the general pattern in southern England, which sees a distinct return passage of birds at the end of the winter period.

123. GLAUCOUS GULL *Larus hyperboreus*

Very rare straggler. This species has historically been more common in London than Iceland Gull, although it has been recorded less frequently than its congener in recent years. At the reservoir both species have occurred with about the same frequency. All records fall within the period 1950-64, with none since:

1950   An adult on Jan 10th.

1955   An adult on several dates between Jan 1st and Feb 26th.

1957   An adult on Jan 12th and 20th.
1958   One on Jan 6th.
1961   Two first-winters on Mar 25th and singles on Mar 26th and
       30th and Apr 9th.
1964   One on Jan 22nd.

The demise of the rubbish dump, active until the late 1960s and immensely attractive to larger gulls during its operative days, has meant the almost total absence of either species over the last three decades.

[GLAUCOUS/ICELAND GULL   *Larus hyperboreus/glaucoides*
The following five records relate to birds of one of these two species that were not specifically identified:

1960   An adult on Nov 20th.
1962   A first-winter on Feb 25th.
1963   One on Mar 18th.
1964   One on Feb 16th.
1979   One, probably a Glaucous Gull, on Feb 19th.]

124. GREAT BLACK-BACKED GULL   *Larus marinus*
Uncommon but increasingly frequent visitor. This species was first mentioned by Bond (1843), but Harting (1866) reported very few records for the reservoir. Glegg (1935) noted it as a scarce species not seen annually in Middlesex, and indeed one on September 18th 1933 was the first for Brent since 1867. Batten (1972) noted that Great Black-backed Gulls had become fairly common in the 1960s, with up to 50 between September and April. Numbers have since declined, no doubt because of the earthing over of the rubbish dump. Nonetheless, the species remains common in the London Area, with counts of over 100 at favoured sites being not unusual. There were very few Brent records in the 1980s, perhaps due to poor coverage, but the 1990s produced the following monthly distribution:

Month	Jan	Feb	Mar	Apr	May	Jun	Jul	Aug	Sep	Oct	Nov	Dec
No.	30	15	9	7	4	5	2	9	9	6	8	12

Birds are now recorded in all months with a pronounced mid-winter peak, low numbers in spring and summer with some evidence of a small increase after the breeding season.

125. KITTIWAKE   *Rissa tridactyla*

Very scarce visitor. Although generally regarded as a marine gull, this species is an occasional passage migrant and winter visitor to the London Area. Harting (1866) listed three 19th century records for the Brent, with three together in May 1859, one in August 1863 and one on April 3rd 1865. Between 1940 and 1962 there were a further 19 records involving 22 birds, most of which were adults, whereas in recent years most have been late summer juveniles. There were no further records until 1984, and all records since are given:

1984	A juvenile on July 22nd and 24th, with another juvenile on Aug 13th.
1990	A juvenile from July 25-30th.
1991	An adult on Apr 7th, with single juveniles on July 25th and Sept 1st.
1992	A juvenile on Aug 1st-2nd and another from Aug 9-14th, on which date its corpse was found.
1994	First-winters on Mar 6th and Nov 19th.
1995	Adults on May 20th and July 1st.
1997	Adults on May 6th and Nov 30th.
2000	One adult on Oct 22nd.

Birds have occurred in all months of the year except June, with a peak in August:

Month	Jan	Feb	Mar	Apr	May	Jun	Jul	Aug	Sep	Oct	Nov	Dec
No.	5	1	2	3	6	-	4	11	2	1	4	2

126. SANDWICH TERN   *Sterna sandvicensis*

Very scarce and irregular visitor. This species was first recorded at Brent Reservoir as recently as 1947, reflecting its status then as a very rare visitor to the London Area with only one 19th century record and no reports in Middlesex until 1926. It has been fairly erratic in its occurrences, with most sightings in the 1960s and records in every month from April to October. All records are given:

1947	One on May 24th.
1951	One on May 15th.
1960	One on July 15th and two on Aug 16th and 19th.
1963	One on June 1st.
1964	One on Apr 18th.
1967	10 flew south-west on Sept 12th, with an immature on the same date and another on Oct 4th.
1968	Seven on Sept 7th.

1973   42 on Sept 9th.
1977   Two on June 19th.
1984   Singles on Sept 25th and 28th.
1989   One on Apr 22nd and four on Aug 26th.
1997   Two on Apr 29th.
1998   In Sept, five on 4th, one on 5th, eight on 12th and two on 19th.
2000   10 on Sept 16th.

The 1973 flock of 42 birds is one of the largest recorded in London. The passage at the reservoir in September 1998 involved the most records in any year and the second highest number of birds, beaten only by the exceptional flock in 1973. It remains a scarce bird at the reservoir, although it is now much more regular in the London Area where, for example, there were 54 records involving 127 birds in 1994.

127. ROSEATE TERN *Sterna dougallii*
Very rare straggler; no recent records. This species very rarely occurs inland, and there have been just 15 records in the London Area to the end of 1997, with the most recent in 1988 being the first for 15 years. The sole Brent record, dating from the mid-19th century, was also the first record for Middlesex:

1866   Two, one of which was shot, on Aug 16th.

128. COMMON TERN *Sterna hirundo*
Common summer visitor and passage migrant. Harting (1866) reported that this species was regularly seen in spring and autumn, sometimes staying for several days. During that period it was only possible to specifically identify birds that were shot as either Common or Arctic Terns, and until recent times it has been best to regard the majority of passage records as relating to 'commic' terns. The largest such flock was 52 on August 13th 1964. Common Terns first bred at the reservoir in 1983 when artificial nesting rafts were provided. The number of pairs breeding has since increased seven-fold, although the success rate has been inconsistent (see table below). The adults do not restrict their feeding forays to the reservoir and during the summer are regularly seen fishing at the ponds on Hampstead Heath or along the River Brent and the Grand Union Canal. The number of breeding terns in the colony has continued to rise, and in 1995 a pair bred nearby at Hampstead Heath for the first time. In 1999 over 100 terns (adults and young) were present in late summer and in 2000 forty four pairs bred, the highest number to date.

Common Tern: Pairs & Younger Produced 1993 - 2000

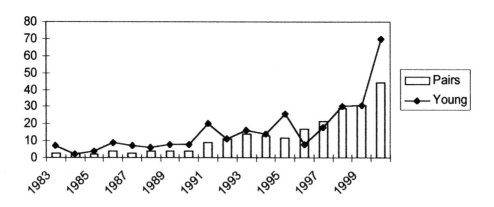

129. ARCTIC TERN *Sterna paradisea*

Scarce and irregular passage migrant. Although most Arctic Terns use coastal routes on passage, migration overland is a recognised phenomenon for this species and sometimes may involve significant numbers. In the London Area the large reservoirs of the Colne and Lea Valleys and the River Thames seem particularly favoured, while in contrast occurrences at Brent have been at best irregular. There are very few recent records of this species, and considering that Harting (1866) described it as less plentiful than Common Tern but noted that small flocks visited annually in spring and autumn, it may well be that Arctic Terns have been overlooked in the past; there were no records at all from 1881-1947. All 20th century records are listed below:

1947	One, possibly two or three, from Apr 23rd-25th.
1957	One on Sept 5th.
1958	One on July 29th and two on July 31st.
1959	Singles on May 4th and 11th and two on July 2nd.
1967	Singles on Oct 14th and 17th.
1977	Two on May 19th and one on June 25th.
1992	An adult and a juvenile on Aug 31st, the latter staying to Sept 12th.
1993	One on May 1st, with two adults and two juveniles on Aug 22nd.
1995	An adult on Aug 9th.
1996	One on Apr 13th.
1997	26 on Apr 26th, one on May 18th and an adult from Oct 9-12th.
1998	Three on Apr 29th, one on May 1st, 27 on 2nd and 22 on 3rd.
1999	Two on Apr 27th and one on June 6th.
2000	Seven on Apr 14th, two on July 27th, eight on Aug 14th, two on Sept 2nd and Sept 5th.

The condensed passage over five days in spring 1998 involved the highest daily total and the highest ever annual total. It reflected a very heavy passage through the London area and south-east England at that time.

130. LITTLE TERN *Sterna albifrons*

Very rare visitor. This is a scarce but annual passage migrant in London but a very rare species at Brent. Harting (1866) referred to Little Tern as the least common of the terns which visited the reservoir, but gave no records. However, Bond (1843) included it in his list as having been obtained at Brent, and Read (1896) stated that specimens taken at the reservoir were in the collection at the Welsh Harp. There were no subsequent records until 1947, after which it was recorded on a fairly regular basis until 1967, but there were no further records until 20 years later and then a futher 13 years before the next occurrence. All 20th century records are given:

1947	One on May 6th.
1950	Six on May 15th.
1954	One on May 9th.
1957	An immature from Aug 24-26th.
1960	One on Apr 29th and two on May 1st.
1961	One on Apr 30th.
1962	One on May 4th and three on June 17th.
1965	An adult and two immatures on July 31st.
1967	One on May 1st.
1987	One on May 16th.
2000	One on May 1st.

131. BLACK TERN *Chlidonias niger*

Scarce passage migrant. Often erratic on passage in Britain, the appearance of Black Terns is closely related to favourable weather conditions emanating from the Continent. Harting (1866) mentioned that it was the most frequently encountered tern after Common Tern in Middlesex, stating that in some years it was very common in the county, but he gave no specific details of any occurrences at Brent Reservoir. The first documented sighting is of five on May 3rd 1928. It was then recorded in 21 years between 1946-95, with the largest flock of 26 on May 11th 1960:

1977	Three on July 5th and two on Aug 21st.
1978	Three on May 18th.
1981	Singles on July 11th and Sept 19-20th.
1982	One on Sept 3rd.

1989   One on June 23rd.
1990   One on May 3rd.
1991   Five on May 29th and one on June 1st.
1992   One on Aug 31st.
1993   One on May 1st and two on May 12th.
1994   Two on May 14th and nine on Sept 15th, when there was an
       influx of 260 birds in London.
1995   One on July 11th.
1996   Three on Apr 23rd.
1997   Two on May 3rd and one on Aug 13th.
1998   Two on Aug 31st-Sept 1st and three on Sept 5th.
1999   One on Apr 29th.
2000   Five on May 7th and one on May 13th.

The Sept 15th 1994 record was part of a large influx into the capital with 260 birds being recorded.

132. WHITE-WINGED BLACK TERN   *Chlidonias leucopterus*

Vagrant. Formerly a very rare vagrant to Britain, this species is now reported annually, with most records occurring in spring and autumn during movements of Black Terns. There were 28 records in the London Area in the 20th century, including the second for Brent Reservoir:

1883   One shot in May.
1996   One in full breeding plumage on July 27th stayed until 17.00 hrs,
       when it flew off north.

The 1883 record was of one reported shot by Sawyer the lock-keeper at the time. When Glegg (1935) published his book it was still the only Middlesex record, he did not include it as an authenticated record as the specimen had not been examined by a competent ornithologist. The observer who found the 1996 individual had gone to the reservoir in the hope of seeing a Little Egret which had been reported flying towards Brent from Hampstead Heath. The previous evening a White-winged Black Tern had been present at Draycote Water, Warwickshire, some 70 miles north-west of Brent, and it is thought likely to have been the same bird.

[PALLAS'S SANDGROUSE *Syrrhaptes paradous*
Vagrant. This Central Asian species is an extreme rarity in Western Europe, and most records have occurred during periodic 'irruption years' when birds moved far to the west of their normal ranges. There has been no such event since the early 20th century, but several noteworthy irruptions prior to that time included influxes in 1863, 1888 and 1908. The one Brent record relates to the first of these major national invasions, which involved hundreds of individuals (Henry Stevenson, writing in The Zoologist in September 1863, recorded the capture of no fewer than 63 specimens in Norfolk and Suffolk alone).

1863   One shot near Neasden in Aug.

Additionally, in Brit. Birds Vol 1, W Wells-Bladen wrote that he saw a Pallas's Sandgrouse flying over Hendon on September 23rd 1907. However, according to LNHS (1963), this record was omitted from subsequent publications, 'presumably on account of the lack of detail'.]

133. FERAL ROCK DOVE *Columba livia*
Common resident. A familiar bird in the area, with flocks of up to several hundred birds mainly centred around the industrial estate near the south bank of the reservoir. Although Harting (1866) did not refer to this species, Dixon (1909) mentioned that there are numerous small colonies all over London, and Glegg (1935) stated that Feral Rock Doves have been known to exist in London since the 14th century.

134. STOCK DOVE *Columba oenas*
Occasional non-breeding visitor. Formerly much more common, Harting (1866) considered Stock Dove as a regular but scarce breeder and occasionally saw parties of up to 12 birds in autumn and winter. In the 1950s flocks of over 100 birds were frequently seen during winter. At present the species is recorded

primarily on passage and in winter, with about 10 records annually. In 1990 a series of records between March 6th and August 19th of up to three birds in the dump/allotments area suggested that breeding was attempted nearby. In recent years up to three were seen regularly from March to September, and in 1997 birds were heard singing on Mar 25th and June 24th.

135. WOODPIGEON *Columba palumbus*
Common resident, passage migrant and winter visitor. Harting (1866) noted that although a few pairs bred each year, this species was most numerous in winter and early spring when large flocks passed over and sometimes dropped down onto the cleared bean and stubble fields. The species is now a common resident and winter visitor, breeding throughout the area. Substantial numbers are sometimes also recorded during migration periods or during cold weather movements, like the huge passage of at least 10,000 birds which flew south-west on December 28th 1960. Recent high counts include 300+ at the Field Studies Centre on January 13th 1990, 1,310 going to roost on November 26th 1994, 863 heading south-west in one hour on October 24th 1996, 400 flying west on November 4th 1999 and 3,300 flying west on November 4th 2000. An albino has been seen on many occasions since March 22nd 1997 until at least October 28th 2000.

136. COLLARED DOVE *Streptopelia decaocto*
Occasional visitor; has bred. The westward expansion of Collared Doves swept across Europe half a century ago, with the first birds reaching Britain in 1955. The first records for the London Area came two years later, when one or two birds were seen at Rye Meads, Hertfordshire, on several occasions in late summer 1957. Brent Reservoir finally received its first on May 6th 1961. There were no more records until one on March 28th 1971, followed by two on April 15th 1972. They remained very rare throughout the 1970s and until 1988, when birds were recorded regularly throughout the year and two pairs bred. A pair nested near the Field Studies Centre the following year, but there were only three records in 1990. There were up to 10 records annually, mainly in spring, each year from 1991-93, and a pair was seen regularly in the summers of 1994-98.

137. TURTLE DOVE *Streptopelia turtur*
Scarce passage migrant. Harting (1866) described Turtle Dove as a summer visitor, arriving towards the end of April and leaving in September, when small flocks occurred in the stubble fields. Dixon (1909) described them as fairly abundant in Wembley, but by the time Glegg published The Birds of Middlesex

in 1935, the species was fairly unusual in the London suburbs and probably ceased to breed in the area about this time, coinciding with the rapid expansion of housing estates. Turtle Doves are now recorded almost every year, on up to four occasions, usually in ones and twos but three were seen on June 10th 1990. The earliest record in recent years was on April 18th 1995, and the latest on September 21st 1991. In 1996 a bird was seen on June 10th and 23rd and heard singing on July 14th near the Field Studies Centre, but most individuals are seen flying over the area.

138. RING-NECKED PARAKEET *Psittacula kramer*

Scarce visitor. This introduced species, which has its British stronghold in the south-western outer suburbs of the capital, is now a near-annual visitor to Brent Reservoir. With counts at the largest roost in Esher, Surrey, numbering almost 1,500 birds, the population in the city must be approaching at least 2,000, and appears to be increasing. All records are given:

1975	One on Apr 6th.
1980	One on Aug 28th.
1981	One on Aug 25th.
1990	One on Nov 17th and Dec 13th.
1991	Singles on Feb 3rd and 17th and on Sept 7th and 21st.
1992	One on Apr 11th and 12th.
1993	One on Sept 18th.
1994	One on May 29th.
1995	One on Sept 22nd.
1996	One on Sept 6th.
1997	One on Jan 12th.
1999	Five in the Eastern Marsh on Aug 30th.
2000	Singles on May 14th and Aug 10th.

Local breeding was recorded for the first time in 2000 when a pair was recorded breeding on Hampstead Heath.

139. CUCKOO *Cuculus canorus*

Passage migrant, chiefly in spring; formerly bred. This species was a regular summer visitor in the last century and remained so until the early 1960s. Since then, although heard from time to time, there has been little evidence of birds holding territory in recent years, However in 1989 a single bird was present from May 24th until June 5th, with two singing birds on June 1-5th. All records for the past ten years are given:

1991	One on May 11th and 19th, and a returning juvenile on July 18th.
1992	One prior to Apr 22nd, five seen between Apr 27th and May 25th, four between July 26th and Aug 16th.
1993	Fourteen bird-days between May 7th and 29th, with three birds on the 18th, in autumn one on Aug 28th.
1994	Singles on Apr 30th and May 29-30th.
1995	One on Apr 29th, four on May 6th, two on May 7th, one on 19th and 21st, and two on 22nd.
1996	Singles on Apr 27th, May 12th and 26th, and June 29th.
1997	Two on May 2nd and one on May 7th.
1998	Singles on Apr 28th and in July on 4th, 11th and 25th.
1999	Singles on Apr 24th and May 16th and 22nd.
2000	Singles on May 14th, 16th and 21st, in autumn singles on Aug 25th and Sept 2nd.

140. BARN OWL *Tyto alba*

Very rare straggler; formerly bred. In the mid-19th century this species was described as the commonest owl at Brent Reservoir (Harting 1866), and it bred regularly in Kingsbury Church and in hollow trees elsewhere. It remained as a resident until the early part of the 20th century, but then disappeared as a regular breeding species. In parallel with its widespread decline nationally it has become a very rare visitor, with only three records at the reservoir since 1960:

1961	One on Sept 11th.
1970	One on May 18th.
1978	One on Feb 15th.

Additionally, one was heard calling nearby from Brook Road at 03.10 hrs on Nov 26th 1973. A record of a bird seen in October 1989 was attributed to an escape, after its owner reported it missing!

141. LITTLE OWL *Athene noctua*

Very rare straggler; formerly bred. As with the last species, this owl was once resident at the reservoir, and was known to have bred from the 1920s to the early 1960s. Since then, however, Little Owls have declined throughout the London Area, and the last record from the reservoir dates back to 1964, when one was seen on several occasions from April to August. Prior to that time, a pair used to frequent an area near the rifle range, and others were seen in gardens in Kingsbury. In view of the sedentary nature of this species, it may be a long time before another is recorded.

142. TAWNY OWL *Strix aluco*

Resident. Tawny Owls were apparently very rare in Middlesex and throughout the London Area during the 19th century, and only one bird was mentioned as occurring in the vicinity of the reservoir – an adult male which was shot at Well Springs, Kingsbury, in spring 1844. However, by 1909 Dixon heard Tawny Owls frequently at Harlesden, and stated that the species could often be heard at Wembley. Today it remains a breeding resident, with up to three pairs present in recent years.

143. LONG-EARED OWL *Asio otus*

Scarce and irregular winter visitor. Harting (1866) talked of a male collected in Colindeep Lane, Hendon, and another two shot at Well Springs, Kingsbury, on December 31st 1862. A further bird was shot in January 1865 in Forty Lane, and in June 1861 some eggs of this species were taken from an old tree in Wembley Park, so the species was clearly not uncommon in the area in the 19th century. Dixon (1909) thought it may possibly breed at Wembley, but offered no evidence to support this statement. Glegg (1935) knew of no satisfactory evidence to prove the recent occurrence of the Long-eared Owl in the whole county of Middlesex. However, Harrison (1931) cited numerous records for the Harrow and Mill Hill area. No records existed for Brent Reservoir and its surrounding open space until 1994, when a roost was discovered which was re-established in the subsequent winter at least. All records are given:

1994   Three on Dec 10th, rising to five by Dec 21st until the end of the year.

1995   Five on Jan 1st and three in Feb and Mar, with the last on Apr 19th. In the second winter period, two from Dec 17th-31st.

1996   Two from Jan 1st-Feb 23rd, and one on Mar 9th.

1997   Two from Nov 29th-Dec 6th, and one on Dec 11th.

144. SHORT-EARED OWL *Asio flammeus*

Occasional autumn and winter visitor. This species was formerly much rarer than its present-day status suggests, with only a few 19th century records and none this century before 1947. It is a winter visitor and passage migrant in variable numbers in London as elsewhere, with numbers fluctuating according to breeding success and the variable availability of its rodent prey; very few are seen in summer in the London Area. All records at the reservoir are given:

1832	One killed near Wembley on an unspecified date between 1828 and 1832.
1840-1	A male and female killed together in a field near the reservoir during the winter (unspecified date).
1866	A few years later two more were killed, but again no year was given (Harting 1866).
1947	One on Mar 15th.
1953	One on Jan 27th.
1958	Singles on Oct 23rd and Nov 9th.
1959	One on Feb 19th.
1974	One on Nov 17th.
1976	One on Oct 16th.
1977	One on Oct 10th.
1978	Singles on Nov 5th, 14th and 25th.
1979	One from Jan 2nd-Apr 14th, with three on Jan 6-7th and two on Feb 18th. In the second winter period, one from Oct 15th-Dec 31st.
1980	Singles on Jan 19th, Feb 9th, Mar 15th and Aug 16th.
1981	One on Dec 27th.
1982	Singles on Jan 3rd, Feb 26th, Nov 26th and Dec 29th.
1983	Three on Jan 3rd, one remaining until Feb 5th.
1984	One picked up injured on Nov 22nd died on 24th.
1985	One on Apr 5th and two on Nov 16th and 21st.
1991	One on Nov 16th.
1992	One on Oct 31st briefly high over reservoir, and one or two on Nov 28th when one flew north over the Northern Marsh and probably another was seen in the Eastern Marsh.
1993	One on Nov 21st after heavy snow.
1998	Singles flew west on Oct 11th, south-west on 14th and north on Nov 1st.

During the post-war period there have been 23 records involving up to 28 birds. No birds were recorded in the 1960s, but records were annual from 1976-85, with up to three birds present continuously from January-April 1979.

145. NIGHTJAR *Caprimulgus europaeus*

Very rare straggler. This was a very uncommon species in the immediate area when Harting (1866) wrote his Birds of Middlesex. However, by the 1870s it bred regularly and Dixon (1909) referred to it breeding at Wembley. Since then it has long since ceased nesting in the area, and there has been only one record since:

1956   One in August, one was flushed on the north bank of the reservoir.

146. SWIFT *Apus apus*

Common summer visitor. This species has always been a summer visitor breeding in the vicinity of the reservoir. Large numbers congregate over Brent in June and July, sometimes numbering several thousand as on July 21st 1987. The first swifts are usually seen before the end of April, with the last lingering until just after mid-September. The earliest arrival dates are April 21st 1958 and 1996, and the latest-ever was on September 20th 1960.

147. ALPINE SWIFT *Apus melba*

Vagrant. In Britain Alpine Swift is typically regarded as an 'overshooting' continental migrant, occurring annually and mainly in spring and autumn. Most records come from the south coast, and it is a very rare visitor to London with 13 records in the 40-year period from 1958-1997.

1841   One with a flock of Swifts over the reservoir in August.

Only two other records exist for Middlesex in the 19th century, at Finchley in 1860 and Staines in August 1895. Harting (1866) stated that the day after the bird was seen at Brent an Alpine Swift was shot at Reading; this was conceivably the same bird.

148. KINGFISHER *Alcedo atthis*

Resident. Kingfishers bred in the area up to the early part of the 20th century, and then declined as a result of river pollution and persecution. The species remained an occasional visitor in autumn and winter. From 1984, around the same time as oil booms and a trash trap were put across Dollis Brook, the species has returned as a breeding resident. At least one pair has been proved or suspected of breeding in most years – a success story of recent times. In some years a second pair is present in the northern marsh and a third pair frequents the River Brent below the dam.

149. HOOPOE *Upupa epops*
Vagrant. This very scarce migrant occurs in small numbers in Britain mainly in spring, with fewer records in autumn and the very occasional breeding record. In London it is not recorded annually, but when birds do appear occurrences conform to the national pattern and spring birds are the norm. The two records of this colourful species at Brent both fall into this pattern:

    1865   One shot at Neasden in Apr.
    1963   One near the rifle range on the north bank on Apr 23rd.

150. WRYNECK *Jynx torquilla*
Very scarce straggler; formerly bred. Harting (1866) described this bird a 'regular summer visitant', generally appearing in about the second week of April, a few days before the first Cuckoo. A decline was in evidence thereafter, reflecting the national position, and it had become scarce in the Lower Brent Valley by the 1890s (Reed 1896). Dixon (1909) stated that it had been recorded from Dollis Hill, Wembley and Kingsbury. A pair were present annually near the reservoir from at least 1923 until 1926, when Wrynecks finally ceased breeding in the area. Since then there have only been two records of migrant birds:

    1956   One on Sept 3rd in a tree by Cool Oak Lane.
    1989   One observed for just 15 minutes on Sept 23rd in the Northern Marsh.

A few migrant Wrynecks are seen in most years in the London Area.

151. GREEN WOODPECKER *Picus viridis*
Resident. This species has exhibited marked population fluctuations in the area over the last 160 years, reflecting the national picture. Up to 1866 it was observed regularly in the area, though not as commonly as Lesser Spotted Woodpecker. It appeared to have ceased breeding regularly by the end of the 19th century, but Dixon (1909) stated that the bird was found in the Wembley district. It remained a regular breeding bird until the 1950s when it suddenly decreased once more, and remained scarce until 1990 when a pair bred near the Field Studies Centre. Since then the species has been resident in small numbers, with at least three pairs breeding in recent years.

152. GREAT SPOTTED WOODPECKER *Dendrocopus major*
Resident. This is another species with a fluctuating population. It was common at the beginning of the 19th century but almost extinct by 1865. Recovery

followed, leading to nesting in the early 20th century, but another decline became apparent in the late 1950s. Described as only an occasional visitor in the early 1970s, the species has increased since the 1980s and has stabilised at between three and six pairs. One or two pairs breed in each of the Northern and Eastern Marshes and at least one additional pair in the vicinity of the Field Studies Centre. This increase was in part due to the maturing willow woodland in the Northern and Eastern Marshes, providing suitable habitat in the form of dead and rotting timber.

153. LESSER SPOTTED WOODPECKER *Dendrocopus minor*

Occasional visitor; regular breeder. This was the commonest of the three woodpeckers throughout the 19th century and remained a regular breeder into the 1930s. Since then it has declined and become a scarce non-breeding visitor, but with birds seen most years. In 1990 a male took up residence in the Eastern Marsh, revealing his presence by calling frequently from the television aerials of nearby houses. A pair bred that year, with another possible territory in the Northern Marsh. In 1991 and 1992 birds were recorded in both the Eastern and Northern Marshes during the breeding season. Breeding may have also occurred in the vicinity in 1993, but disappointingly there were no further breeding season records and the bird reverted to its status as an occasional autumn and winter visitor. In 1997, however, the species was once again reported drumming and calling in the Eastern Marsh during the summer.

154. WOODLARK *Lullula arborea*
Very rare straggler. The species became extinct as a breeding bird at nearby Barn Hill prior to the 1860s, and there were no records at the reservoir until 1958. Harting (1866) blamed the extinction on the London bird-catchers,

although a national decline had already started. The species remained at a low level until the 1920s, when it began to increase in many counties including the London Area. This increase lasted until the 1950s and early 1960s, after which another decline took place. It is only in the past few years that another increase in the British population is becoming apparent. It is worth noting that the majority of records at the reservoir occurred during periods of greater national abundance, and included records of winter flocks. All records are given:

1958   One on Apr 12th.
1959   One on Aug 31st.
1960   Six on Jan 17th and five on Jan 22nd.
1961   One on July 30th and 12 on Dec 28th.
1962   One on June 14th.
1971   One flew south-west on Feb 28th.

155. SKYLARK   *Alauda arvensis*

Passage migrant; formerly bred. Formerly a common resident, this species is now only a migrant in unpredictable numbers, with October as the peak month for passage in the autumn. Occasionally large numbers are counted in cold weather movements; for example 1,250 were observed flying south in five hours on January 1st 1962. In the 1970s five or more pairs bred on the allotments, other pairs were located on the north bank and occasionally a pair bred on the Neasden side of the reservoir. As recently as 1988 four pairs were believed to have bred, yet the following year only a single pair were recorded on the Northern Marsh census and there were just two spring records in 1990 of a single singing male, with no evidence that it managed to find a mate. A single bird was reported singing in 1997 on April 13th. This catastrophic decline reflects the national pattern, with a reduction of more than 50 per cent in the population over the past 25 years.

156. SAND MARTIN   *Riparia riparia*

Passage migrant. In the 19th century this species bred at a number of Middlesex sites, though not at the reservoir. However, Harting (1866) commented on seeing 'an immense flight of these birds on the ground near Kingsbury Reservoir' in August 1863, and estimated 'that there must have been about six hundred birds congregated there'. Harting additionally mentions that the nearest breeding colonies to the reservoir were at Pinner in some chalk-pits and on Lord Mansfield's estate in Hampstead 'where an old sandbank is completely riddled with their holes. Dixon (1909) noted that 'in autumn especially large gatherings congregate over such large sheets of water as the Welsh Harp'. The national population crash in 1969 greatly affected numbers for over 20 years, although the species now seems to be back to pre-1969 levels. Today Sand Martins are conspicuous 'double' migrants at Brent, with counts in recent years of up to 200 in a day in autumn and 31 in spring, when there is generally a much lighter passage. The earliest arrival date was March 5th 1977, and the latest departing bird was on October 8th 1988.

157. SWALLOW *Hirundo rustica*

Passage migrant. Swallows were familiar summer residents in the area until at least the first decade of the 20th century, and probably later. In 1907, for example, Kendall wrote that the species was still common in Willesden and nested in Neasden and Wembley. Though regular nesting has long since ceased, Swallows are still common passage migrants in spring and autumn, and up to 200 or more birds can be counted passing through the reservoir in a day. The earliest record was on March 27th 1993 and the latest on October 29th 1959. Harting (1866) mentioned a pure white specimen which was shot some years prior to 1866, and Glegg referred to a cream-coloured bird shot near Kingsbury in the 19th century which was in Bond's collection, though no date was given.

158. HOUSE MARTIN *Delichon urbica*

Common summer resident. Harting barely mentions this species in his 1866 account merely remarking that it was: 'A common summer visitant, arriving, like the Swallow in April, but generally later than that bird, and leaving in October'. For many years this species nested on houses in streets near the reservoir. In the 1990s, however, it has declined markedly and now only breeds in very small numbers in West Hendon under the eaves of shops on the Broadway. Maximum concentrations over the reservoir have numbered in excess of 400 birds on several occasions in August and September. The earliest record in recent years is of 24 on April 8th 1995, and the latest was a bird on October 28th 1993.

[PURPLE MARTIN

Harting (1866) referred to two birds reputedly obtained at the reservoir in September 1842, but stated that 'I have received such unsatisfactory information respecting these birds that were it not for Mr Yarrell's mention of them, I should not have noticed the species in this catalogue'. An American species, there are no accepted records of Purple Martin in Europe to date.]

159. RICHARD'S PIPIT   *Anthus novaeseelandiae*

Vagrant. This Siberian species occurs in Britain annually, chiefly as a very scarce autumn 'reverse migrant' in the Northern Isles and along the east and south coasts. Formerly much rarer, the numbers occurring increased from the mid-1960s and the species was no longer considered by the British Birds Rarities Committee after 1982. In addition to the sole Brent record, there were 11 other London Area records up to the end of 1991, following the first in 1956 (Hardwick and Self 1991).

> 1963   One seen on October 19th was watched for an hour from 10.15 hrs on the old rubbish dump.

This bird, found by Leo Batten, was observed at ranges from 20-50 yards on the ground in grass, on a stone fence and on a 12-foot high bush. The original description is included on page 183 of this publication. The record, belatedly accepted by the BBRC, was the fourth for the London area.

160. TREE PIPIT   *Anthus trivialis*
Scarce passage migrant. Tree Pipits occur annually at Brent, but in very small numbers in contrast to their former status in the area, and they are getting scarcer. Harting (1866) described the species as an 'annual summer visitant, arriving in April and common enough throughout the summer months'. Dixon (1909) noted it a regular summer visitor to Wembley, Kingsbury and Hendon.

Harrison (1931) recorded a marked passage at the reservoir in late April and again in August and September in the period 1925-1930. Prof. Warmington recorded a single pair occasionally at Brent in summer during the 1920s-40s, but had no record of successful breeding. In both 1969 and 1970 a pair held territory for much of the summer on nearby Barn Hill. Since 1987, when the annual Brent bird reports began, there have only been 21 records involving 18 birds. These are in the months of April (seven birds), May (one bird), August (six birds) and September (12 birds). Records for the past ten years are listed:

1991	Singles on Aug 27th, May 19th and Sept 7th.
1992	Two on Apr 26th and Sept 27th.
1993	Two on Apr 17th.
1994	One on Sept 30th.
1995	Singles on Apr 29th and Sept 15th.
1996	One on Aug 31st.
1997	Singles on Apr 26th and Aug 30th.
1998	One on Aug 30th, two on Sept 12th and one on 13th.
1999	One on Aug 26th, two on Sept 24th and one on 29th.
2000	One on Sept 9th.

161. MEADOW PIPIT *Anthus pratensis*

Common migrant and winter visitor, very occasional breeder. Harting (1866) described it as a common resident throughout the year. This sentiment was echoed by Dixon (1909) who stated it to be a widely distributed resident in the London area and who said that it would be impossible to mention all the places in the more rural suburbs where the species nested. However, according to the LNHS (1964), there appeared to be very little evidence of breeding in the first two decades of the 20th century in London. Although remaining a common visitor to Brent Reservoir in spring, autumn and winter, Meadow Pipit is now rare in summer. In 1930 a pair bred just south of Cool Oak Lane Bridge, breeding took place again in 1957, and in 1974 a pair held territory from May to August on the north bank. It is far more familiar as a migrant, with numbers regularly passing over during spring and autumn migration. The recent highest totals have been as follows:

1995	42 flew north on Apr 3rd, followed by 59 north on Apr 8th and 91 south on Oct 5th.
1996	85 flew north on Mar 23rd, and 67 were logged on Sept 27th.
1997	120 flew north on Mar 23rd, 44 went north on Mar 30th, and 40 flew south-east on Sept 21st.
1999	122 flew south on Sept 25th, 141 went south on 26th and 59 again flew south on 29th.

162. ROCK PIPIT   *Anthus petrosus*

Irregular passage migrant. This generally coastal species is now a regular passage migrant and winter visitor in small numbers in the London area, where birds typically favour the foreshore and adjacent marshes of the Lower Thames. At Brent, however, where there is less suitable habitat, Rock Pipits are only very occasional autumn, winter and early spring visitors. There is no evidence as to the subspecific identity of birds occurring at the reservoir, but there has been specu-lation that some, perhaps most, of the birds occurring in the London Area are of the Scandinavian subspecies *littoralis*, rather than nominate British race *petrosus*. All 19th century records are given, subsequent records are summarised by decade:

    1845   Seven killed by Bond in Oct.
    1866   Two on Mar 20th.
    1950-59 Five records of five singles.
    1960-69 16 records of singles one of two on Apr 1st 1960.
    1970-79 Five records of singles and one of two on Oct 15th 1971.
    1980-89 Three records of singles.
    1990-99 11 records of singles and one of two on Oct 22nd 1995.

Birds have occurred in all months from October to April except January, with a very marked peak in October:

Month	Jan	Feb	Mar	Apr	May	Jun	Jul	Aug	Sept	Oct	Nov	Dec
Birds	0	1	9	3	0	0	0	0	0	27	11	4

163. WATER PIPIT   *Anthus spinoletta*

Very rare and irregular passage migrant. Formerly considered to be a race of Rock Pipit, this montane breeder from continental Europe is a regular passage migrant in small numbers and a localised winter visitor to the London Area. It occurs alongside Rock Pipit in the Lower Thames Marshes, but is also more regularly found at inland sites such as cress beds, where birds sometimes winter in small numbers. However, lack of suitable habitat means that it is a very rare passage migrant at the reservoir, with a total of only seven individuals recorded in five years, and the first as recently as 1961:

    1961   Singles on Apr 14th and 22nd, the latter in summer plumage.
    1962   One on May 7th in summer plumage.
    1984   Two on Oct 6th.
    1986   One on Oct 12th.
    1991   One on Apr 6th.
    2000   One on Nov 4th.

164. YELLOW WAGTAIL *Motacilla flava*

Passage migrant; formerly bred. Both Harting (1866) and Glegg (1935) commented that the bird was a common summer visitor and bred at the reservoir. Harting commented on the difficulty in locating the nest and eggs as they were so carefully concealed 'It is very compact in form and is usually placed in a hole in the ground (oftentimes the depression made by a horse's hoof) with tall herbage'. Regular observations after 1945 showed that between three and 10 pairs of Yellow Wagtails bred at Brent Reservoir each year up to 1962. However, after that date a rapid decline took place, coinciding with the destruction of their main breeding habitat by the municipal rubbish dump on the northern banks of the main reservoir. Two pairs bred in 1963, but there were no further breeding records until 1967 and 1968, when one pair bred in an area adjacent to the northern arm of the reservoir. Breeding has not taken place since then, due to the loss of wet grassland to scrub, and the species is now only a regular spring and autumn migrant in small numbers. Totals of six on September 6th 1988 and seven on April 24th and 27th 1997 are the highest daily counts of the species in recent years. This is in contrast with its previous status as an abundant spring and autumn migrant when, especially in August, over 150 individuals were counted on some days. In 1945, several hundred were present at the end of August. The reduction of passage birds reflects the national decline of this species, as well as the loss of suitable habitat at the reservoir. The earliest spring record was of one on March 30th 1959, and an exceptionally late individual was recorded on November 29th 1960.

In addition to the British race *flavissima*, three other subspecies have been recorded at the reservoir:

• Blue-headed Wagtail *M f flava*

The nominate continental race is the second most widely recorded form of Yellow Wagtail in Britain, and many years ago was formerly fairly numerous at the reservoir, especially on spring passage when there were up to six records each year. However, following the general decline of the species Blue-headed Wagtails have become very scarce at Brent. On May 11th 1950 a male at the reservoir appeared to be paired with a female Yellow Wagtail. Until 1997 when one occurred on April 26th, the last documented record was as long ago as 1964. This race has become scarcer in the London area.

• Grey-headed Wagtail *M f thunbergi*

This Scandinavian race is a scarce migrant in Britain, mainly in spring, and has been recorded on two occasions at the reservoir. In May 1864 an immature was shot by Mr W H Power, who commented: 'It was not the plumage or the size of the bird that made me think it was a Grey-headed Wagtail, so much as the note, which first attracted my attention, being certainly different from that of the yellow species, and this induced me to shoot the bird in order to examine it.' A male on April 7th 1945 was the only other record.

• Sykes's Wagtail *M f beema*
Individuals resembling this rare Central Asian race, which is characterised by its pale blue-grey head with white supercilium, throat and lower border to the ear coverts, were claimed on April 30th and May 6th 1950 and April 14th 1963.

165. GREY WAGTAIL *Motacilla cinerea*
Scarce resident. Formerly a regular visitor from September to April, and occasionally at other times, Grey Wagtail has now become a year-round resident. Its breeding was possibly under-recorded, but mention by Glegg (1936) of a pair breeding near the reservoir in 1929 indicates that their summer presence was not too regular. The Silk Stream and River Brent are the favoured breeding sites. In recent years at least one pair has bred annually, but two or three pairs were present in the summer of 1984 and two pairs produced young in 1999. There is a marked autumn passage, especially in October when up to six may be seen in a morning.

166. PIED WAGTAIL *Motacilla alba yarrelli*
Scarce resident. This familiar city bird is surprisingly scarce at the reservoir, at least in modern times. In the last century it was described by Harting (1866) as a 'common species, resident throughout the year, but most numerous in the autumn when it may be observed in small parties of seven or eight. Very few were to be seen throughout the winter.' It is still the most numerous in the autumn but numbers on any one day in recent years have not exceeded 15, compared with counts of up to 200 in some autumns in the 1950s and 1960s. Its present breeding status is uncertain, but at least one pair breeds in the vicinity of the reservoir. In 1975 a pair bred successfully in a greenhouse in the London Borough of Brent central nursery between pots of geraniums.

• White Wagtail *M a alba*
The nominate continental race is an occasional passage migrant, especially in the spring. Harting (1866) mentioned nine individuals between 1841 and 1862, and added that his friend Frederick Bond 'succeeded in shooting three of the birds, two males and one female, and very kindly gave me one of the males'. Birds have occurred in March (3), April (27), May (7), August (1) and September

(16). It is interesting to note that in 1960 and 1997 when the water level was low there were many records.

167. DIPPER *Cinclus cinclus*
Very rare straggler. Not surprisingly this species is a great rarity at the reservoir with just two records, separated by well over a century. A breeding species associated in Britain with the fast-flowing rivers of the northern and western uplands, the Dippers which very occasionally occur in south-eastern England are often found to be of the migratory nominate continental race *cinclus*, which is characterised by its black belly.

> 1862   One in spring.
> 1990   One on March 26th and 31st, seen in flight near Cool Oak Lane bridge.

The 1862 individual, at the Silk Stream near Colindeep Lane, Hendon, was described by the observer as 'like a wren in shape and action, and flew like a kingfisher'. The rather brief views of the 1990 bird were by an observer familiar with the species; on neither occasion was it possible to make any specific racial identification. This record was not accepted by the LNHS records committee as insufficient detail was submitted.

168. WREN *Troglodytes troglodytes*
Common resident. This species has always been numerous in the reservoir recording area, reflecting its status in the rest of London. However, numbers are severely depleted after cold winters. Breeding bird censuses showed the Wren to be the sixth commonest passerine in scrub habitats in the late 1960s and 1970s. It was the second commonest in the Eastern Marsh, but after a series of mild winters it became the dominant passerine on the census plots by 1975, and retained this position throughout the 1980s and 1990s with up to 43 territories in the Eastern Marsh (1990) alone. Numbers of territories in other years have been as low as 17 in 1977, when there were snow showers in April and a cool late spring.

169. DUNNOCK *Prunella modularis*
Common resident. A familiar breeding species whose status at Brent and in the rest of London does not appear to have changed. Its population is more stable than that of the Wren; it is the third commonest passerine in the scrub woodland habitats in the area, and on average the fourth commonest in the marshland census plots. The number of territories mapped in the Eastern

Marsh varied between 11 (1992) and 19 (1975). In December 1961, following an eruptive dispersal of Dunnnocks throughout eastern England in November, numbers rose at the Brent. On December 28th, just prior to severe wintry weather, an influx of c 60 birds was noted near the Field Studies Centre; this included two albinistic birds, one of which was completely white.

170. ROBIN *Erithacus rubecula*

Common resident. The status of this familiar species appears to have changed little over the last 160 or so years. Harting (1866) wrote that it was 'commoner even than the last [Dunnock] owing perhaps to a current superstition that it is unlucky to kill a Robin, or to take its eggs. Hence it lives unmolested, while the nest of Hedge Sparrows, 'Jenny Wrens' and other small birds are plundered without remorse'. In woodland and scrub habitats at the reservoir Robin was second only to Blackbird in abundance. In a census plot of 9.7 ha there were on average 24 Robin territories compared with 31 Blackbirds and 18 Dunnocks. In the Eastern Marsh study plot of 11.7 ha, the number of Robin territories varied between eight and 18, and it tended to be outnumbered by six other species.

171. NIGHTINGALE *Luscinia megarhynchos*

Rare passage migrant. In common with many other parts of London, this species ceased breeding in the vicinity of Brent Reservoir in the early part of the 20th century as the suburbs encroached on its habitat. Nightingales still bred at Mill Hill and Harrow until the late 1920s at least although the last Hampstead breeding record was in 1899. Harting (1866) described the species as a regular summer visitor to Middlesex, arriving towards the end of April and departing in August. Many were taken by London bird-catchers and were sold for 18 shillings a dozen. Read (1896) described Nightingales as a summer visitor to the Brent valley, not by any means rare but said to be not so common as formerly; he recalled seeing and hearing many at Wembley Park on April 29th 1894. Today the species is a very occasional spring and autumn migrant, though it is doubtless overlooked. The only records since breeding ceased are given below:

1959	One on July 6th.
1962	One on July 16th.
1964	Singles on Aug 5th and 27th, the latter trapped and ringed.
1990	One on Aug 17th.
1992	A singing male on May 3rd.
1995	A singing male on Apr 28th.
1998	One flushed from waterside vegetation in the Northern Marsh on Apr 27th.

The 1995 bird was seen near Staples Corner and struggled to make itself heard against the rush-hour traffic.

172. BLACK REDSTART *Phoenicurus ochruros*

Rare passage migrant. The first record of this species for Britain was a specimen shot in a brickfield at 'Kilbourn' on October 25th 1829, only a few miles southeast of the reservoir. According to the LNHS (1964), 'In 1926, three years after the beginning of its continuous history as a British breeding species, the Black Redstart began to breed in Middlesex … with three pairs taking up their abode within the Palace of Engineering in the year after the Wembley Exhibition', a short distance west of Brent reservoir. At least three pairs bred there annually until 1941, with a fourth confirmed in 1937, but despite this and the fact that Black Redstarts colonised other parts of the city, the first record at the reservoir was not until 1954. Its rarity since then, compounded by a 32-year gap in observations after the fourth occurrence in 1963, is somewhat puzzling. All records are listed.

1954	A male in June.
1958	A male on Sept 23rd.
1959	A female on Apr 10th.
1963	Females on Apr 6th and 19th.
1995	A male on Apr 13th.
1997	A female on May 3rd, and an immature female on Aug 30th.
1999	A male on Apr 17th.

In addition, one was seen in nearby Hendon on October 31st 1937.

173. REDSTART *Phoenicurus phoenicurus*

Scarce passage migrant. Once a regular summer visitor, according to Harting (1866) Redstarts arrived in the second week of April and remained into the first week of September. Read (1896) described it as a not very common summer visitor 'but doubtless breeds in holes of willows and other old trees by the Brent as I have observed both old and young birds flitting along the hedgerows in the late summer'. By 1909, when Dixon wrote The Bird Life of London, the species had suffered a widespread decline. Dixon stated that the 'Redstart cannot be described as common or even of frequent occurrence in the Metropolitan Area. There are few places where it breeds except in the remote suburbs, and even there it is a local one'. While Glegg (1935) and Harrison (1931) mentioned that it occasionally still bred at Stanmore Common, it had ceased nesting around the reservoir at the turn of the century. It remains an occasional spring and autumn migrant, and all records since 1960 are given:

1960 Males on Apr 8th and 27th and May 1st.
1961 One on Oct 1st.
1962 Singles on Aug 16th and 18th, and two on 24th, one of which
      was trapped and ringed.
1963 Single males on Apr 19th and May 6th.
1964 One on Aug 24th was trapped and ringed.
1965 A male on Apr 14th, and three on May 2nd.
1966 Singles on Apr 23rd, Aug 31st and Sept 16th and 18th.
1986 One on Sept 20th.
1990 Single immatures near the Field Studies Centre on Aug 19th
      and the old cycle track on Aug 25th.
1991 A female/immature in the Northern Marsh on Sept 21st.
1992 Single females on Apr 26th and May 12th.
1993 Singles on Sept 26th and Oct 2nd.
1994 A female on Apr 30th, a male on Aug 29th, two females on
      Sept 24th and a male on Sept 25th.
1995 A female on May 9th.
1996 A female on Apr 27th.
1997 One on Sept 2nd, and a female on Sept 6th.
1998 Females on Apr 26th, Aug 30th and Sept 24th.

The gap of 20 years between 1966 and 1986 without a single record is hard to explain, although there are mitigating factors. The crash of Redstarts, Whitethroats and Sedge Warblers in 1969 caused by the Sahelian drought in their African wintering grounds accounts for fewer birds on migration, and there were also fewer observers in the 1970s. Coverage at the reservoir has increased considerably since the late 1980s, and the species has since recovered from its population crash.

174. WHINCHAT *Saxicola rubetra*

Passage migrant. This species was a common summer visitor in Harting's day, being particularly numerous in some years such as 1861. It remained a breeding bird by the reservoir until at least 1926 and at Hendon and Wembley Park into the 1940s. The subsequent decline has been reflected throughout the London area, where it has ceased breeding as urbanisation took hold. Today it is a regular double passage migrant at the reservoir, although a pair did breed in 1960, rearing one young. One bird had also been seen on June 19th 1959. Exceptionally early and late birds were seen on March 30th 1960 and November 2nd 1982 respectively. The passage of Whinchats through the Brent has declined markedly since the 1930s and 1940s. In the 1980s they were particularly scarce, with only a few birds seen each year, although the species has since increased in its occurrences: this was partly due to the construction of a 'bund' in 1990 to receive silt dredged from the reservoir. This created a very attractive habitat for migrant chats, and was followed by a dramatic increase in records (including 19 bird-days between August 23rd and September 12th 1991 alone). All records for the past ten years are given:

1991   Many records, with spring maxima of three on May 18th and autumn maxima of four on Sept 1-2nd.
1992   One or two present from Apr 26th-May 5th, and singles on Sept 13th and 19th.
1993   One on Aug 23rd.
1994   One on Apr 23rd, two on Apr 30th and one on Sept 4th.
1995   Two on Apr 29th, two on May 8th, one on Sept 20th and one on Oct 8-9th.
1996   Singles on Apr 25th and 27th, May 5th (female) and 13th, Aug 25th and Sept 1st, with five on Aug 31st.
1997   Two on May 3rd and singles on May 13th and Sept 6th.
1998   A male on Apr 27th, two birds on Aug 28th, one on 29th, two on Sept 5th, one on 20th and one on Oct 9th.
1999   Singles on Apr 24th and in Sept on 21st and 25th.
2000   Singles on Sept 2nd and 9th.

175. STONECHAT   *Saxicola torquata*

Passage migrant and winter visitor; former breeder. Stonechat was a breeding resident at Brent in the last century, although it was less common in winter. Harrison (1931) observed this species as a scarce and very erratic breeder, and cites one nest at Hendon in 1929. A pair bred successfully on the slopes of Barn Hill in 1943. A marked decline took place in the London Area, particularly after 1933, following a series of cold winters. Today it remains a scarce breeding bird in the region. Stonechats have been irregular visitors to the Brent ever since, with none being reported in some years (particularly in the late 1980s and early 1990s). Yet in other years it is quite common with, for example, up to 10 present in the winter of 1960-61. Up to six then wintered from October 11th 1961 until cold weather at the beginning of 1962 and again in 1963 caused a reduction in numbers. Only a few single birds were then seen for the rest of the decade. Numbers then slowly increased to at least four in 1974, although these birds were just passing through. A pair then bred in 1978 and 1979 with two young raised in the latter year. Since then usually only one or two birds have been seen each year mainly just on one day in early spring or late autumn. Records for the past ten years are listed below:

1993   One on Sept 4th.
1994   Singles on Feb 18th, Sept 4th and Oct 2-3rd, five juveniles on Sept 29th, and two birds on Sept 30th.

1995	Two on Sept 28th, a male and female on Oct 28th, and a male again on 29th.
1996	Singles on Mar 25th and 28th and Oct 5th.
1998	A pair on Oct 9th.
1999	One on Feb 28th.
2000	Pair present with Dartford Warbler on March 4th.

176. NORTHERN WHEATEAR *Oenanthe oenanthe*

Passage migrant. Harting (1866) commented that the Wheatear 'remains with us about six months in the year, from the middle of March to the middle of September'. He stated that its favourite haunts included old gravel and chalk pits and rabbit warrens, where it made its nest in a deserted burrow. It must have ceased breeding in the area soon after Harting wrote his book, as Read (1896) described it as 'rare in our district'. Today the species no longer breeds in the London Area, although breeding was suspected near the reservoir in 1944 as a pair were seen between April 15th and May 11th and a young bird was present on June 20th. Wheatear is now a regular double passage migrant, the earliest dates being March 12th in both 1961 and 1995 and the latest November 1st 1959. The largest count on any one day is 17 on March 28th 1965.

All records for the past ten years are summarised below, showing the variation in numbers from year to year:

1991	Spring passage spanned Mar 30th-June 9th, with some 28 bird days and a peak of six on Apr 26th, including five at Woodfield Park football pitch. Autumn passage involved four birds.
1992	An early spring passage started with three on Mar 21st, one remaining to 31st. More followed with two on Apr 1st and one on 8th, a female on 19th, eight birds on 26th, further singles on 27th and May 2nd, and two birds on May 4th.
1994	Singles on May 3rd (female), 7th and 22nd.
1995	Six on Apr 29th.
1996	In spring, six (three males) on Mar 24th, three on 25th,

one on 30th, four on Apr 7th, three on 14th, a female
on Apr 19th and 21st, two females on 25th and a
female May 6th. In autumn, a female on Aug 14th, two
on 26th and one on 31st.

1997   In spring, single birds on Apr 1st, 4th, 11th, 23rd, 25th, 30th
and May 3rd, with two on Apr 26th. Autumn passage
saw one on Aug 14th and two on Sept 9th.

1998   In spring, singles were seen on Apr 10th, 12th, 27th and
28th and May 8th. Autumn singletons were recorded on
Aug 16th and 25th and Sept 3rd and 13th.

1999   Recorded in spring only, with singles on Mar 28th, Apr 2nd, 17th
and 24th, and May 1st.

2000   Single birds on Apr 1st, 8th, 21st and 24th and on Aug 27th and
Sept 9th.

• Greenland Wheatear   *O o leucorrhoa*

Birds showing characters of this larger race, which is typically a later migrant
in spring, have occurred as follows:

1926   One on Apr 23rd.
1928   One on May 13th.
1947   One on May 6th.
1948   One on May 24th.
1960   One on May 19th.
1961   One from May 21-26th.
1963   Two on May 5th.
1964   Two on May 7th.
1999   One on May 15th.

It is also possible that the more recent May individuals were of this race, but
none has been subspecifically identified.

177. RING OUZEL   *Turdus torquatus*

Scarce passage migrant. Harting (1866) described this species as 'a passing
visitant, appearing in spring and autumn'. He further commented on the partiality
of Ring Ouzels to ivy berries, noting that 'a male bird, shot at Kingsbury on April
18th 1864, had the stomach filled with them'. Dixon (1909) stated that 'In
Surrey, the bird is by no means a very rare one on passage, especially on the
higher grounds. In Middlesex it similarly occurs, and has been recorded from
Kingsbury, Kilburn, Hampstead, Hendon and Edgware'. They were clearly
more frequent then than they are now, but despite this there do not appear to

be any documented records from the reservoir this century until 1953. Since that date there have been only 12 records involving 16 birds. They have been more regularly recorded in the past 10 years with six records, four of which were in April. All records in the 20th century are given:

1953   One on Apr 22nd.
1960   Males on Oct 6th and the late date of Dec 3rd.
1971   Two males and a female on Apr 6th.
1972   One on Sept 7th.
1973   A male on Apr 24th.
1981   A male on Oct 24th.
1988   A male on Apr 29th.
1989   One on Oct 2nd.
1991   An immature male on Oct 12th.
1994   A female on Apr 11th.
1995   A male on Apr 21st.
1997   A female on Apr 26th.
1998   A male on Oct 3rd.
2000   A female from April 5th-7th.

178. BLACKBIRD   *Turdus merula*
Common resident. Blackbird has always been a common resident at Brent Reservoir, and it is one of the most numerous breeding birds in scrub and woodland areas with densities of up to 3.7 pairs per hectare. It is outnumbered by Wren and Dunnock on the Eastern Marsh census plot, but remains dominant in the Northern Marsh plot as this contains proportionally more scrub. Large communal roosts used to occur throughout the year in the bushes on the wall of the dam and in the Field Studies Centre, with peak numbers of up to 2,000 occurring in late autumn. Recoveries from ringing studies carried out between 1964 and 1972 (Batten 1973) showed that most of the birds came from gardens in Kingsbury to the Field Studies Centre and from Neasden to the bushes on the dam. By 1972 over 6,000 Blackbirds had been ringed at roost, and these had produced 235 recoveries. All but four were recovered within the London Area, and only one in 18 had moved outside the roost catchment areas of about 200 hectares, suggesting a highly residential population. Only one individual was recovered abroad: a bird ringed on February 10th 1968 which was found dead in Sweden in October 1969. Considering that in national terms about one in 11 recoveries of the species refer to birds of continental origin, it strongly suggests that continental Blackbirds are either usually scarce in the area or do not use the communal roosts. The latter seems more likely, as observations suggest there are occasional influxes of migrant Blackbirds in autumn. Further studies (Batten 1977) showed that some interchange

between roosts occurred. Of 269 birds caught at the roost on the dam, six birds were caught which had been ringed at the main roost; and of 340 birds caught at a roost in the Eastern Marsh, one bird had been ringed previously at the main roost. Subsequent changes in vegetation in the Field Studies Centre from scrub to woodland, and the removal of scrub from the back of the reservoir dam, have resulted in much more dispersed roosts in recent years.

179. FIELDFARE   *Turdus pilaris*
Winter visitor and passage migrant. Harting (1866) stated that Fieldfares generally arrived in either the last week of October or the first week of November, and stayed until the third week of April and occasionally into May. A pair remained in the neighbourhood of Kingsbury throughout the summer of one year prior to 1866, but did not breed. In some years Fieldfares pass over the area in large numbers: examples of this phenomenon include 1,250 in two hours on November 4th 1961; 1,500 in a five-hour period on January 5th 1963; 800 south on January 10th 1967; and 272 on October 30th 1993. The numbers remaining in the area during winter tend to be far fewer now except in severe weather. In some years small numbers (50-70) used to roost in the main Blackbird roost, usually in cold weather. The earliest arriving birds were two on the remarkably early date of August 19th 1984, and the latest departure was one on May 19th 1970.

180. SONG THRUSH   *Turdus philomelos*
Resident. Until recently this species was a common resident and winter visitor. It was outnumbered by Blackbirds in suburban gardens by six to one, and at the main thrush roost by eight to one. In the scrub and woodland there were just over two pairs of Blackbirds to every pair of Song Thrushes, and the same ratio was apparent in the marshland census plots in most years in the 1970s. From the late 1970s, however, the ratio has decreased to sometimes as low as three to four Blackbirds for each Song Thrush. This reduction in numbers has been reflected throughout the country, with a national decline of 50 per cent in the last 25 years which has resulted in this species being added to the Red List of species of high conservation concern. The Song Thrush population has been shown to be more mobile than the local Blackbirds, as seven out of 18 recoveries came from sites more than three miles away: these included Mill Hill, Langley, Slough, Ealing, Regent's Park and East Putney.

181. REDWING   *Turdus iliacus*
Common winter visitor and passage migrant. Redwing is the commoner of the two winter thrushes at Brent Reservoir, although a century ago Read (1896)

described it as not so numerous as Fieldfare. Birds usually begin arriving in early October, typically slightly before Fieldfares, and are still present well into the following March, although they often leave a little earlier than that species. The earliest arrival date is September 25th 1993, and the latest departure is April 29th 1995. A huge passage occurred as early as October 5th 1966, with about 400 moving over per hour during the day, with a few Fieldfares among them. On October 10th 1992, 1,456 flew over and on Oct 12th 1997 there were some 3,600, with most passing through in a 1.5-hour period. On the same day more than 12,000 flew over nearby Hampstead Heath. Sometimes large movements are associated with cold weather: at least 3,000 passed over in a six-hour period from 09.00 hrs on January 14th 1960; c 700 in five hours on January 5th 1963; 300 east on January 8th 1963; 300 south on January 10th 1967; and 200 on January 6th 1996. In the past birds sometimes used the main thrush roost in mid-winter, with birds flying in from Barn Hill/Fryent Way.

182. MISTLE THRUSH *Turdus viscivorus*

Resident. This has always been the least common of the resident thrushes because of its large territorial requirements. There is no evidence of any marked change in status in the area since Brent Reservoir was constructed in the 19th century, despite the urbanisation which has occurred since that time. In a typical year there are two or three breeding pairs around the reservoir. There is some evidence of flocking in the autumn, the largest party being 20 on September 5th 1998 in Woodfield Park.

183. CETTI'S WARBLER *Cettia cetti*

Very rare straggler. Cetti's Warbler was unknown in Britain as recently as the mid-1960s. However the expansion of the species' range on the Continent saw the arrival of the first at Titchfield Haven in 1961 and this heralded an influx which, after the first breeding occurred in 1972, saw it quickly established as a localised resident in south and south-east England. This species was first recorded in the London area in 1975 and peaked in 1981, when up to 11 singing males were recorded, mostly in the Lea Valley at Rye House RSPB Reserve. However, the freezing weather of the following winter all but wiped the species out in the South-East, and it remained absent from many of its former haunts. It has made something of a comeback since then, but reflecting its continued scarcity in the London Area there is just one record at Brent:

1990   A singing male in the Eastern Marsh from Apr 19th-22nd.

This unusually obliging individual, found during a Common Birds Census visit, was one of three singing males in the London Area in spring that year.

184. GRASSHOPPER WARBLER *Locustella naevia*

Scarce passage migrant; has bred. Harting described this species as a 'regular summer visitant though not particularly numerous as a species'. He frequently observed it at Willesden, Hendon and Kingsbury. It was still recorded in these districts by Dixon (1909), although Read (1896) had described it as a rare summer visitor to the Lower Brent valley. Harrison (1931) stated that it was probably regular on passage at Brent Reservoir and may have nested, and cited a late record of three on September 21st 1929. Glegg (1935) stated that it was a scarce visitor to Middlesex and that it had probably bred, but no nest had been found in recent years. Since then it certainly has decreased further and although birds are heard singing on migration in spring in various places in the London Area, it is unlikely that more than a handful stay to breed. Nesting at the reservoir was last proved in 1964 when a pair raised at least one young. Owing to the skulking habits of this bird a number must go through undetected, especially in autumn. All 20th century records are given:

1946	One on May 10th.
1953	One on Aug 17th.
1956	Singles on May 18th and Sept 11th.
1957	One on June 8th.
1959	Three on Aug 27th.
1960	One singing every evening from June 17th-July 9th.
1964	One pair bred and raised at least one young.
1970	One singing between May 4th to Aug 3rd, and another present on Sept 13th.
1981	One singing on May 2nd.
1991	Singles on Apr 28th and May 27th put in brief vocal appearances.
1992	Singles on Apr 26th, May 3rd and June 26th.
1994	One on Apr 23rd.
1995	One on May 3rd.
1997	One on Apr 26-27th.

185. AQUATIC WARBLER *Acrocephalus paludicola*

Vagrant. This Eastern European breeder is annual in small numbers in Britain in early autumn, mainly along the south coast from Sussex to Cornwall, and to a lesser extent in south Wales, in August. It is very rare inland, and as might be expected is extremely unusual in the London Area: there have been just 11 records, the last on August 12th 1981 at Rainham Marsh. The Brent individual was typical in date, if not location:

1955	One on Aug 28th.

The bird was found by G Warburg and seen later the same day by Prof. Warmington, and the record is described by the observers in detail in Brit. Birds 49: 327-328, from which the following extract appears. 'The bird stayed on top of the grass in full view for some moments, and G.W. was at once struck by its bright yellowish colour and by its striking head-pattern with buff stripes over the eyes and a broad, buff stripe down the middle of its crown. Before any other details had been noted it disappeared into the sedge, uttering a short, rather loud 'teck'. About 20 minutes later the bird was found again in the same place but only briefly seen. G.W. was struck by the fact that this bird behaved exactly like an Aquatic Warbler he had seen only 8 days previously in France: both stayed for some moments in full view on top of the grass and the note in each case was exactly the same. Later that day E.H.W. visited the same area at G.W.'s request. After an hour's search he found the bird and, apart from having good views of the head-pattern, noted that it was also prominently streaked on the upper-parts, including the rump, while there were distinct marks on the under-parts as well. The bird seemed to him to be much more buff in colour than any Sedge Warbler, and the central crown-streak was much broader and more clearly defined than is the case with young Sedge Warblers'.

186. SEDGE WARBLER *Acrocephalus schoenobaenus*

Common summer visitor and passage migrant. Historically, Sedge Warblers appear to have been fairly common visitors to the reservoir, Harting (1866) implying this in his description of this species as 'a summer visitant, arriving in April and leaving in September'. Harrison (1930) noted that 'a few usually arrive in April at the Brent' but that 'a very marked passage' is especially apparent in early May, when they can be abundant. Census areas and techniques have varied since the 1970s, with not all suitable habitat surveyed, but the overall recent trend is unfortunately one of a marked decline. Despite the inconsistency of the censuses, the various peaks and troughs are at least partly explained by the severe droughts in the wintering quarters of the species in Africa. In recent years the 18+ pairs in 1989 represents the greatest breeding success. Since 1991 there have been at least five pairs, but no more than 10 in any single season. Like the Whitethroat this species also suffered severely from the Sahel droughts in 1969 and the 1983/4 winter, and the breeding pattern reflects this: there were just two pairs in 1984. It is interesting to note that both Sedge and Reed Warblers were equally common as recently as the late 1970s. On passage, Sedge usually arrives at least a week or two before Reed, this being reflected in the earliest-ever arrival date of April 5th 1993; autumn departure is also earlier than that species, with the latest recorded on October 1st 1944.

187. REED WARBLER *Acrocephalus scirpaceus*

Common summer visitor and passage migrant. Harting (1866) described this species as being local and seldom seen in north and north-west Middlesex, although common along the Rivers Thames and Colne. Harrison (1930) commented on a decrease within recent years, mentioning that in 1929 only three localities within Harrow district were occupied. This pattern appears to have continued throughout the middle of the 20th century, with just sporadic breeding records. The dramatic increase in numbers of this summer resident since the early Seventies reflects a similarly dramatic growth in the size of the main Eastern Marsh reedbed, after the 1974 draining of the reservoir; this reedbed now measures over two acres in area. This has resulted in a steady rise in breeding activity since 1975, peaking in 1990 with 43 singing males recorded. There has been a continued slow decline since, but while the reedbeds have fewer pairs others have moved into new habitats; Reed Warblers now also breed on the dump, in the allotments, and in the Japanese Knot-weed behind the dam. Other small areas of reed have become established in the Northern Marsh and these too have their breeding Reed Warblers. In spring the first birds typically arrive in late April, with the earliest recorded date on April 13th 1997, and in autumn the last usually depart by late September, with the latest on October 12th 1991.

188. DARTFORD WARBLER *Sylvia undata*

Rare straggler. The only record for Brent Reservoir is of a male found early morning on March 4th 2000. It remained all day in low scrub in the company of two Stonechats. Following a series of cold winters in the 1980s this species crashed in numbers but has subsequently recovered. It has now significantly expanded its range from the lowland heaths of southern England and has reached East Anglia and Wales. Dartford Warbler is an annual visitor to the London Area and often over-winters.

2000   A singing male on March 4th, north bank, western end.

189. LESSER WHITETHROAT *Sylvia curruca*

Summer visitor and passage migrant. In the 19th century Harting (1866) considered this species to be one of the commonest warblers, along with Whitethroat. However, Harrison (1930) described its comparative status as rather scarcer: 'In most years I expect to find about one nest of Lesser Whitethroat to four nests of Common Whitethroat, and this ratio holds for most of the districts.' Censuses since the last in the 1960s have indicated a fairly stable breeding population of between three and six pairs. However, there has been a shift in the distribution of territories; numbers have dropped around the Field Studies Centre as it has matured from scrub to closed canopy woodland. At the same time increasingly suitable habitat on the allotments and the dump have led to an increase in territories. In spring the first birds generally arrive in late April and early May, with the earliest recorded date on April 21st 1991. There is usually a strong autumn passage, with peak numbers present at the end of August and early September, mainly around scrub on the dump and in the disused allotments. Ten birds on August 31st 1996 was a noteworthy count; the latest recorded date is October 3rd 1998.

190. WHITETHROAT *Sylvia communis*

Common summer visitor and passage migrant. All commentators from the 19th and early part of the 20th centuries describe this species as a very common warbler. However, numbers of this summer resident crashed nationally in 1969, after several years of severe drought in the Sahel wintering grounds in sub-Saharan Africa, with numbers remaining low over the next two decades. Since 1990 there has been a steady recovery in the numbers of breeding birds, surpassing their previous levels in recent years. There were up to 20 pairs in both 1996 and 1997, with an impressive 22 singing males recorded on April 27th 1996 and 25 on May 5th 1997. As with Lesser Whitethroat, the old allotments and the Northern Marsh scrubland hold the greatest number of birds both breeding and on passage. Birds typically arrive from mid-April, with the earliest-ever on March 23rd 1957; most have departed by early-mid September, with the latest date on October 5th 1995.

191. GARDEN WARBLER   *Sylvia borin*

Summer visitor and passage migrant. It is interesting that Read (1896) noted this species to be commoner than Blackcap along the Lower Brent Valley, especially in 1896 when there were five nests in the area. Harrison (1930) considered Garden Warbler to be locally common, though shy and skulking. Prof. Warmington, a regular visitor to the reservoir, had noted a marked increase at nearby Mill Hill in 1929 and 1930. In contemporary times Garden Warbler has been a summer resident in small numbers, and although it probably breeds in most years, this is often hard to prove. The species is also a regular passage migrant in small numbers; four singing males on April 26th 1997 was the highest recent total. The earliest and latest records are April 19th 1997 and September 11th 1993.

192. BLACKCAP   *Sylvia atricapilla*

Common summer visitor and passage migrant; regular in winter. Harting (1866) noted that this was an uncommon summer visitor, arriving in early April and departing in about the last week of August. Read (1896) described it as fairly common, though less so than Garden Warbler. Subsequently, Prof. Warmington (Harrison 1930) commented on the change in status at nearby Mill Hill: 'The Blackcap is increasing and was especially plentiful in 1930.' Between 1958 and 1967, however, this was a very scarce species; breeding remained unproven despite occasional territory-holding. Blackcaps were more often seen on passage; 22 were trapped in the autumn of 1966, for example. Today the species is a common summer resident, double passage migrant and occasional winter visitor in small numbers. Over the last decade breeding activity has been stable with 10-12 pairs. Large numbers can be present in late April and early May, with up to 29 singing males being recorded. In 1999 a leucistic female was seen paired with a normal male on May 29th.

193. WOOD WARBLER   *Phylloscopus sibilatrix*

Rare passage migrant. Harting (1866) described this species as somewhat local in the breeding season and Glegg (1930) commented on a probable decrease since Harting's day. Read (1896) noted the collection of an individual from beside the reservoir in April 1867 by a Mr Power. Harrison (1931) alluded to an increase in the Harrow district in 1929 and 1930; these appear to have been bumper years for warblers. Three records exist for the 1960s, including singles on April 8th 1960 – a remarkably early individual found at

Woodfield Park amongst a significant fall of migrants – and on July 30th 1961 and two on August 30th 1960. There is an anecdotal record of a singing bird in the Northern Marsh from May in the early 1980s, though the general dearth of records is somewhat mystifying. On nearby Hampstead Heath birds are found in both spring and autumn, and may remain on territory for a few weeks in April and May. The closed canopy woodland in the Field Studies Centre would appear to be very suitable for this species.

> 1867   One collected by Power in Apr.
> 1960   One on Apr 8th and July 30th, two on Aug 30th.
> 1961   One on July 30th.

194. CHIFFCHAFF   *Phylloscopus collybita*

Common passage migrant, winter visitor and occasional breeder. This species was considered to be commoner than Willow Warbler by Harting (1866). However, later commentators like Glegg (1935) noted a decrease. Several pairs which bred in 1970 were the first since at least the mid-1950s (Batten 1972). Recent census results indicate one pair proved breeding in 1988, up to five pairs in 1989 and four singing males in 1990, with possible breeding also in 1991. Two territories were held in both 1992 and 1993 but with no breeding confirmed. More recently three or four pairs have been reported breeding. On migration the strongest passage is noted in autumn, peaking in early September with sometimes up to 30 birds around the reservoir, particularly in the allotments and Northern Marsh. Wintering birds occur with regularity with sometimes up to 10 birds present in mild winters.

On April 13th 1997 an apparent Chiffchaff x Willow Warbler hybrid was found on the north bank; the bird was rather imperfectly singing both songs, and had pale legs and a short primary projection.

Occasionally birds showing characteristics of the races *abietinus* and *tristis* are present (the latter sometimes proposed as a separate species, Siberian Chiffchaff).

• *Phylloscopus collybita abietinus*
> 1992   One seen on Dec 19-20th.
> 1997   One on Dec 24th.

• *Phylloscopus collybita tristis (Siberian Chiffchaff)*
> 1989   Two present, first found on Nov 25th, over-wintered to
> new year.

1990   Over-wintering bird present until March 4th. Single bird noted on Nov 3rd.

1991   Single on Dec 31st.

1992   Single on Dec 19-20th, with second bird of *abietinus* type.

2000   One over-wintered from Nov 25th until at least Dec 25th.

195. IBERIAN CHIFFCHAFF *Phylloscopus brehmii*

Vagrant. Until the late 1990s this warbler was considered to be a form of Common Chiffchaff *P collybita*, but analysis of differences between the two, including mtDNA and vocalisations, has led to its recognition as a full species. Aside from song, however, distinctions between the two are marginal in the field, so this is crucial in the identification and acceptance of individuals of the species in Britain. The bird at Brent was the first British record, there have since been four further records accepted.

1972   A singing male was observed and tape-recorded on June 3rd.

This individual was originally found on the south bank in front of the factories adjacent to Neasden Recreation ground by John Wood who alerted Leo Batten. Batten had the foresight to tape the song, and this was to prove conclusive to its acceptance by the national records committees. He described the distinctive vocalisations as follows: 'The call was quite unlike that of either the Willow Warbler or the Chiffchaff, being more reminiscent of a young chicken. The usual song consisted of about 10-12 chips, the first five or six being delivered at a slower rate than the remaining ones. The whole song lasted 2-2.5 seconds.' A fuller account is to be found on page 186 and is fully written up in a *British Birds* article to be found in Vol. 93 No.7.

196. WILLOW WARBLER *Phylloscopus trochilus*

Common summer resident and passage migrant. This species was apparently less numerous than the Chiffchaff in Harting's day. Glegg (1935) noted an increase, while Harrison (1931) described this species as the commonest *Phylloscopus* warbler. Censuses since the late 1960s have recorded 10-15 pairs in most years, although 1989 was an exceptional year with approximately 20 pairs present. Birds typically arrive from early April (earliest date March 28th 1996) and are present into mid-September (the latest being three on September 28th 1999). An unusual record concerns one observed from January 4-9th 1977, with a Chiffchaff present for comparison on 4th.

197. YELLOW-BROWED WARBLER *Phylloscopus inornatus*

JPPW

Very rare straggler. Although this Siberian migrant is regular in small numbers on the east coast in autumn, it is much prized at inland sites and the sole Brent record was also the first for Middlesex.

    1994   One from Sept 18th-20th.

The bird was very elusive and was seen by just five observers during its three-day stay. It was originally found adjacent to the rifle range, and was watched for just two minutes. Despite much searching it was not relocated until early evening behind the Field Studies Centre, where it was seen again briefly over the next two days. At the time there was a notable influx of this species on the east coast, and at least 130 individuals were recorded (Evans 1997). The same autumn another was recorded nearby at Kenton, Middlesex, on October 11th. See account on page 187.

198. GOLDCREST *Regulus regulus*
Autumn passage migrant and winter visitor; irregular breeder. Harting (1866) considered this a rare breeding species in the 19th century, with just one record. Harrison (1930) noted that the severe frosts of February 1929 seriously

Plate 11

A. Common Terns, an increasing breeding species, June 2001, (Leo Batten)

B. Kittiwake, a scarce visitor, July 1990, (Bob Watts)

C. Long eared Owl, a winter visitor between1994-1997, (Leo Batten)

Plate 12

A. Kingfisher, a re-established breeding
resident April 1995, (Leo Batten)

B. Reed Warbler a regular breeding
summer visitor, (Brad Charteris)

C. Dartford Warbler on March 4th 2000, the
first for the area, (Leo Batten)

D. Fox, a common predator of birds, (Leo Batten)

affected this scanty population. In recent times a pair has regularly bred in the large yew trees growing in the churchyard. Two juveniles seen in the Cemetery on July 18th 1993 indicated successful breeding, and the species has probably bred at this locality since. Otherwise, it is a regular autumn passage migrant, with a few birds over-wintering. The biggest total in recent years was 26 on October 28th 1990, more typically 10-15 are present in autumn.

199. FIRECREST *Regulus ignicapillus*
Rare, but increasing, passage migrant. The first record was not until 1958. Subsequently this species has been a rare passage migrant, but it is now recorded almost annually. Nearly all recent records have been from the mature willow woodland area of the Eastern Marsh. All records are given:

1958   One on Apr 9th.
1969   One female on Apr 5th.
1974   Two on Nov 4th.
1990   One from Nov 3rd-Dec 1st at least proved frustratingly elusive as it consorted with a tit flock in Eastern Marsh.
1992   One on Oct 8th and Nov 1st.
1993   One on Oct 23rd, with possibly a second individual heard on 31st.
1994   One on Nov 26th.
1995   One on Oct 15th and a second which over-wintered from Nov 23rd until the year end.
1996   One from Jan 1st-Mar 30th.
1997   One called in Braemar Avenue on Jan 24th; another was in a tit flock in the Eastern Marsh on Nov 9th.
1999   One from Oct 20th-Dec 24th at least, with two on Nov 17th.
2000   One on Jan 2nd, one from Nov 26th until Dec 26th at least.

The long-staying 1995-96 bird initially frequented sallows on the boundary of the East Marsh. Later in the winter, following some severe weather, it moved into an area of mixed woodland heavily overgrown with ivy that presumably gave it a food supply and shelter during the hardest weather. Since that date Firecrest has over-wintered in most years and always in that area.

200. SPOTTED FLYCATCHER *Muscicapa striata*
Regular passage migrant in small numbers. A species in heavy decline, apparently not just over recent decades. In Harting's era (Harting 1866) the species was noted as a regular summer visitor, in some years very common while in others scarce. Harrison (1930) describes it as perhaps the most abundant

summer migrant bar [Common] Whitethroat. An occasional breeder up until the early 1970s, it is now a regular double passage migrant in small numbers, especially late May/early June and mid-August to late September. The best count in recent years was eight individuals frequenting the willow canopy around the Northern Marsh on September 16th 1990.

201. PIED FLYCATCHER *Ficedula hypoleuca*

Scarce passage migrant. This bird is an occasional passage migrant. Harting (1866) comments that 'in May 1842, a male of this species was shot at The Hyde, which is between Kingsbury and Hendon'. It was an occasional Middlesex breeder in the late 19th century. Glegg (1930) mentions breeding pairs in 1866 and 1868 on nearby Hampstead Heath. All available records are given:

1956	One on Aug 20th.
1964	One in Aug.
1966	One on Aug 24th.
1967	One on Aug 11th.
1971	One on Sept 25th.
1984	One on Aug 16th.
1990	A female on Apr 28th, briefly in the Eastern Marsh.
1993	An immature male in Eastern Marsh on May 8th.
1995	One on Aug 28th.
1996	A male in the Northern Marsh on Apr 16th, then a female at the nearby dump on Apr 27th.
1997	A male in the Northern Marsh on Apr 26th.

Other North London sites such as Hampstead Heath and Alexandra Palace record Pied Flycatcher far more frequently than at Brent Reservoir.

202. BEARDED TIT *Panurus biarmicus*

Rare winter visitor. This was an exceptionally rare bird in the 19th century. Read (1896) mentions one on the River Brent at nearby Stonebridge Park, watched for 15 minutes on June 3rd 1896. At the reservoir itself it was first recorded in 1965. The species became a regular winter visitor in the late 1970s and throughout the 1980s, but these days it is once again a rare winter visitor to the reservoir, with the last record in 1991. All records are itemised:

1965	A pair on Oct 25-26th.
1971	Fifteen-plus on Oct 17th, with 17 on the 20th. On the former date six individuals were ringed, and two were re-trapped at

Wimblington Marsh, Cambridgeshire, 102 km north, on Dec 4th. There were further records of two on Nov 20th and one on Dec 25th.

1972 Singles on Jan 30th, Feb 5th, 6th, 19th and 26th, with two males and a female on Dec 10th.

1973 Singles on Oct 28th, Nov 17-18th, Dec 9th and 15th. The last date refers to a female that was ringed.

1974 One on Jan 1st, with two on 20th, four on Oct 14th and a minimum of three on Dec 30th.

1975 Four on Jan 3rd, with three on 9th.

1976 One on Oct 25th.

1977 A pair on Mar 25th.

1978 A male on Nov 5th, then two males and a female on several dates from Nov 24th-Dec 22nd.

1979 Three on Jan 10th and 13th; two on Feb 9th; nine on Oct 17th; and two on Nov 2nd.

1980 Fifteen-plus on Oct 19th, about half of them males; one male and two females from Dec 7-31st.

1981 One male and two females on several dates from Jan 1st-Mar 2nd, and on Nov 15th, Dec 24th and 27th, with single females on Nov 1st and Dec 30th.

1982	Singles on Jan 9th and Sept 23rd.
1985	Female on Jan 2nd.
1986	One female on Jan 2nd, a pair on 5th and two from Dec 21-31st.
1987	At least two present from Jan to March with three on Mar 14th.
1988	A pair on Nov 2nd, then one male and two females from Nov 12th until the year end, with four on Nov 25th and Dec 5th.
1989	Two females and one male present from 1988 until Mar 11th.
1991	One heard briefly on Oct 12th.

203. LONG-TAILED TIT *Aegithalos caudatus*

Increasing resident. Harting (1866) describes it as a common species found throughout the year and observed in parties of five to ten or more in autumn and winter. However, it was lost as a breeding bird from the early 20th century until the mid-1970s. Harrison (1930) notes its patchy distribution, recording it as scarce at nearby Hendon and Mill Hill. It is now a resident breeder in small numbers and slowly increasing, averaging four to six pairs over the last decade. Post-breeding flocks can reach 50-plus birds, as on August 1st 1994 by Cool Oak Lane Bridge and 60-plus on October 6th 1997. It is the common-est species in mixed winter flocks, with up to 50-plus present in recent years, notably in the Eastern Marsh on December 11th 1993.

204. MARSH TIT *Parus palustris*

Rare straggler. Harting (1866) states that it was uncommon but occasionally observed on the banks of the reservoir. However, he could not rule out Willow Tit, which was not formally described until 1897. To a lesser extent this is also the case with later commentators, such as Harrison (1930) who describes it as a scarce and local breeder in the nearby Harrow district. Over the past decade there has been a marked decline in the London area, from a minimum of 59 pairs in 1993 to just 18 in 1995. Indeed, by the latter year the species was believed to be extinct in Middlesex, with no records at all for the year. All definite records are given:

1960	One in September.
1966	One on Oct 29th.
1967	One on Jan 29th.
1987	Two on Sept 4th.
1988	One on Mar 3rd.

205. WILLOW TIT *Parus atricapillus*

Occasional and decreasing passage or winter visitor. This species was not described until 1897 when type specimens were collected at Coldfall Wood, Finchley. This species has undergone a significant decline in numbers in recent years at the reservoir, as it has throughout the London Area. The London Bird Report goes as far as describing this species' plight as 'absolutely desperate', with just 12 sites reporting the species in 1995, compared with 17 the year before. First recorded breeding in 1957, it did so consistently from the mid-1960s until the early 1970s. Numbers in London have declined dramatically in the past 20 years and it is now almost extinct. All recent records are given:

1957	First recorded breeding with certainty.
1960	Three on May 1st.
1964	One to three present from Aug 11th-Oct 31st; three were ringed in this period.
1965	One pair bred.
1966	Two present from at least July until the end of the year; both were trapped and ringed.
1967	Two from Jan to July.
1968	At least two pairs present and singing, juvenile seen on July 19th and 28th.
1969	Present throughout the year, with a juvenile caught in the first week of Aug.
1970	One pair probably bred.
1971	Two pairs present and singing on Feb 21st and Apr 19th.
1972	Two pairs present and singing.
1974	One on Nov 30th.
1976	One on Nov 13th.
1979	One on Dec 8th.
1980	Singles on March 15th and Aug 16th.
1983	Present in the breeding season, with one on Nov 26th.
1987	Recorded four times by the ringing group between Aug and Sept.
1988	Two or three from Nov 22nd-Dec 20th.
1989	One on May 28th; juvenile on July 1st.

206. CRESTED TIT *Parus cristatus*

Vagrant. Harting (1866) describes one shot in the spring of 1860 in a small spinney near Cool Oak Lane: 'Mr W. Warner, the lessee of the fishery at Kingsbury, has a small collection of birds shot in that neighbourhood. On looking through this collection, I was agreeably surprised to find a specimen of the Crested Tit.' This is most likely to have been a wandering bird from the Continent.

207. COAL TIT *Parus ater*
Scarce resident. Harting (1866) describes this species as a resident, most numerous in the autumn and winter. Its status remains unaltered, with one pair breeding annually in Birchen Grove Churchyard. Exceptionally, in 1970 at least seven pairs bred locally (Batten 1972), three in the Field Centre and the other four on nearby Barn Hill. Records away from the cemetery are unusual, so 1995 proved remarkable in yielding five such occurrences. There were a further three records in the Eastern Marsh during summer/autumn 1997 and 1999.

208. BLUE TIT *Parus caeruleus*
Common resident. This beloved garden bird has always been a common resident, since first mentioned in the literature of Harting (1866). When ringing studies were undertaken this often proved the commonest catch, as 204 processed in 1987 testifies. During the 1990s the population has remained relatively stable, with an average of 20-25 pairs per annum. Exceptional flocks have included 50 on August 26th 1990.

209. GREAT TIT *Parus major*
Common resident. The status of this species has not changed since the 19th century. In the 1990s there appears to have been a slight decline in breeding numbers with 10-15 pairs recorded annually. The highest recent count was 30 on August 26th 1990.

210. NUTHATCH *Sitta europea*
Scarce visitor, mainly in winter. It has never been a common species, and in Middlesex it suffered from a patchy distribution even in Barrett-Hamilton's era (1893). It formerly bred at nearby Barn Hill/Fryent Country Park [until 1963], which may have accounted for wintering birds. This species demonstrates a remarkably sedentary nature given that barely five miles away there are 20-plus territories on Hampstead Heath. All records for recent years are given:

1961	One on Aug 16th.
1985	One on Nov 16th.
1988	Several winter records from the Field Studies Centre.
1989	Likewise reported in winter.
1990	A juvenile in the Eastern Marsh on June 16th was most unusual; another was in the Nursery on Dec 5th.
1995	One adult on June 20th in the Northern Marsh.
2000	One on May 31st and one on Dec 17th.

211. TREECREEPER   *Certhia familiaris*

Occasional visitor. Harrison (1930) describes it as quite common. Now only an occasional visitor and occasional breeder, having ceased breeding regularly in the early 1950s, with just two records reported by Batten in the 1960s. The species remained scarce during the 1970s and 1980s and the breeding records in the 1980s appear to have been a temporary phenomenon. All recent records are given:

1986	A family party seen on July 26th.
1987	Three pairs believed to have bred.
1988	Two records in Apr and one on Dec 20th.
1989	Single record on Nov 26th in the Northern Marsh.
1990	Breeding not proven, but up to two between Mar 10-18th, then several in the Eastern Marsh from Nov 4th.
1991	Just two records on Feb 3rd and Dec 15th.
1992	Singles on Jan 4th and 19th, with a pair in the Northern Marsh on Apr 12th followed by further singles on Apr 18th and 20th.
1993	A single at Birchen Grove Cemetery on Sept 11th was followed by sightings of a single in the Eastern Marsh on Nov 3rd and 21st and Dec 11th.
1994	One on Sept 24th.
1995	One in a tit flock in Oak Wood on Dec 22nd.
1996	At least two in Birchen Grove Cemetery on Aug 31st.
1997	Present from Jan 2nd-Apr 26th (seven records) and from Sept 22nd-Dec 8th (five records); two present on Jan 26th and Apr 7th, 14 records of 16 birds.
1998	One on Jan 2nd and 10th, then June 21st.
2000	One on Dec 5th.

212. PENDULINE TIT   *Remiz pendulinus*

Rare straggler. A juvenile male was found in the afternoon of November 16th 1996 in the Northern Marsh reedbed. It was seen very well the following morning by 15 observers from the main hide in the Eastern Marsh. The bird was seen until early afternoon but only once again later in its stay, briefly from the main hide in the Eastern Marsh on November 22nd. This is the second record for London. Almost a year later and only 50 metres away from where the 1996 bird was found, three birds were found feeding on Typha at 10.15 hrs in the fog. Present for just two hours always in the Northern Marsh, they were seen flying off calling at 12.15 hrs.

1996	Juv. Male on Nov 16th and again on Nov 22nd.
1997	Three, probably female and two juveniles for two hours on Nov 2nd.

An account of these occurrences is given on page 188.

213. RED-BACKED SHRIKE *Lanius collurio*

Rare passage migrant, formerly bred. This species has been a great rarity since it ceased breeding in the 1940s. During the 19th century it was a common summer visitor, usually arriving about the first week of May and remaining until the end of August. Its decline appears to have coincided with urbanisation and a change in farming practices. Harrison (1930) refers to E. H. Warmington's observations of a decrease at Mill Hill and a total disappearance from the Kingsbury area within the previous five-six years. The last confirmed record of breeding, and the only record of breeding in the 1940s in the area, comes from 1945 when a male was seen on July 7th and there was a pair with three juveniles on 31st. That year there were still at least 28 pairs breeding in the London Area, where they continued to breed until the last proven pair in 1969. The only Welsh Harp record since involves one from September 25-26th 1971. This was a first-year bird which was on the old boat-house fence at the end of the Eastern Marsh.

214. GREAT GREY SHRIKE *Lanius excubitor*

Rare winter visitor. Harting (1866) described this species as a winter visitant of rare occurrence. Apart from the record listed Harting also mentions a male shot at Wembley Park in January 1841 and one of two birds obtained in the winter of 1851 was from Kilburn. Glegg (1935) mentions birds seen at or near the reservoir in 1868 and 1870 and further records nearby of one seen at Hampstead in November 1877 and one shot at Pinner in November 1883. There was then a gap of fifty years until Glegg's book was published in 1935 when there were no further records. This dearth of records continued and the next record in the area was not until 1952. There have been ten records to date, all of which are listed:

1854	Harting (1866) reports that 'this bird, when first seen, was flying along the brook between Hendon and the Hyde, in pursuit of a small bird'.
1868	One seen near Kingsbury Church in the winter.
1870	One seen at Brent Reservoir in November.
1952	One on Oct 7th.
1953	One on Feb 21st.
1954	One on several dates between Jan 24th-Mar 20th.
1967	One on Apr 15th.
1974	One on Dec 1st and 15th.
1975	One on Jan 2nd, 3rd and 5th and on Mar 30th.

This species is also increasingly rare in a London context as a passage migrant and a winter visitor. In most years there are only one or two records.

215. JAY *Garrulus glandarius*

Scarce but increasing resident. Commoner now than in the 19th century, Harting (1866) notes as nowhere numerous, while Glegg (1930) comments on an upturn in the population. Resident, breeding in small numbers with winter visitors and occasional irruptions from the Continent augmenting numbers. For example, 28 on December 28th 1984 was the largest concentration in London that year. In the 1990s two-four pairs bred annually.

216. MAGPIE *Pica pica*

Common resident. Batten (1972) notes that it was very scarce in the 1950s but that at least six pairs bred in 1970. It appears to have declined from the late 19th century as Harting (1866) notes that it was 'not unusual to see five or six in company'. By 1930 it only nested in one Harrow district locality (Harrison 1930). Over the past decade breeding numbers have fluctuated but 1990 saw a record 20 pairs, and the largest flock of 50-plus on October 6th; 30-plus on November 30th 1997 was also notable.

217. JACKDAW *Corvus monedula*

Occasional visitor, mainly in autumn and winter. In the latter half of the 19th century Harting (1866) considered this species to be a thinly distributed breeding species. Over the next several decades there appeared to be an increase, which was noted by both Glegg (1930) and Harrison (1930). Breeding ceased in the late 1940s/early 1950s. However, it was still regularly seen in the early 1960s; in 1962 up to 12 were present throughout the year, mainly near the Dump. Numbers then declined during the 1970s and 1980s. More recently there has been a significant increase in records and it has bred nearby at Alexandra Park and Kenwood. The most exceptional flock recently was of 33 birds on the West Hendon Playing Fields on October 17th 1993. The Jackdaw is a common breeding resident around the country fringes of London, but it is a much scarcer breeder in the suburbs.

218. ROOK *Corvus frugilegus*

Rare visitor. A dramatic reversal in fortunes has occurred between the Rook and the Carrion Crow. Harting (1866) refers to 11 rookeries in Middlesex, each containing c 20 nests, in a 5x3 mile study area. Glegg (1930) notes a probable decrease from Harting's era but Harrison (1930) comments on an astonishing level of variation. Using Harrow on the Hill as his epicentre, he notes 84 nests within a four-mile radius in 1928, and 55 in 1929. Using a five-mile radius in 1930 he notes a remarkable 361 nests. Closer to the reservoir itself, the four pairs nesting at Barn Hill in 1929 had deserted the site by 1930. It appears that the Rook was seriously affected by rapid land development as the area became urbanised up until 1929, and by 1930 had reacted to the changing environment by deserting the area. It was last recorded breeding at the reservoir in 1959 when there were just two pairs in tall elms around West Hendon Playing Fields. Subsequently it was regularly recorded in all months until the early 1970s. Batten (1972) reports flocks of up to 100 in the autumn and winter. A flock of 140 was present near Staples Corner on July 24th 1961, together with 12 Carrion Crows and one Jackdaw. All recent records are listed:

1990   One on July 8th.
1993   One on Apr 12th.
1995   One flew south, low over the main reservoir, at 08.00 hrs on the morning of Apr 10th.
1996   One over Eastern Marsh at 10.15 hrs on Mar 30th, two east over the allotments on Oct 5th.
1997   One near Eastern Marsh on Mar 15th, 22nd and 25th; then two on Mar 30th and Apr 6th.
1998   One flew west on Nov 7th.
2000   One on Apr 29th and May 1st, two on Oct 8th and three on Oct 14th.

Rook is a scarce spring and autumn migrant in the inner suburban areas of London. Elsewhere, breeding surveys indicate a stable population after a period of decline in the late 1980s and early 1990s.

219. CARRION CROW *Corvus corone*
Common resident. Carrion Crow has not always been common at the reservoir. According to Harting (1866) it was generally distributed, but nowhere common. Both Glegg (1930) and Harrison (1930) note an increase, but it was still relatively uncommon though flocks of up to 15 occurred in October and November around Barn Hill (Harrison, 1930). Nowadays, apart from resident pairs it is likely that large numbers of nearby breeding and non-breeding birds are attracted to a large roost in the Eastern Marsh, which is maintained throughout the year. There are several counts of over 300 roosting individuals from February-March, with 334 on March 19th 1992 and 550 on February 5th 1999 the biggest counts to date. West Hendon Playing Fields also attract large concentrations, particularly in the autumn and winter. This was the site of a corvid massacre on September 7th 1996 when about 200 birds were illegally poisoned after eating poisoned bait.

• *Corvus corone cornix* (Hooded Crow)
Rare straggler. This subspecies has been recorded on a number of occasions, but not since the closure of the Dump. It became commoner in the 19th century

and during the first half of the 20th. Harting (1866) noted six Middlesex individuals killed in 15 years, while Harrison (1930) mentions that several were present around Elstree during January 1930. Periodically, there appear to have been small movements from the Continent. All records since 1952 are itemised:

1952   One from Dec 20-21st.
1953   One or two from Jan 2nd-Mar 3rd.
1955   One in Dec.
1960   One from Jan 24th-Apr 3rd; one from Nov 14th-Dec 22nd.
1963   Two on Jan 23rd.
1967   One from Apr 13-16th.
1971   One from Nov 5-7th.
1972   One from Nov 11-14th.
1973   One on Jan 14th.

This is now an extremely rare bird in London, with the most recent record in the capital in 1991.

220. RAVEN *Corvus corax*
Rare straggler. Formerly a regular breeding species in Middlesex. Harting (1866) states that it bred regularly at Enfield up to 1846. In recent times an unsurprisingly rare crow due to its mainly western and northern British distribution. Just one record:

1962   One flew north-east at 11.15 hrs on Aug 19th 1962.

There were just three London records in the 20th century, all prior to the Brent individual.

221. STARLING *Sturnus vulgaris*
Common resident. Its status has changed since the 19th century. Both Glegg (1930) and Harrison (1930) note marked increases in the London Area. In the 1970s juveniles roosted regularly in the Eastern Marsh in large flocks, sometimes of several thousand strong, which came in from the surrounding district. Since the loss of the rubbish dump these flocks no longer occur. No data is available on the breeding population but it would appear to be considerable. There has been no noticeable change in breeding numbers in recent years. Sizeable roosting and feeding flocks include c 1,500 in 1990, 1,000 on Feb 12th and 200 on Nov 30th 1992, 800-plus on Jan 16th 1993 and 600 on West Hendon Playing Fields on Jan 11th 1994. However, the highest count by far of recent years was of 5,000-plus going to roost towards Central London on Aug 5th 1992.

222. HOUSE SPARROW *Passer domesticus*
Common but declining resident. Harrison (1930) notes this was a species that benefited enormously from the increase in houses. More recently its story has been one of decline and inexplicable absence. The Brent logbook has been bereft of information on this species but in recent years it commonly bred in gardens adjoining the reservoir. More recently there has been a significant drop in numbers of this species, mirroring a national decline and at certain times of the year it appears to be completely absent from the reservoir. The reasons for this national decline are as yet unclear although a number of theories have been suggested including loss of nest sites due to modern building practise and pollution from cars.

223. TREE SPARROW *Passer montanus*
Rare visitor. Known only as a winter visitor until 1866, Glegg (1930) noted it as a not uncommon breeder. It was first recorded breeding in Middlesex in 1871 at Hampstead, and numbers increased annually from then on. Between 1881-83 Power reported large numbers near the reservoir, apparently breeding (Read 1896). At least 12 nest-boxes were occupied in 1910 in the Brent Valley Bird Sanctuary (Glegg 1930). It bred regularly in small numbers up until the mid-1960s, with numbers increasing in the autumn and winter when flocks of 100-plus were frequently recorded

(Batten 1972). However, during the 1960s there was a very rapid reduction in records and since 1966/67 there have been no records involving more than five birds. This reflects the substantial national decline over the last few decades, and its present status is that of an occasional visitor. All records since 1957 are noted:

1957　Present, but no details.
1958　One pair bred; otherwise few seen.
1959　Occasionally seen from Jan-Mar and Oct-Nov; up to 120 present on rubbish dump in Dec.
1960　Up to 60 seen on the rubbish dump during the winter.
1961　Three pairs bred, and 300 were counted around the reservoir on Dec 27th.

1962 Two pairs present in the summer; no large flocks, but present all year.
1963 One pair present in the summer.
1964 One on May 30th; 20 seen during the winter.
1965 Two or three pairs bred; up to 30 present in winter.
1966 None seen in the summer; 20 seen on Oct 23rd.
1967 Eight to twelve seen on Oct 21-22nd.
1984 Five on Jan 28th and one on Feb 1st.
1991 One on Oct 6th.
1992 Four briefly from the North Bank on Sept 10th.
1996 Two on Oct 6th.
1997 One on Jan 11th and another over Woodfield Park on Apr 26th.
2000 One calling in flight Eastern Marsh Oct 22nd.

224. CHAFFINCH *Fringilla coelebs*

Autumn passage migrant, breeder and winter visitor. Read (1896) noted it as one of the commonest residents in the Lower Brent Valley. Formerly a regular breeder in small numbers, Batten noted a few pairs breeding in the late 1950s. This small breeding population was maintained until the late 1960s, with four pairs in the Field Studies Centre in 1968 declining to two in 1969 and the last recorded breeding (one pair) in 1971. Occasional summer records persist in the Eastern and Northern Marshes but no territories were established until 1998 when two birds held territory, followed by four in 1999. The mid-1960s also witnessed a reduction in the number of wintering birds, with never more than 25 reported. There were still occasional significant movements, for example, 150 were seen flying south on October 5th 1966. The present status is as an autumn passage migrant and winter visitor in small flocks and now in most winters 10-15 birds are present at the reservoir. Numbers peak in the autumn with 193 west on November 1st 1998 by far the most significant movement of recent years.

225. BRAMBLING *Fringilla montifringilla*

Autumn passage migrant and occasional winter visitor. Its occurrence appears always to have been irregular. Read (1896) commented on its near-annual occurrence in the autumn near Kingsbury. Harrison (1930) recorded it as an occasional winter visitor, mentioning an E. H. Warmington record from April 21st 1929. Up until the 1970s occasional flocks were seen near the rubbish dumps. The earliest autumn date concerns three on September 30th 1995, with a singing male on April 23rd 1984 the latest of spring. All records since 1958 are given:

1958	Present from Jan 4th-Apr 16th, maximum of 35 from Mar 9-28th down to 15 on Apr 1st and then four until 16th.
1960	Three on Jan 14th, with c 40 near the rubbish dump on 16th increasing to c 60 on 17th and 30 from 23-30th. Then 25 on Feb 6th, 18 on 13th, 55 between Feb 20th-Mar 4th, with 20 on Mar 10th, 10 on 22nd and four on Apr 4th the last.
1962	One or two from Jan-March.
1963	Fifteen on Jan 5th, 10 on 6-7th, 12 on 8th, six on 12th and two on 13th.
1964	Two on Oct 17th.
1965	Five on Oct 2nd.
1967	One on Jan 10th.
1968	Three on Dec 28th.
1971	Six on Feb 7th.
1983	Nine on Nov 15th.
1984	Eight on Jan 28th, five on Feb 4th with three on 23rd and a singing male on Apr 23rd.
1985	Two on Feb 23rd.
1990	One male on Mar 18th.
1995	Three flew south-west on Sept 30th.
1996	One on Oct 6th, two on 21st, and 15 NE over the main reservoir on Dec 28th.
1997	Sixteen flew north on Oct 12th, one on Nov 2nd and another on Dec 13th.
1998	One flew west on Nov 1st; one on Nov 7th.
1999	One at a bird table behind the dam on Nov 5-6th.
2000	Three on Jan 7th, one on Apr 2nd and one on Nov 4th.

226. SERIN *Serinus serinus*

Vagrant. A singing male was heard in the Allotments area and briefly seen in flight on April 26th 1991 and then showed all day to an appreciative crowd on the 27th, singing from a variety of low perches in the Allotments. This was the Welsh Harp's first recorded twitch. About 50 birders successfully twitched this 10th record for London. Interestingly, the majority of London's records relate to singing males; no doubt a number of females and immatures have gone unde-tected. See account on page 190.

227. GREENFINCH *Carduelis chloris*

Common resident, passage migrant and winter visitor. Its status appears unchanged since Harting's era but there appears to have been a small decline in its London status over the past decade. Between four-ten pairs have been recorded annually over the past decade, with an impressive westerly movement of between 200-250 on Aug 29th 1992 easily the most significant count.

228. GOLDFINCH *Carduelis carduelis*

Scarce breeder and autumn passage migrant; scarce in winter. Historically this species has seen mixed fortunes. Harting (1866) commented on the species seldom being seen, though he notes that it had once been common: 'a few may be seen in autumn and in the early spring but they do not remain to breed here as formerly'. Due to the captive bird trade it became virtually extinct as a breeder (Harrison 1930). Glegg (1930) notes an increase but at a local level [this seems to contradict Harrison]. As a partial result of earlier persecution it was not until the 1940s that numbers started to increase, and it did not again become a regular breeder until the late 1950s (Batten 1972). Breeding records are very scattered and include a number of records from suburban streets surrounding the reservoir. Three or four pairs have been the average over the past decade, with an exceptional 10 pairs in 1990. Sizeable autumn flocks are attracted by the ripe thistle-heads but these have decreased significantly from 40-60 in the early 1990s to seldom more than 20-30 in recent years. Fifty-five flew south on October 11th 1997. It is regularly recorded in winter but numbers are low with usually less than 20 present.

229. SISKIN *Carduelis spinus*

Passage migrant and winter visitor. Read (1896) considered this species to be locally rare while other commentators in the 19th and early 20th century deemed it an occasional visitor. Harrison (1930) notes it to have been a regular winter visitor to the nearby Harrow district. Numbers vary considerably from year to year but the first are usually seen in early September, with larger flocks from December to February, and the last hanging on in some years into May. The largest winter flock of recent years numbered 120 on Jan 2nd 1986, but this was exceptional. One on July 6th 1997 was an unusual record.

230. LINNET *Carduelis cannabina*

Declining and irregular breeder, autumn passage migrant and winter visitor. An annual but declining breeder, concentrated mainly in the Allotments area. Historically never particularly common, Read (1896) informs us that small flocks were present in the winter but that it was scarce in the breeding season. Glegg (1930) alludes to an increase from the early 20th century. Batten (1972) noted flocks of over 100 as being not infrequent in the autumn and winter, especially near the rubbish dumps. The last flock of this magnitude appears to have been 100-plus on October 12th 1980. However, in recent years flocks have rarely exceeded 50, with 40 on February 22nd 1987 and 40-plus on November 7th 1992 the largest flocks in recent years. There has been a further decline in the past few years, with typical winter maxima of 20-25. This mirrors its breeding decline from eight to ten pairs between 1988-1991 to no more than two or three pairs since. There was no evidence of breeding in 1999 or 2000.

231. TWITE *Carduelis flavirostris*
Rare winter visitor. Harting (1866) comments that in October 1864 'several were taken alive by some bird-catchers near Kingsbury Reservoir, from whom I purchased two pairs for my aviary'. Additional birds were seen in October and November 1865. In modern times there have been just six records, all of which are listed:

1954	One on Jan 31st.
1960	One on Mar 30th.
1961	One on Apr 28th
1962	One flying north-west and calling on Dec 30th.
1964	One female on March 23rd.
1996	Fifteen flew east towards Brent Cross on Dec 7th; there were no significant London records at this time.

Rainham Marsh still represents this species' London stronghold despite a considerable decline in wintering numbers to single figures.

232. LESSER REDPOLL *Carduelis cabaret*
Scarce winter visitor and passage migrant. Recent taxonomic changes have resulted in Lesser Redpoll being separated from Mealy Redpoll which is now placed with Greater (Greenland) Redpoll *C.f. rostrata* and Icelandic Redpoll *C.f. islandica*.

Lesser Redpoll appears rather commoner today than in the 19th century, apart from during the 1890s and 1900s when it bred. Harting (1866) alluded to just five occurrences while Read (1896) noted it as an occasional visitor. An increase in breeding numbers was commented upon by Glegg (1930). Thereafter, up until the 1970s, it was unknown as a breeder. An increase became apparent in the 1960s, and Batten (1972) reported summer records in both 1969 and 1970. An upturn in fortunes in the late 1980s included one pair breeding in 1987, with notable flocks of 17 on January 11th 1986, 12 on September 30th 1988, six on December 17th 1988 and 10 on October 18th 1997. A singleton on June 17th 1990 could have indicated nearby breeding. Its status in the past decade has returned to pre-1960s levels.

233. MEALY REDPOLL *Carduelis flammea*
Very scarce winter visitor. Harting (1866) included this species in his county avifauna on the authority of Mr Bond who obtained some specimens from Kingsbury several years prior to 1866. Bond also saw several in that neighbourhood in the autumn of 1861 and some of them were afterwards taken by the London bird-catchers. It is not certain whether these birds were inside or outside of our recording area. This species was known to the London bird-catchers by the name of Stony Redpoll.

The species' status in the London area was rather uncertain when the Birds of the London Area was published in 1957 and revised in 1964. Then it was considered that the species passed through the area each year unrecorded. Its present status is as a regular autumn and winter visitor usually in small numbers. In 1966 however well over 100 were reported. There are just two recent records for the reservoir which may refer to the same bird.

> 1965   One on Oct 17th and 28th.

234. CROSSBILL *Loxia curvirostra*
Rare irruptive visitor. Always scarce in Middlesex, Harting (1866) claimed it had nested in the county but Glegg (1930) could find no evidence to substantiate this. Even in irruption years it put in few notable appearances owing to the scarcity of conifers. Harrison (1930) notes a significant flock of c 60 in August 1927 at Northwood. There are seven records of this irruptive species for the reservoir itself, involving 32 individuals. All are listed:

> 1955   One in March.
> 1966   One on Nov 25th.
> 1990   Eight flew west near the Field Studies Centre early on Aug 26th, part of a national influx.
> 1997   Flocks of three-plus and nine on July 19th, 10 on 21st and nine on 26th.

The 1997 records were all flying south-east and each was observed from early to mid-morning, this reflected a huge influx into Britain, with flocks of up to 200 in other parts of London, notably Black Park to the west of London.

235. BULLFINCH *Pyrrhula pyrrhula*
Scarce breeder, with increased numbers in winter. Prior to Harting's publication (1866) it was a very common breeder. During the 1860s and 1870s, although it was frequently observed in winter and early spring, it was seen seldom at

other times. It again became a regular breeder in the 1880s and 1890s. Harrison (1930) referred it to as fairly common but unevenly distributed. Its chequered history continued in the 1950s when it ceased to breed for several years, but it currently breeds in small numbers. In early January 1962, up to 40 birds foraged for food in small flocks. These were mostly northern immigrants of the larger and brighter nominate race, probably from Scandinavia. Over the past decade breeding numbers have remained relatively stable at four or five pairs, with winter immigrants boosting numbers, although rarely to more than 12.

236. HAWFINCH *Coccothraustes coccothraustes*
Very rare visitor. Extinct as a breeding species since the beginning of the 20th century though Glegg (1930) commented on an increase between 1866 and 1910. The first record for a number of decades was one seen in flight over the Allotments on November 1st 1991. Three miles to the east, this species returned to the Highgate area as an occasional breeder in the early 1990s.

> 1991   One in flight over the Allotments on Nov 1st.

237. LAPLAND BUNTING *Calcarius lapponicus*
Very rare winter visitor. Always a rarity in Middlesex, Harting (1866) refers to one Middlesex record. At the reservoir itself there have been three records involving three birds, as itemised:

> 1892   One shot on Oct 25th, shown to Swann by Cole.
> 1959   One on Dec 13th.
> 1961   One on Dec 19th was flushed from the old rubbish dump near the Northern Marsh and flew east, calling once.

238. SNOW BUNTING *Plectrophenax nivalis*
Rare winter visitor. Harting (1866) mentions two records: 'In October 1862 I purchased from a bird-catcher a pair which he had taken near Kingsbury Reservoir, in company with Bramblings. An adult male was shot at Kingsbury on February 8th 1865 by Mr Charles Wharton, and recorded by him in 'The Zoologist' for April 1865. This last-named was feeding in company with some Larks and Meadow Pipits among the dead weeds collected on the edge of the Reservoir.' Harting alluded to one more Middlesex individual, while Glegg (1930) referred to a further four records between 1870-95. Some of these may be the same as those in Mr Warner's collection shot by Hudson in 1888 (Read 1896). In 1933, four were seen together on November 5th. All records since are listed:

1949 Singles on Nov 28th and 30th,
      with a female on Dec 9th.
1950 Male on Nov 5th.
1956 Two flew south on Jan 31st,
      with singles on Oct 18th, Nov
      4th and 28th.
1958 Male seen in flight on Dec 6th.
1960 Two on Oct 22nd.
1962 One on Jan 7th, two males on
      Nov 11th, single on Nov 17th
      and female on Dec 28th.
1963 One on Jan 7th.
1985 A male on Nov 13th.
1996 A male appeared high from
      the west on the morning of
      Nov 23rd, flew low over the Eastern Marsh, and left to the east.

JPC

Interestingly on the same day as the 1996 occurrence a male joined a female at King George V Reservoir.

239. YELLOWHAMMER *Emberiza citrinella*

Occasional passage migrant or winter visitor. Once considered the commonest bunting in the district, though not especially plentiful (Read 1896). Glegg (1930) informs us that the status remained unaltered from Harting's era. Once it was a regular visitor from the Barn Hill/Fryent Country Park area. Up to 11 pairs bred at Fryent Country Park in the late 1960s/early 1970s, but this population declined when cattle ceased to be grazed there. Now, records are less than annual, mainly in winter or on passage. The last major influx appears to have coincided with that of Bullfinches in early January 1962 when there was a peak of seven on January 3rd. Over the past decade there has been a decline in numbers breeding within the London Area. All records since 1991 are listed:

1991 Pairs near the main hide in the Eastern Marsh on May 9th
      and July 26th.
1992 A female near the Allotments on May 15th, another flying over
      calling on Nov 1st.
1993 A female in the Allotments on Mar 7th.
1995 One on Apr 15th; one flying south-west on Nov 6th.
1997 One flew east on Mar 15th.
2000 Singles heard calling on Nov 18th and Dec 25th.

240. CIRL BUNTING *Emberiza cirlus*
Extremely rare straggler. No records for more than 100 years. At least three Middlesex records exist from the 19th century (Harting 1866). Joseph Warner shot one at Blackbird Farm (at the head of the reservoir) in the autumn of 1859, and there was a nest with three eggs at nearby Wembley Park in May 1861. Batten (1972) also refers to a nest from 1871 at Hendon. Always a scarce breeder within Middlesex, Harrison (1930) refers to breeding records from Harrow in both 1927 and 1928. It is very rarely recorded in London these days.

    1859   Joseph Warner shot one at Blackbird Farm in the autumn.

241. ORTOLAN BUNTING *Emberiza hortulana*
Vagrant. Three records relate to four individuals. In 1956 Eric Simms flushed a bird from the dense growth of sedge along the northern bank of the River Brent, where it flows into the reservoir. 'It rose with a loud call, and then concealed itself in some willows at a height of 3-4 feet above the ground. It returned later to the sedges where I had it under observation at a range of 15 feet for some ten minutes. It called twice with a clear incisive z-tick - really a monosyllabic call but with a slurred sibilant z.' (Brit. Birds 1957). This sighting coincided with a heavy passage of associated species on the east, south and Irish Sea coasts, including a sprinkling of Ortolan Buntings.

    1867   Two in early May.
    1868   One in Oct.
    1956   Female at 12.05 hrs on Sept 2nd.

242. REED BUNTING *Emberiza schoeniclus*
Scarce breeder and winter visitor in low numbers. Historically referred to as resident but not common by Read (1896) and locally common by Harrison (1930). Breeding numbers have declined sharply from 19-plus pairs in 1988 to just two or three pairs now. Winter roosts used to be significant, especially in severe winters; 150 on February 10th 1960 and 50-plus at roost on Dec 27th 1981 bears testimony to this. Nowadays they disappear in the late autumn and return in early March, with a few birds seen occasionally during the winter, eight over-wintered in 1998.

243. CORN BUNTING *Milaria calandra*
Rare visitor. In the 19th century it was a resident species with some dispersal in the winter. Read (1896) considered it to be local. By Glegg's era (1929) it was

a much decreased species. Batten (1972) noted that there were seven records for the 1960s, but it is now a rare visitor. It is in serious decline nationally, and the closest known breeding birds are at Tyttenhanger Gravel Pits. All available records are itemised:

1960   One on Jan 6th, two on Mar 4th and a male in song in June and July.
1962   One on Jan 6th.
1963   One on Oct 26th.
1966   One on Jan 19th flew south.
1967   One on Jan 19th.
1982   Five in the Field Studies Centre on Jan 17th were observed perched in hawthorns for several minutes before flying off south-west.
1997   One seen and heard near the Dam on Nov 15th.

ESCAPES

1. PELICAN sp.   *Pelecanus sp.*
1991   One in flight on the evening of June 19th.

A 'dark' individual observed in flight over the hide could have been one of the Pink-backed Pelicans (*P. rufescens*) wandering around southern Britain at that time.

2. WHITE STORK   *Ciconia ciconia*
1990   Two drifted west over the Field Studies Centre on Aug 1st.

It is more than likely that these were the two immatures that had escaped from Whipsnade Zoo and were seen later the same month as far apart as Norfolk and Dorset.

3. BLACK SWAN   *Cygnus atratus*
1988   One present from Aug 23rd until the year end.
1989   Two or three present all year, with a maximum of five on Nov 25th.
1990   One present for most of the year, occasionally joined by a second individual. Five were present on Nov 17th.

1991   A female from Mar 15th until the year end.
1994   Two on Apr 3rd.
1997   One on Mar 22nd.

In 1989 a pair attempted to breed but the nest was flooded and the eggs lost. A pair was intermittently present the following year, but there was no attempt to nest. In 1991 a male Mute Swan was seen displaying to a female of this species.

4. BEAN GOOSE *Anser fabalis*
1988   Single on Sept 11th.

5. PINK-FOOTED GOOSE *Anser brachyrhynchus*
1990   One on Mar 27th may have wandered from Hampstead Heath.

6. WHITE-FRONTED GOOSE *Anser albifrons*
1945   A tame individual from Feb 4th-Mar 11th.

7. BAR-HEADED GOOSE *Anser indicus*
1993   Five on May 22nd, with three on Nov 24th and 29th.
1999   One on Mar 28th.
2000   Two on May 31st.

8. SNOW GOOSE *Anser caerulescens*
1984   One blue phase on May 25th.

9. BARNACLE GOOSE *Branta leucopsis*
1959   Single present from Oct to the year end.
1960   Single present from Jan until Apr; the previous year's individual.
1961   Single on June 10th.
1970   Single on June 8th.
1978   One on Mar 5th.
1984   Singles on Sept 3rd and from Oct 28th-Nov 4th.
1985   Single on Jan 5th.
1990   Tame individual seen on two dates; June 17th and Aug 9th.
1992   Single on Jan 17th.

1993　Two flew into the Eastern Marsh in the early morning of May 15th.

1994　Singles on July 6th and Oct 6th, the latter feeding among Canada Geese in Woodfield Park.

1995　Two on May 20th.

1996　One on May 9th.

1999　One from Mar 28th-Apr 27th.

10. RUDDY SHELDUCK　*Tadorna ferruginea*

1950　Two on May 9th.

1969　One on Feb 1st.

1978　Female on Feb 24th.

1994　Single on the evening of May 27th in the Northern Marsh in immaculate plumage, unringed and fully-winged.

1996　Two on June 12th.

11. CAPE SHELDUCK　*Tadorna cana*

1978　Single on Feb 26th.

1995　Six on Sept 23rd had been seen earlier flying W over Tottenham Cemetery.

12. MUSCOVY DUCK　*Cairina moschata*

1993　Single on May 2nd.

1994　First found on Mar 21st in the Northern Marsh, this individual shifted to the Eastern Marsh where it was frequently observed loafing on a raft until June 5th.

1997　One on Jan 26-27th.

2000　Singles on Jan 15th and 29th.

13. RINGED TEAL　*Callonetta leucophrys*

1990　Single present from Sept 23-29th.

14. WOOD DUCK　*Aix sponsa*

1982　A male present on Nov 23rd and again from Dec 26-31st.

1983　A male present all year.

1984　Male present all year.

1985　One male on Jan 3rd.

1989　Two males present from March 26-27th.

15. YELLOW-BILLED PINTAIL   *Anas georgica*
   1997   One on Dec 6th, 14th and 19th.
   1998   One on July 11-12th.
   1999   One on Apr 30th and May 1st.
   2000   One on May 16th.

16. BAHAMA PINTAIL   *Anas bahamensis*
   1975   Single on Apr 5th.
   1994   A leucistic individual first observed on Aug 23rd in the Eastern
          Marsh was last seen on Oct 16th.
   1995   Presumably the 1994 individual present from July 28th-Sept 15th.

17. CHILOE WIGEON   *Anas sibilatrix*
   1979   Single on Sept 22nd.
   1989   Male from July 30th-Oct 10th.
   1996   Pair on Dec 21st.
   1998   One on Feb 15th.

18. AUSTRALIAN SHOVELER   *Anas rhynchotis*
   1995   Male of the New Zealand race *variegata* from Dec 28-31st.
   1996   Same individual remained until Feb 4th.
   1999   One on Jan 1st.

19. RED-CRESTED POCHARD   *Netta rufina*
   1991   Female on Mar 9-10th fed with Mallards close to Cool Oak Lane
          Bridge.

20. ARGENTINE BLUE-BILL   *Oxyura vittata*
   1997   Male from May 16th-June 8th, displaying to Ruddy Ducks.

21. EAGLE sp.   *Aquila sp.*
   1963   One on Aug 26th was thought by the observer to have been a
          Tawny Eagle *Aquila rapax*. It was watched drifting N on flat
          wings at a moderate height.

22. CROWNED CRANE *Balearica pavonina*
   1974   Single on Sept 28th.

23. COCKATIEL *Nymphicus hollandicus*
   1991   A leucistic individual walked around the tern rafts on Aug 17th.
   1992   One on Apr 11th.
   1994   An individual in the Northern Marsh on Aug 12-13th.
   1996   Singles on July 14th and Aug 17th.
   1997   Singles on Apr 8th and July 6th.
   1998   One on July 19th.
   1999   One on July 25th.
   2000   One on April 29th.

24. BUDGERIGAR *Melopsittacus undulatus*
   1988   Single on Aug 27th.
   1989   Single 'blue' in the Northern Marsh on Aug 10th.
   1998   One 'blue' on June 6th.
   2000   One on April 21st.

25. GREY PARROT *Psittacus erithacus*
   1990   Single on Apr 29th.

26. SENEGAL PARROT *Poicephalus senegalus*
   1997   One from Aug 8th to Sept 6th was then seen on Hampstead
          Heath.

27. FISCHER'S LOVEBIRD *Agapornis fischeri*
   1997   One on rooftops by Welsh Harp Playing Fields on June 22nd.

28. MACAW sp. *Ara sp.*
   1994   A dog warden reported that a red macaw had visited his
          compound situated near the rifle range.

29. BARN OWL *Tyto alba*
   1989   One in Oct related to an escaped individual. A group member
          spoke to its owner a couple of years later.

30. PEKIN ROBIN (RED-BILLED LEIOTHRIX) *Leiothrix lutea*
   1994   One on Apr 24th discovered at 18.45 hrs in the vicinity of the
   New Hide. A scratchy, Sylvia-like song alerted the sole observer.
   Despite being highly mobile and elusive it was eventually well
   watched for about two minutes. Not relocated subsequently.

31. RED-HEADED BUNTING *Emberiza bruniceps*
   1967   Male present on Aug 13th and Sept 8th.

32. ORANGE-CHEEKED WAXBILL *Estrilda melpoda*
   1979   One on Sept 30th and Nov 2nd.

33. COMMON WAXBILL *Estrilda astrild*
   1991   Pair present between July 12-14th, with three on Aug 9th and
   up to three present until Sept 13th. Often observed in the lush
   vegetation of the Eastern Marsh.

34. AVADAVAT (RED MUNIA) *Amandava amandava*
   1967   Single on Aug 10th, with four on 15th and nine on 17th. Finally,
   four were observed on Oct 6th.

35. JAVA SPARROW *Padda oryzivora*
   1967   Single on Aug 1st.

36. NAPOLEON WEAVER *Euplectes orix*
   1970   Single on Oct 11th.

37. BLACK-WINGED RED BISHOP *Euplectes hordeacea*
   1980   One from Oct 12-30th.

References

Batten, L. A., 1959. Kestrel catching a fish. Brit. Birds, 52: 314.

Batten, L. A., 1972. The past and present bird life of the Brent Reservoir and its vicinity. Lond. Nat. 50: 8-62.

Batten, L. A., 1973. Population dynamics of suburban Blackbirds. Bird Study, 20: 251-258.

Batten, L. A. & Wood, J. H., 1974. Iberian Chiffchaff at the Brent Reservoir. Lond. Bird Rep. 37: 78.

Batten, L. A., 1977. Studies on the population dynamics and energetics of Blackbirds Turdus Merula Linnaeus. University of London: PhD thesis.

Barrett-Hamilton, G. E. H., 1892. Harrow Birds. Harrow.

Bond, F., 1843. Note on Water-birds occurring at Kingsbury Reservoir. Zool. for 1843 p102-103.

Chandler, R. J. & Osborne, K. C., 1977. Scarce Migrants in the London Area 1955-74. Lond. Bird Rep. 41: 73-99.

Dixon, C., 1909. The Bird-life of London. London.

Evans, L. G. R., 1997. Rare Birds in Britain 1994. LGRE Public. Ltd.

Glegg, W. E., 1930. The Birds of Middlesex since 1866. Lond. Nat. 9: 3-32.

Glegg, W. E., 1935. A History of the Birds of Middlesex. London.

Harting, J. E., 1866. The Birds of Middlesex. London.

Harrison, T. H., 1931. Birds of the Harrow District 1925-1930. Lond. Nat. 10: 82-120.

Homes, R. C., (Ed.) 1957. 1964. The Birds of the London Area since 1900. London.

Hudson, W. H., 1898. Birds in London, Green, London. New edition, 1969, David & Charles Reprints, Devon.

London Natural History Society. 1936-1998. Lond. Bird Rep. 1-63.

London Natural History Society. 1921-1935. Lond. Nat. 1-15.

London Natural History Society. The Birds of the London Area, revised 1964 London.

Read, R. H., 1896. The birds of the Lower Brent Valley. (Reprinted from the Report and Transactions of the Ealing. Nat. Science Soc. for 1896).

Simms, E., 1957. Ortolan Bunting in Middlesex. Brit. Birds 50: 118-19.

Warburg, G. & Warmington, E. H., 1956. Aquatic Warbler in Middlesex. Brit Birds, 49: 327-8.

Welsh Harp Conservation Group. 1987-2000. Welsh Harp Report. 1-10.

EARLIEST AND LATEST DATES OF REGULAR MIGRANTS

Summer Migrants	*Arrival*	*Departure*
Hobby	Apr 15th 1995	Oct 23rd 1994
Common Sandpiper	Apr 3rd 1996	Oct 20th 1997
Common Tern	Apr 3rd 1998	Sept 20th 1997
Swift	Apr 21st 1958	Sept 24th 1994
Sand Martin	Mar 5th 1977	Oct 8th 1988
Swallow	Mar 27th 1993	Oct 29th 1959
House Martin	Apr 8th 1995	Oct 28th 1993
Yellow Wagtail	Mar 30th 1959	Nov 29th 1960
Redstart	Apr 8th 1960	Oct 2nd 1993
Whinchat	Mar 30th 1960	Nov 2nd 1982
Wheatear	Mar 12th 1961	Nov 1st 1959
Sedge Warbler	Apr 5th 1983	Oct 1st 1944
Reed Warbler	Apr 13th 1997	Oct 12th 1991
Lesser Whitethroat	Apr 21st 1991	Oct 3rd 1998
Whitethroat	Mar 23rd 1957	Oct 21st 1996
Garden Warbler	Apr 19th 1997	Sept 21st 1995
Willow Warbler	Mar 28th 1996	Sept 28th 1999
Spotted Flycatcher	May 3rd 1997	Oct 10th 1995

Winter Migrants	*Departure*	*Arrival*
Water Rail	May 20th 1984	Aug 23rd 1994
Fieldfare	May 19th 1970	Aug 19th 1984
Redwing	Apr 29th 1995	Sept 25th 1993
Siskin	May 13th 1997	July 6th 1997

JPPW

WADERS AT THE WELSH HARP

When the reservoir was built in the 1830s it was the only large body of water near London other than the Thames and remained so for most of the 19th century. The large Lea Valley and Staines group of reservoirs were not built until the end of the 19th and the early 20th century. Such a stretch of water was an obvious attraction to waterbirds and the Victorian naturalists who sought them, usually with a shot-gun. It was built to top up the canal system and so had extensive gravel and mud banks exposed each autumn, especially after a hot dry summer. This mud and gravel acted as a magnet for passing waders, in particular on their return autumn passage, and many of the early county records for scarce waders came from the Kingsbury Reservoir as it was then called. Pectoral, White-rumped and Spotted Sandpiper were all recorded in the middle of the 19th century and Little Ringed Plover, Little and Temminck's Stint were recorded nowhere else in London until after 1900.

The function of the reservoir as a canal top-up continued until the 1960s, as did the frequent occurrence of waders. Since then the water has been kept at a constant level apart from occasional lowering for maintenance. Apart from on the rare occasions when the level is lowered and mud is exposed, waders are now much less frequent.

Recently some management work in the Eastern Marsh has established a permanent shingle bank and some muddy edges. These and the tern rafts attract a few waders each year during spring and autumn passage periods. The table overleaf shows when, during a year, the waders in the systematic list have been most frequently recorded and is divided into half-monthly periods.

Summary of Passage Wader Records

Units in bird-days

SPECIES	Ja 1	Ja 2	Fe 1	Fe 2	Mr 1	Mr 2	Ap 1	Ap 2	My 1	My 2	Jn 1	Jn 2	Jy 1	Jy 2	Au 1	Au 2	Se 1	Se 2	Oc 1	Oc 2	No 1	No 2	De 1	De 2
Oystercat.	-	-	6	-	-	1	4	1	3	1	1	1	1	1	5	-	-	-	-	-	-	1	1	3
LRP	-	-	-	-	-	1	3	4	8	5	12	10	6	4	2	6	3	-	-	-	-	-	-	-
Ringed P.	-	-	1	-	6	2	1	1	16	2	-	1	1	5	30	61	50	10	2	5	1	1	2	-
Sanderling	-	-	-	-	-	-	-	1	1	-	1	-	-	-	-	-	3	6	1	2	-	-	-	-
Little Stint	-	-	-	-	-	-	-	-	4	1	7	-	-	-	11	-	11	10	1	2	-	-	-	-
Tem. Stint	-	-	-	-	-	-	-	-	3	-	-	1	-	-	3	2	10	-	2	-	-	-	-	-
Knot	2	-	-	1	(5)	1	-	-	-	-	2	-	-	-	-	-	4	3	-	1	-	-	-	-
Cur. Sand.	-	-	-	-	-	-	-	-	-	-	-	-	-	2	8	8	9	37	-	-	-	-	-	-
Dunlin	6	1	4	-	1	-	1	-	2	3	-	-	2	4	5	4	6	2	4	-	1	2	-	8
Ruff	-	-	1	1	-	2	-	-	-	5	-	-	-	-	6	20	7	7	16	15	-	-	-	-
Bl-t Godw	-	-	-	-	-	-	-	36	1	-	-	-	-	3	8	-	-	2	-	-	-	-	-	-
Br-t Godw	-	-	-	-	-	-	-	12	6	-	-	-	-	-	-	-	1	1	-	-	-	-	-	-
Whimbrel	-	-	-	-	-	-	-	-	7	-	-	-	-	2	2	1	-	-	-	-	-	-	-	-
Curlew	1	-	-	1	2	3	-	4	1	-	-	9	-	17	2	22	7	2	-	2	-	-	-	-
Spotshank	-	-	-	-	-	-	-	-	-	2	1	-	-	-	12	10	4	4	-	-	-	-	-	-
Redshank	18	9	1	-	1	10	4	4	3	2	5	9	4	23	7	9	-	-	-	-	-	-	1	3
Grnshank	-	-	-	-	-	-	-	4	6	9	18	16	18	21	63	57	43	7	1	-	-	-	1	-
Green San.	-	-	-	-	-	-	1	3	2	-	1	-	1	4	11	19	-	1	-	-	-	-	-	3
Wood San	-	-	-	-	-	-	-	-	-	3	-	-	4	20	20	25	7	-	-	-	-	-	-	-
Turnstone	-	-	-	-	1	-	1	1	4	7	-	-	-	-	2	1	2	-	-	-	-	-	-	-
Others	-	1	-	-	-	-	1	1	4	-	8	-	-	-	1	1	3	1	-	-	-	-	1	-
Total species	27	11	13	3	14	20	16	72	73	39	47	38	59	106	190	246	170	93	27	27	2	4	5	17
No. of Species	4	3	5	3	6	7	7	7	18	11	8	6	10	12	17	15	17	15	7	6	2	3	3	4

Includes most passage wader species. Excluded are winter-occurring species and undated records eg. Jack Snipe, Common Snipe, Woodcock, Pectoral Sandp., White-rumped Sandp., Golden Plover. Additionally Common Sand. has also been excluded due to the volume of records and difficulty in assessing bird-days.

WHEN AND WHERE TO WATCH BIRDS AT BRENT RESERVOIR

by Andrew Self

Spring

Towards the end of March the regular birdwatchers at the reservoir will start looking forward to the first summer arrival. By this time the over-wintering Chiffchaffs will already be in song around the reservoir and may be joined by the odd Blackcap but the first migrant is usually the Wheatear which will most often be found on West Hendon Playing Fields, either early in the morning before the dog walkers are out or pitching in during the late afternoon. Alternatively it will be a lone Sand Martin, swooping low over the water before continuing north to its breeding grounds.

In most years, few other migrants appear before April but this month will only be a few days old before the first pair of Common Terns appear. Their arrival is very spread out and not until the end of May will all the colony return. The early ones ignore the rafts for a week or so but will soon evict the Canada Geese who always try to raise a few young there but rarely succeed. The geese will then move to the pools at the back of the Northern Marsh where they are usually successful unless the water levels fluctuate too much and wash out their nests. Also in the first week of April Willow Warblers will return, especially to the area of scrub on the old rubbish tip which is simply known now as the dump. This is a particularly good spot for migrants, especially warblers.

By the end of April most of the summer visitors have arrived and it is around this time that the annual Spring Birdcount is held. This is when many of the local and other birdwatchers spend the whole day recording as many birds as possible. The current day record is 80 species and, with lots of people looking, many unusual birds have been seen including two Marsh Harriers, Pied Flycatcher, Ring Ouzel, Wood Sandpiper and Grasshopper Warbler. The hides act as a focal point for the day and many an hour is spent scanning the skies hoping for something to fly over.

The hides overlook the Eastern Marsh and offer excellent views of displaying Great Crested Grebes and the Common Tern colony on the rafts. Both hides also give views of the wader bank. Wader passage is very erratic at Brent and really needs low water levels to attract them down although several species have been seen on the rafts including Sanderling, Grey Plover and Whimbrel. The only waders which are recorded annually are Lapwing, Little Ringed Plover, Dunlin, Snipe, Greenshank, Redshank, Common Sandpiper and Green Sandpiper.

Summer

A busy time of the year, with about 50 species breeding regularly. The Common Terns will have hatched their first chicks by the beginning of June and the noise level of the colony will start to increase. Added to this cacophony of sound will be the ceaseless begging calls of dozens of Coot and Great Crested Grebe chicks. Away from the open water, there will be seven or eight species of warbler in full song. The disused allotments and dump are the best places to observe most of these except for the Sedge Warbler, which is mainly found at the dam end of the North Bank. By mid-June the return passage of waders will have started, usually with Redshank and Green Sandpiper. There can also be other surprises, with both Spoonbill and White-winged Black Tern turning up in July in recent years.

Autumn

Joining the early returning waders are Black-headed Gulls, which start to arrive from mid-June. However, the peak numbers are not seen until August when 4-5,000 can be seen roosting on the main reservoir in the evenings. This is a good time to look for Mediterranean Gulls, with three seen in 1998. The best place to watch the roost is by the jetty on the North Bank as the gulls appear from all directions. A feature of recent autumns has been the arrival of Black-necked Grebes, which always turn up on the main reservoir.

Duck numbers increase rapidly in August and usually peak in September; it is worth looking for Garganey in the Eastern Marsh among the Teal and Shoveler. Migrant raptors are also worth looking for, with Honey Buzzard, Marsh Harrier and Osprey all seen in the 1990s. More commonly observed though will be Hobby. Warbler passage is generally uneventful although the numbers of Chiffchaff build up in September. A few Wheatears are found most years on the playing fields and Whinchats should again be found on the dump or the North Bank. One or two Redstarts are seen most years but tend to be very elusive; the hedges running down the cricket pitch can be a good bet. Also on the hedges will be a few Spotted Flycatchers but they can turn up almost anywhere. Another favoured place for them is the hedge just south of the Sea Cadet base, appropriately known as 'flycatcher corner' since both Spotted and Pied Flycatchers were found there on an Autumn Birdcount. The latter event is held either at the end of August or the start of September, with the highest count being 78 species on September 5th 1998.

Later on during this month the visible migration picks up with Meadow Pipits and hirundines seen heading south. The occasional Tree Pipit is usually heard flying over as are regular Yellow Wagtails. A good place to stand is by the top football pitch, which is at the head of the main slope from West Hendon Playing

Firecrest

Fields. It was from here that 3,600 Redwings were counted along with 16 Bramblings and many other finches on October 12th 1997. It is from this time onwards that a few Rock Pipits are also recorded flying over every year. When the first migrant Goldcrests start to appear it is then time to look for Firecrests. One or two have been found in most recent autumns; the best place to search is in the tit flocks in the Eastern Marsh. They have also been known to over-winter here. The star bird of November has been Penduline Tit which was twice discovered in the Northern Marsh although its preferred food, Bulrush, is widely spread around both areas of water.

Winter

This season is at its best when it is very cold and there is snow or ice. Then all sorts of birds may turn up, especially duck with Smew being quite reliable although not in the high numbers that made this reservoir famous for them in the past. Goldeneye and Goosander are frequently seen and Slavonian and Red-necked Grebes can put in the occasional appearance. A Bittern sometimes over-winters in Eastern Marsh but can be very tricky to see; waiting patiently in the hides hoping to see one fly over the reed bed in the late afternoon is probably the best bet. Wild swans have been seen recently with both Whooper and Bewick's observed in 1997. Water Rails are regular and can be found in both marshes but are more often heard than seen. In the late 1990s a roost of Long-eared Owls formed with up to five birds seen. As they are very prone to disturbance, they are best left alone during the day but can be seen hunting over the uncut grassy areas around the reservoir at dusk. Siskins and Redpolls are generally quite scarce but are best looked for on the Alders in the Eastern Marsh, particularly in front of the factories. This area of willow carr is also the best bet for over-wintering Chiffchaffs and Goldcrests.

RECENT ADDITIONS TO THE RESERVOIR'S LIST OF BIRDS

• GREAT WHITE EGRET

Account, May 13th 1997   *Andrew Self*

On May 13th I received a telephone call at 16.50 from Jan-Paul Charteris saying that he and Max Wurr had seen a Little Egret at 16.30. It had flown out of a creek in the main reedbed, then around the reservoir before landing briefly on the shingle shoreline. It then flew towards the North Marsh. I dashed out to look for it and arrived within 10 minutes. After wandering around a couple of times I could not see any sign of it and presumed that it must have flown off. I went to the hide to read the account in the log book.

At 18.05 I suddenly saw an egret flying over East Marsh at tree-top height. I was ecstatic at having seen the 'Little Egret', but when I put my bins up to watch the bird I immediately noticed that it had an obvious large orange bill. I then realised that it was too large to be a Little Egret and checked the feet to see that they were not yellow. I knew then that I was looking at a Great White Egret!

It flew past the trees heading east and I ran out of the hide to look for it, but it had disappeared. I made a few phone calls, just in case it returned, and although several of us waited until dark it did not come back. As well as being the first record for Brent Reservoir, this is also the first record for London.

Description

Plumage: All pure white; no plumes noted on head.
Bill: Long and dagger-like, orange-yellow in colour.
Legs and feet: Uniform blackish, projecting a long way beyond body in flight.
Size: In flight, looked about the same as Grey Heron. JPC saw the bird land briefly next to a Grey Heron and also said that it was the same size.

• BLUE-WINGED TEAL

Account, December 9th 1995 - January 30th 1996   *Andrew Self*

On December 9th 1995 I was birding at the reservoir with Roy Beddard and Andrew Verrall. It was extremely cold and a lot of the reservoir had iced over. There had also been an increase in duck numbers which I stopped to look at in the North Marsh. I could see that the Teal numbers had gone up, so I proceeded to count them. As I went along the line of Teal that were on the edge of the reedbed one of the preening birds suddenly flashed a bright blue forewing. My immediate thought was Blue-winged Teal and I dashed off after RB and AGV. We walked closer to the ducks and had prolonged views of the bird in question and were able to confirm its identity before it was eventually flushed by a noisy group of canoeists who were trying to break the ice. It flew overhead towards the main reservoir, but in poor light we were unable to relocate it that afternoon.

Fortunately, it reappeared the next day in front of the main hide although it kept disappearing into the fog! With the news out, about 50 birders came to see it that day. It was also seen by RB on 12.12.95 then it apparently went. However, it was refound on 28.12.95 and eventually stayed until 30.1.96. It often went unseen during this time and after a while we found it lurking in the back pools of the North Marsh with a few Teal and it is likely that it retreated there for most of December when the ice had melted. At all times it was a very wary bird and it fed with either Teal or often Shoveler, and never showed any signs that it had escaped from captivity.

Description

Head:	A steep forehead and flattish crown, rather square at the rear. A dark brown cap and neck, pale brown supercilium, prominent blackish-brown eye-stripe. White eye-ring which was broken at the sides. Pale oval loral spot at the base of the bill.
Bill:	Longer than Teal; slightly more spatulate; all black.
Size:	About 5-10 per cent larger than Teal.
Legs:	Dull yellow and unringed.
Body:	Darker brown than Teal.
Wings:	Sky-blue forewing with white line along greater coverts; secondaries looked blackish. Underwing showed large white central area, dark leading edge and slightly duller trailing edge.

• HONEY BUZZARD

Account, July 30th 1994   *Andrew Self*

It was 10.50 am on July 30th and I was on the North Bank with Roy Beddard, Will Griffin and David Watson, looking at Purple Hairstreaks. DW noticed a raptor behind us being mobbed by Common Terns. As we turned round to look at it, its large size and shape initially made us think of Common Buzzard. It continued coming closer and drifted overhead about 30 metres up. We realised the wing shape was wrong for Common Buzzard and as it circled around on flat wings I could see three bars on the tail and the bird was identified as a Honey Buzzard. After circling around for about two minutes it drifted off northwards.

Description

Head: Brown and rather pigeon-like, small but protruding well out in front of the wings.

Wings: Long and straight, especially the trailing edge of the secondaries, which lacked the bulging 'S' shape of Common Buzzard. It had moulted its inner primaries and new ones were only half-grown. Wings held flat all the time it was circling overhead. Outer primaries formed five 'fingers'.

Underparts: Breast, belly and wing coverts boldly streaked dark brown.

Tail: Long with two narrow bands at base and wider sub-terminal band.

• GOSHAWK

Account, March 23rd 1997   *Jan-Paul Charteris*

At 06.55 on March 23rd I was scanning the North Marsh when, glancing up, I saw a raptor come into view from behind some tall trees. It was flying at a height of approximately 20 metres and at this stage was in direct flight. Its large bulk and slow relaxed wingbeats were immediately obvious. It didn't at first strike me as being a hawk, but some other larger raptor. It quickly began to soar, which it did for about four minutes and it was then that I began to suspect it was a Goshawk.

Description

The body itself was distinctly heavy with a prominent, barrel-chested appearance. The wings were broad-based and bulged slightly at the secondaries before tapering to relatively pointed (but still fingered) wing-tips. The wings were proportionately longer and the tail shorter compared to Sparrowhawk.

The tail was very broad-based and when spread (when the bird was soaring) was very rounded. When the bird was in direct flight, the tail was closed and unlike Sparrowhawk's, tapering outwards from a broad base to a slightly narrower tip. A striking feature were the very prominent white undertail coverts. These appeared 'fluffed-up' (as if in display) and from some angles appeared almost to 'wrap' around the sides of the tail. This had the effect of exaggerating the broad tail base still further.

Other than the undertail coverts, the only other striking plumage feature was a contrasting hooded appearance caused by the prominent dark head against the white throat. The rest of the underparts simply appeared greyish with the primaries being far more finely barred than Sparrowhawk. The upperparts were uniformly slate grey-brown.

After about four minutes of soaring the bird flew purposefully NW. In direct flight the wing beats were slow (slower and more relaxed than a Carrion Crow) and were not really reminiscent of a Sparrowhawk's 'flap-flap-flap-glide' flight. Glides were generally interspersed between periods of flapping flight but the bird would often break the glide with one or two random wing beats.

It was about 1.5 times the size of a normal female Sparrowhawk (one of which I had watched about 10 minutes earlier being mobbed by a Carrion Crow), with proportionately a much greater bulk. The Goshawk was noticeably larger and bulkier than the particularly large female Sparrowhawk present in the area.

An interesting footnote is that one of the local dog walkers with a keen interest in falconry also saw a bird that he recognised as a Goshawk on the same day.

• RING-BILLED GULL
Account, March 23rd 1996 *Andrew Self*

On March 23rd I had been in the hide watching a very heavy passage of gulls, some of which were dropping in and landing on the reservoir (c 2000 had flown over by midday). I headed over to North Marsh with Leo Batten as there is often a good number of gulls roosting there.

As we stopped in the North Marsh I put my bins up to look at the closest gulls that were standing on a large bit of rubbish in the reservoir. One of them was head-on and its head was very white. It then stuck its bill out which was yellow with a striking black band and I said almost disbelievingly that it looked like a Ring-billed Gull. Leo and I watched it for about a minute then it was flushed by an aggressive Lesser Black-backed Gull. We carried on watching it flying around quite close for several minutes before it gained height and drifted off southwards.

Description
Head: Appeared all-white with no streaking noted. It had a slight dark smudge in front of the black eye.
Bill: The most striking feature, yellow with a solid, sharply-defined black ring and a pale tip. It was quite a thick bill and had straight parallel sides. It was obviously stronger and thicker

than that of Common Gull, but was shorter and lacked the red spot and pronounced gonys of Herring Gull.

Mantle:	Pale grey, paler than Common Gull.
Size:	About 20 per cent larger than Common Gull; smaller than pursuing Lesser Black-backed Gull in flight.
Legs:	Pink.
Wings:	Not seen in perched bird, as obscured by Common Gull.
In flight:	Saddle and greater coverts same pale grey colour; Common Gulls showed contrasting darker grey saddle.
Tail:	Showed series of vertical black lines instead of solid sub-terminal black band of Common Gull. Also, lines went up side of tail, further making a 'U' shape. Light brown flecks on rump.

• RICHARD'S PIPIT

Account, October 19th 1963   *Leo Batten*

The bird was first seen flying into a bush where it perched in full view on a twig for several minutes about 12 feet above the ground. Two Reed Buntings were also present in the same bush at the time. My first impressions were of a rather large, quite dark, long-tailed pipit, longer than the nearby Reed Buntings. I watched it for an hour from 10.15-11.15 whilst it moved around various habitats; these were grassy footpaths, the rubbish dump and a reedbed. It also perched on a stone and a fence. It was observed at ranges from 20-50 yards, often viewed through my telescope.

For most of the time the bird remained solitary but did associate with three Skylarks and flew around with them at times, breaking off every now and again, flying 300-400 yards and circling back. The flight was slightly undulating, here the tail looked noticeably long. On one occasion the bird hovered for a few seconds about 30 feet from the ground rather like a Skylark, then plummeted down to the ground. It called frequently in flight even when flying without being flushed. It was always the same note which was rather similar to the chirrup note of the Skylark but slightly harsher. Whilst on the ground, it assumed an upright stance, even when walking – rather like the stance of a Wheatear.

Description

Size:	Distinctly larger than Reed Bunting and Meadow Pipits; slightly longer even than Skylark but not so plump. All these species were present nearby at times so a direct comparison was possible.
Shape:	Rather like a plump wagtail with a relatively slightly shorter tail and with very long legs. On the occasion when it was seen on

the grassy footpath, it stood well clear of the blades of grass which were 1.25-1.5 inches high. The gait consisted of walking with occasional periods of short runs, but less jerky than Meadow Pipit.

Upperparts:	Forehead and crown dark brown, heavily streaked brown-black. Nape and neck brown streaked inconspicuously brown-black. Mantle and back dark brown with more heavily and bolder brown-black streaking. From a distance this varying intensity of streaking gave a lighter half-collared effect on the nape and neck. Rump not seen well but no streaking was discernible.
Head:	Dark crown contrasted with a thick light supercilium which was distinctly visible at a range of 50 yards through binoculars. The lores were pale. Ear coverts dark brown, sides of neck buff, streaked dark brown. Iris was black-brown.
Underparts:	Off-white, unmarked except for streaks on upper breast and throat. The chin was unmarked and a purer white than the rest of the underparts. A conspicuous malar stripe extended from the lores along the sides of the chin to the streaking on the flanks and lower belly. The thighs were a dull white colour.
Wings:	Coverts were dark chestnut-brown with buff edges. The tips of the median and greater wing coverts were a lighter buff – almost white – and gave the appearance of a double wing bar.
Tail:	Dark brown with conspicuous white outer feathers.
Bare parts:	Bill was relatively longer and stouter than a Meadow Pipit and was grey-brown in colour. Legs and feet were orange-brown.

• CETTI'S WARBLER

Account, April 19-22nd 1990 *Roy Beddard*

On April 19th 1990 I was coming to the end of a mid-week evening Common Bird Census of the Eastern Marsh and my mind was switching to the Conservation Group meeting due to start in a few minutes time. I was walking along the track where the large hide is now situated when I heard a loud and abrupt burst of song coming from some osier bushes 30-40 metres behind me. The song didn't register for a few seconds, but then I stopped dead in my tracks and realised that I had just heard the characteristic outburst of a Cetti's Warbler! The question was, what to do? I was due at the meeting in about 20 minutes time. However, I had yet to see the bird so I hurried back to the osiers and waited ... and waited ... and waited. Forty-five minutes had passed and I began to think that I had imagined it and just hadn't been paying attention. Then from the middle of the bush about five metres away came that familiar outburst of song, and there was the bird. No mistake, it was a Cetti's alright. I watched it fly off into a nearby tangle and disappear. I rushed off to my meeting, 30 minutes late, and gave the news to the other Conservation Group members. It was too late to go back and search that evening but thankfully the bird was there the next morning and stayed for a few days longer. Two or three days later I went back to see the bird again and this time I heard it singing from the island opposite the willow screen that preceded the small hide. I watched it distantly from 30-40 metres away and it then took off and flew directly towards me landing on the top of the willow screen that I was standing behind! In all the bird stayed for just four days.

At that time the Kent Stour Valley population had been decimated in successive cold winters and the Lea Valley pocket had peaked at 11 singing males in 1981 and by 1990 had declined to three pairs. There have been no records at Brent since.

Description

Size: Similar to Reed Warbler in length.
Shape: Medium-sized warbler, rather portly and short-necked; short
            rounded wings and broad tail (often raised).
Head: Similar pattern to Reed Warbler; narrow and indistinct super-
            cilium; dark lores and eye-stripe; greyish ear-coverts.

Bill:	Shortish and narrow; two-toned; dark upper mandible, paler yellow-flesh lower mandible.
Underparts:	White throat; greyish breast; flanks and belly darker rusty tinge; short dark brown undertail coverts.
Upperparts:	Uniform red-brown wings, mantle and upper-tail.
Legs:	Orange-brown.
Call:	Song unmistakable, a loud explosive outburst of metallic notes, typically tchip … tchippee, tchip … tchipee, tchippee tchip, tchip.
Behaviour:	Active in tangled undergrowth and willows, but often difficult to see due to habit of singing from middle of bush and then immediately moving to a new position; flicked wings and tail; tail often cocked.

• IBERIAN CHIFFCHAFF

Account, June 3rd 1972   *Leo Batten*

The bird was first found by J H Wood, his attention being attracted by a loud and clear song coming from some willows adjoining the reservoir. After several minutes the bird was located at the top of a group of willows. The size and general appearance of the bird resembled a Willow Warbler, but the legs appeared blackish.

After being informed of the bird's presence I visited the site with JHW in the early afternoon. The song and several of the call notes were recorded on a cassette recorder and a more detailed description taken. The bird was very active, remaining at the tops of the willows – a height of some 15-20 feet. Eventually it was seen well from all angles and the following description was taken.

Description

Head:	Olive-brown, with a distinct creamy-white supercilium which terminated well beyond the eye. A dark line ran through the eye, broader behind than in front.
Upperparts:	Olive-brown.
Wings:	From certain angles an indistinct yellow bar was detected along the tips of the primary coverts. JHW could not detect any bar on the greater coverts although I detected a slight indication of one and felt it was due to possible wear to the tips of the greater coverts (it was no more distinct than the wingbar on a small number of Chiffchaffs that I have seen).
Underparts:	Washed greyish with a light ill-defined yellow band across the breast. This yellow area was slightly better marked on the lower sides of the neck. The undertail coverts were light yellow contrasting with the light creamy-grey lower belly.

Legs: Appeared dark brown in good light.

Shape: Looked rather dumpier than Willow Warbler and Chiffchaff.

Vocalisation: The bird sang and called frequently. The call was quite unlike that of Willow Warbler or Chiffchaff, being more reminiscent of a young chicken. It was uttered several times in a disconnected sequence and sounded rather similar to the one repeated in the rapid warbling song. It was also not unlike the chiff in the Chiffchaff's song. A tic-tic-tic call was also heard on one occasion. The usual song consisted of about 10-12 chips, the first five or six being delivered at a slower rate than the remaining ones, with the whole song lasting 2-2.5 seconds.

It was not until seven weeks later that the bird was finally identified as an Iberian Chiffchaff from the recordings of its song and comparison of sound spectrograms. Both observers visited the area on subsequent occasions but the bird was not encountered again.

This bird was accepted as a Chiffchaff of the race *ibericus* by the LNHS records committee. It was the first record of this race in the British Isles. As this was just a race of Chiffchaff the record was forgotten about for nearly 25 years until research showed that this form merited being a separate species: Iberian Chiffchaff (Helbig et al). Since then this record has been submitted to the British Birds Records Committee and the British Ornithological Union Records Committee who have now accepted this occurrence at Brent Reservoir as the first record of this species in the UK.

Ref: Helbig et al. Ibis 138: 650-666.

• YELLOW-BROWED WARBLER

Account, September 18-20th 1994   *Andrew Self*

At 10.20 on September 18th I was walking around by the rifle range. The only migrants I had seen that morning were one Chiffchaff and a few hirundines, and I felt that it must be time to go home as there was nothing much around. However, that all changed when I approached a small oak tree and heard a familiar call. It was a particularly distinctive disyllabic tsee-swee, rising on the second syllable. It is a call I have heard many times on the Isles of Scilly and I immediately recognised it as that of a Yellow-browed Warbler. I went into a state of panic as I knew that this was a rare bird in London. I decided to wait until I had seen it properly before I put out the news so that at least I could make a description.

I glimpsed the bird in the tree a couple of times and I was able to make out the obvious supercilium and two wing-bars. I managed to 'pish' the bird out onto an open branch where it stayed long enough for me to make some notes.

I then left the area to alert other birders. Within 15 minutes there were five of us searching the immediate area but we could not refind it. We continued to search further afield but still were unable to relocate it. The same evening Brad Charteris was in the woods behind the Field Centre when he saw it. It was also seen in the same place briefly on each of the following two days.

Description

Head: Olive-green with broad whitish supercilium with a pale yellowish wash which stretched back well beyond the eye almost to the nape. It also had a thin dark eye-stripe of the same length.

Upper-parts: Bright olive-green mantle and wings. Two wing-bars, on median and greater coverts, both whitish with a touch of yellow.

Tertials: Dark with white fringes.

Underparts: Silky white.

Shape: Like a small dainty Willow Warbler.

• PENDULINE TIT

Account, November 16th 1996   *Andrew Self*

I received a telephone call in the evening of November 16th from Jan-Paul Charteris saying that he had heard and briefly seen a bird flying around the reedbed in the Northern Marsh that afternoon. After checking up on the call he believed that it was probably a Penduline Tit. I then phoned Roy Beddard who told me that he had been checking the reedbed for Bearded Tits earlier that day when he heard an unusual call. He later phoned me back after listening to a tape of the call of Penduline Tit and said that was what he had heard. We arranged to meet up in the hide at Brent the following morning after doing the monthly WeBS count.

Sunday morning was wet and rather dismal. At 9.15, Roy and I were sitting in the main hide when we heard a very distinctive call – a high pitched almost metallic descending tzzzzeeeeooooooo – which I recognised instantly as Penduline Tit. We looked hard but could not see any sign of it so we searched all the likely areas. It called several more times during the morning but it still remained hidden. I guessed that it was feeding on the bulrushes so I returned to the main hide with RB to scan them. At 11.40 it called and suddenly appeared on a close patch of bulrush heads just 10 metres away. It was pulling the bulrushes apart and feasting on the seeds within allowing us to get excellent views. We were able to age it as a juvenile as it lacked the dark mask of an adult.

It remained feeding in the same area on and off for an hour and a quarter during which time about 15 people managed to see it. It usually called before putting in an appearance and flew out of the reedbed or willows onto the bulrushes. It was not seen later in the afternoon. It was searched for extensively on Monday 18th and Tuesday 19th but not seen – perhaps not surprisingly as the weather was abysmal with lots of rain and sleet. I searched for it later in the week when the weather had improved but to no avail. On Friday 22nd, JPC heard it call in the same place then saw it fly over towards the main reedbed at 14.45. After this final sighting it was not seen again.

Description

Size:	Similar to Blue Tit.
Shape:	A very upright bird, slimmer than Blue Tit.
Head:	Light grey with beady black eye, slightly paler on forehead and just behind the eye. Short black streak on forehead just reaching to crown (possibly due to matting of feathers).
Bill:	Steely-blue colour, small and sharply pointed, like a small version of a Goldfinch's bill.
Underparts:	White throat, pale peachy/buff breast, belly and undertail coverts.

Upperparts:	Rich apricot mantle, dark brown wings, tertials dark centred with broad pale edges; tail dark brown and markedly forked.
Legs:	Steely-blue.
Call:	Very distinctive – a short-carrying, sharp, descending long note – tzzzeeeooooooo. Much sharper than other birds that can call similarly, for example Robin, which also lacks the opening high start to the call.
Behaviour:	Clung on to bulrush stems and pecked at the seed heads and ate the seeds within. It became easy to see where it had been feeding because of the state of the bulrushes.

On November 2nd the following year came a further record of three birds, found within 50 metres of the previous year's occurrence.

• SERIN
Account, April 26th 1991   *Bill Oddie*

After a hard night's filming, I was aroused from my lie-in by sunshine, a light south-easterly breeze and the irresistible lure of Brent Reservoir – albeit that it was after lunchtime and the day was surely past its best. My circuit seemed to confirm this, as there was very little warbler song. However, a little pack of five Wheatears following the grass cutter on the football fields was more encouraging and inspired me to go round once more. Nevertheless, by half past four I was heading back to my car.

As I passed the allotments, I was day-dreaming about what I should have seen in such Mediterranean weather conditions, when I became aware that the accompanying soundtrack was strangely appropriate. Above the wheezing of the local Linnets, I could hear a sibilant twittering that I definitely associated more with the Med than the North Circular – Serin! Even as I muttered its name, the bird shot past me and disappeared through the poplars on the far side of the canoe club. The view was brief and end on but diagnostic: lemon-yellow rump and a couple of tinkly calls. I trotted back to the hide to put the sighting in the log and was also able to grip off – sorry, I mean tell – Roy Beddard, who was just arriving. Alas, the bird did not reappear that evening.

However, the next day, I rang Birdline South East and heard the joyous news that a male Serin was singing heartily back in the allotments. To be honest, I was rather relieved as single-observer in-flight-only records are often treated with a little scepticism! I certainly couldn't resist nipping back to join in my first Brent twitch. I'm happy to say that the bird performed beautifully on Saturday, but it apparently didn't fancy the Sunday crowds any more than I did and it was not seen or heard again.

Chapter 5
The Natural History of Brent Reservoir

Flora, by Leslie Williams

Change is the key to the flora and the vegetation of Brent Reservoir and its surroundings. This is because, of all the habitats present, only the remnant hedgerows and small areas of old grasslands on gravels pre-date the construction of the reservoir. Even the marshland flora has had to establish, or re-establish, since the two rivers were dammed. Indeed, since the early 19th century the whole area has changed from one of rural farmland with riverside meadows, to one where the land use is dominated by suburbia, industry and recreational facilities.

The vegetation of the reservoir area can be considered as several broken, concentric arcs. Starting from the reservoir itself, one passes through swamp, marshland, willow woodland, gravel grasslands and, beyond that, an array of habitats.

The open water of the reservoir supports few if any plants, possibly due to the lack of light, in turn the result of turbidity causing the suspension of alluvium in the water. Swamp occurs where the soil is flooded throughout the year; and typically supports tall emergent plants, usually in single-species colonies. There is a narrow band of swamp vegetation around the reservoir, though this widens on the south-eastern shore where there is a large bed of Norfolk or Common Reed *Phragmites australis*. Elsewhere, the swamp includes Bulrush *Typha latifolia* and Lesser Bulrush *Typha angustifolia*, Sea Club-rush *Bolboschoenus maritimus* and a small quantity of Reed Sweet-grass *Glyceria maxima*.

The division between the swamp and the marshland can be arbitrary, but whilst the marshland soil is permanently waterlogged, the summer water level is seldom much above the surface. The marshland plants include Alder *Alnus glutinosa*, Water-pepper *Persicaria hydropiper*, Crack Willow *Salix fragilis*, White Willow *Salix alba*, Osier *Salix viminalis*, Grey Willow *Salix cinerea*, Meadowsweet *Filipendula ulmaria*, Great Willowherb *Epilobium hirsutum*, Indian Balsam *Impatiens glandulifera*, Hogweed *Heracleum sphondylium*, Gipsywort *Lycopus europaeus*, Water Mint *Mentha aquatica*, Hard Rush *Juncus inflexus*, Soft Rush *J effusus*, Compact Rush *J conglomeratus*, False Fox-Sedge *Carex otrubae*, Remote Sedge *C remota*, Hairy Sedge *C hirta*, Cyperus Sedge *C pseudocyperus*, Pendulous Sedge *C pendula*, Tufted Hair-

Plants
Plate 13

A. Common Reed, an expanding species in the area, (Leo Batten)

B. Yellow Iris. a common marshland plant, (Leo Batten)

C. Fringed Water Lily, present in one canal in the mid 1990s, (Leo Batten)

D. Flowering Rush, a declining species of the marshes, (Leo Batten)

Plate 14

A. Marsh Marigold, a scarce early spring plant in the area, (Leo Batten)

B. Gorse, recently reintroduced in to the area, (Leo Batten)

C. Southern Marsh Orchid, a newly discovered plant for the area, (Leo Batten)

D. Spotted Orchid, locally distributed around the reservoir, (Leo Batten)

grass *Deschampsia cespitosa*, Reed Canary-grass *Phalaris arundinacea* and Yellow Iris *Iris pseudacorus*.

On the landward side of the marshland, some of the wetland species extend into wet willow and other damp woodland. These woodlands are dominated by Crack Willow *Salix fragilis*, which together with several other willow species forms an extensive belt around the eastern ends of the two arms of the reservoir. On the woodland floor, species include Lesser Celandine *Ranunculus ficaria*, Remote Sedge *Carex remota*, Pendulous Sedge *Carex pendula* and Giant Fescue *Festuca gigantia*.

A narrow belt of Taplow Gravels occurs intermittently along the northern and southern shores of the main arm of the reservoir. Where this is above the marshland, it supports acid grassland dominated by Red Fescue *Festuca rubra* and Common Bent *Agrostis capillaris*, together with Yorkshire Fog *Holcus lanatus*, Sheep's Sorrel *Rumex acetosella*, Common Bird's-foot Trefoil *Lotus corniculatus* and Burnet Saxifrage *Pimpinella saxifraga*.

Beyond the Taplow gravels there is an assortment of habitats in the adjacent open spaces. The remnant hedgerows were the field boundaries when the area was farmed, and these can be traced on 19th century and earlier maps. One of these hedgerows is the parish boundary between Kingsbury and Hendon, and now the borough boundary between Brent and Barnet. It was a green lane too, part of the original route of Wood Lane, and once continued to a bridge over the River Brent. When the reservoir is drained, the stumps of the hedgerow trees and fenceposts can still be seen in the reservoir. The hedgerows continue to support much of their earlier flora.

Grassland habitats vary from those of the sports pitches, to an imitation 'chalk downland' at Neasden Recreation Ground. There, an area of crushed rubble has been seeded with a 'wildflower mixture' and includes a variety of species seldom found in this area of London, for example Salad Burnet *Sanguisorba minor*, Hawkweed Oxtongue *Picris hieracioides* and Quaking-grass *Briza media*. Several areas of rough grassland occur around the reservoir, for example where grasslands have been left uncut, and on former rubbish tips. Where the ground has been disturbed, the rubbish tips have provided many interesting 'weed' plant records, though few of these become established. A succession from rough grassland to scrub and secondary woodland is a common feature.

Large areas of alluvium may be exposed during times of drought, as in 1919, or when the reservoir was drained in 1984. Alluvium was also exposed in bunds constructed to take material dredged from the reservoir, as with that adjacent to Staples Corner in 1989 and at West Hendon in 1990. The vegetation that developed on the drained alluvium included species characteristic of such circumstances and some which were not usually noted in the marshland, such as various goosefoots and docks, including the Marsh Dock *Rumex palustris* and the Golden Dock *Rumex maritimus*. Collections of willows are developing on the lower side of each bund.

No account of the reservoir's flora would be complete without mentioning the orchids, of which five species have been recorded. Of these, a single Pyramidal Orchid *Anacamptis pyramidalis*, grew for several years in the eastern marsh, far from its typical habitat of dry chalk downland. There is evidence that the Southern Marsh Orchid *Dactylorhiza praetermissa*, which was first noted at the reservoir in 1988, is now spreading. Coppicing of young willows to create more open marshland appears to benefit this species, and this habitat may also benefit the Common Spotted Orchid *Dactylorhiza fuchsii*. The Bee Orchid *Ophrys apirera* made an appearance on rough grassland in the early 1990s. The Broad-leaved Helleborine *Epipactis helleborine* grows in the wet woodland.

With so much developmental change and ecological succession, the conservation of the flora and the habitats will be enhanced by active management. Several species are obviously undesirable, for example Japanese Knotweed *Fallopia japonica*, which has spread to cover much rough ground and damp woodland. The Giant Hogweed *Heracleum mantegazzianum*, a massive plant with equally massive flowerheads, and a cousin of the indigenous hogweed, is a danger on public health grounds, as contact with its sap causes blistering of the skin and often permanent skin damage. As with most other species that are deemed to be weeds at the reservoir, control may best be effected by removing smaller, satellite colonies, before trying to control the main infestations. The logic behind this is that mathematically, the smaller a colony, the greater will be the proportional spread outwards.

Other species also require management. The swamp and marshland habitats at the reservoir are probably the most important in terms of nature conservation. Without management, the growth of willows in these habitats, will shade much of the flora of these habitats. Annual management is required to control willows in the beds of Common Reed. Since the early 1980s, belts of willow have grown along the shores of the main arm of the reservoir, adjacent to the Welsh Harp Open Space and Neasden Recreation Ground. These need to be controlled if the marshland and swamp habitats are to be extended, rather than lost. However, the management of trees in such prominent locations can be controversial with local visitors; and it is important that opportunities are taken to explain the long-term objectives at the reservoir. Likewise, oak scrub has reduced the area of old gravel grasslands together with their associated ant-hills. Elsewhere, the emphasis is on conserving and creating woodland, for example the Crack Willows of the eastern and northern marshes, and woodlands around the outer perimeter of the adjacent open spaces.

Ironically, there are few ponds near to the reservoir. Yet the creation of ponds in clay or Taplow Gravels would do much to increase the aquatic flora and be of benefit to amphibians. One other improvement, though exceedingly expensive, would be to de-silt the alluvium from the reservoir, thus providing a greater volume of (clearer) water, which would allow more aquatic and emergent plants. However, even without the finance for such a project, there is much that can be done to enhance the vegetation and important habitats at the reservoir.

Reference

Readers interested in a fuller account of the flora of the Brent Reservoir are referred to the article by Williams, Warren and Hutchinson in The London Naturalist, No. 74, 1995 pp 61-75. This contains a species list for the Reservoir.

Yellow Iris

Botanical surveying at Brent Reservoir, by Leslie Williams

The flora of the reservoir area was first noted in Trimen and Dyer (1869), and their records reflect that of the then rural area. Other records have been reported in The London Naturalist during recent decades, and by Kent (1975) and Burton (1983). Salisbury (1921) described the vegetation which grew on the exposed [mud] of the reservoir floor during a drought in 1919. Botanical survey work has also been undertaken in the grounds of the Welsh Harp Field Centre, and by the Welsh Harp Conservation Group in 1971 and 1981. John White, curator/botanist of the Westonbirt Arboretum, surveyed and noted the willows of the reservoir area in 1982. Ward and Pilcher (1989) described the vegetation of the reservoir, though their list of the flora appeared to be an unchecked compilation of previous lists.

Surveys of the flora of the reservoir were undertaken during the 1980s and early 1990s. Williams, Warren and Hutchinson (1995) detailed it following a survey undertaken between 1983 and 1995. Further records have been made since then, and are included in this article. The survey was centred on the reservoir including the adjacent wetlands, and open spaces to the south and the north. These open spaces were Neasden Recreation Ground, on the southern side of the reservoir, and the Welsh Harp Open Space, Woodfield Park and West Hendon Playing Fields to the north of the reservoir. The grounds of the Welsh Harp Field Centre were included, as were areas of wasteland between the reservoir and the Edgware Road. Hedgerows in Silver Jubilee Park, adjacent to the West Hendon Playing Fields, were included, but the amenity and sports grasslands there were not otherwise surveyed. Excluded from the survey were all allotment sites (at Birchen Grove and Cool Oak Lane), nurseries (at Birchen Grove and Wood Lane), school fields, and sports pitches at Woodfield Park.

Much of the survey was undertaken during opportunistic visits, while a more systematic series of visits were undertaken during 1994 by all three authors. The results also noted records made by other recorders and those published elsewhere. Species records from earlier sources were reviewed and several unconfirmed records were excluded. The order and scientific names of species follows Stace (1991). Dates and/or references are given for records by other recorders, for records before 1983 or where the dates were notable. A subjective indication of frequency is given using the ACFOR scale of abundant, common, frequent, occasional and rare. It was obvious from the large number of casual, persistent and naturalised species, that much of the flora of the reservoir had been introduced.

Mammals of the Welsh Harp, *by Andrew Self and Clive Herbert*

In order to ascertain the status of the mammals at the reservoir, a survey was carried out in 1995 (Herbert). This, along with personal observations from several regular watchers at the site, has been used to give a brief summary of the mammals of the Welsh Harp.

Hedgehog *Erinaceus europaeus*
A common mammal at the reservoir, but rarely noted due to its nocturnal habits. The remains of one that had been eaten by gypsies was found when there was an encampment at the Northern end of the reservoir in the late 1980s (J. Colmans pers obs). Two road casualties were found on Cool Oak Lane on May 7th 1995.

Mole *Talpa europaea*
Although rarely seen, its presence is betrayed by the molehills that can be found among the grassy areas around the reservoir, for example at least 10-plus fresh hills were located around the perimeter of the sports pitches on Neasden Recreation Ground in 1995 (Herbert). With the occasional dead one that is found, these sightings point to it being fairly common although they are never recorded on the largest expanse of open grassland at the West Hendon Playing Fields which may well be due to the underlying substrate being dumped material unsuitable for burrowing.

Common Shrew *Sorex araneus*
Of all of the small mammals at Brent, this is the species most likely to be found dead.

Water Shrew *Neomys fodiens*
One was seen on October 23rd 1995 by the cycle track in the Northern Marsh (Herbert). It was considered to be in atypical surroundings so its actual status at Brent cannot be confirmed, although it was recorded on the canal behind the dam in the 1960s (per Batten).

Daubenton's Bat *Myotis daubentonii*
The only record of this species is from September 1937 when a group of 12 was seen, one of which hit a martin species and fell into the water (Fitter). Not recorded when bat detectors were used in 1978 and again in 1985/86 and 1995.

Noctule Bat *Nyctalus noctula*
Recorded twice during the 1995 Bat Survey. Both appearances were after dark and both individuals left the area quickly so it was considered that they do not roost locally and that the area only constitutes a minor foraging area (Herbert).

One was recorded feeding over the open water. Additionally, one was seen flying over the northern reservoir in the evening of September 8th 1960 with two smaller bats.

Leisler's Bat   *Nyctalus leisleri*
The first and only record of this bat at the reservoir was on June 24th 1999. This sighting has yet to be confirmed.

Pipistrelle Bat   *Pipistrellus pipistrellus*
All individuals located in the Bat Survey were of the 55 kHz genotype. Fairly common and widespread around the reservoir. The largest number recorded together was at least eight immediately north of Cool Oak Lane Bridge. No roost sites were found but the appearance of several at dusk around the Field Centre is suggestive of a nearby roost. Pipistrelles of the 45 kHz genotype have been located in several areas around the reservoir in 2001.

Whiskered Bat   *Myotis mystacinus*
There is one old record from Hendon (Fitter) that may be within our recording area.

Bank Vole   *Clethrionomys glareolus*
Recorded from four separate areas in 1995 (Herbert).

Field Vole   *Microtus agrestis*
The small rodent most often seen or heard around the reservoir. The large expanses of unmown grassy areas near the dam and by the Northern Marsh, as well as areas like the disused allotments, provide a perfect habitat for these voles. Their abundance also attracts predators such as Kestrels and owls. Indeed, when pellets from overwintering Long-eared Owls were examined they were found to exclusively contain the remains of this species (A. Self, pers obs).

Wood Mouse   *Apodemus sylvaticus*
The only species trapped in all five transects in the 1995 Mammal Survey (Herbert).

House Mouse   *Mus musculus*
This species was not recorded in the 1995 Mammal Survey as the traps were mainly laid out around the 'wilder' areas of the reservoir. It is undoubtedly present within the recording area, probably in many of the houses and sheds as well as many of the factories bordering the Eastern Marsh.

Grey Squirrel   *Sciurus carolensis*
The most commonly observed mammal at the reservoir. This species is recorded from all areas of the reservoir from the woodlands to back gardens where it can regularly be seen raiding bird tables in the winter.

Common Rat *Rattus norvegicus*
Widespread at the reservoir, it is most often observed near the bridge on Cool Oak Lane, feeding on scraps that visitors have left out for the birds.

Fox *Vulpes vulpes*
Regularly seen around the reservoir even during the daytime. There are territories in East Marsh, North Marsh, the Field Centre and possibly elsewhere. They have often been seen from the hides as they walk through the reedbed and have been known to take ducks and feral geese as well as Moorhen eggs although these observations represent just a fraction of their actual diet.

Stoat *Mustela erminea*
No longer present at the reservoir, this species was last known to have occurred in the 1960s, although it was only occasionally seen.

Weasel *Mustela nivalis*
Like the preceding species, Weasels are no longer reported at Brent although their smaller size could mean that they are still overlooked. The latest records are from the 1970s when they were not infrequently seen (L. Batten, pers obs).

Muntjac *Muntiacus reevsi*
One or two have been reported, although no precise details are known (Creasey).

References

Creasey, P.   (1987) Mammals of the Reservoir. Welsh Harp Report 1987.

Fitter, R. S. R.   (1949) A Check-list of the mammals, reptiles and amphibia of the London Area: 1900-1949. The London Naturalist 28: 98-115.

Herbert, C.   (1995) Bat Survey Report: Brent Reservoir (Welsh Harp).

Herbert, C.   (1995) Small Mammal Survey Report: Brent Reservoir (Welsh Harp).

Editor's note
Clive Herbert is Mammal Recorder for the London Natural History Society and any records of mammals at the reservoir should be sent to him at 67a Ridgeway Avenue, East Barnet, Herts EN4 8TL (Tel/Fax 020 8440 6314).

Reptiles and Amphibians, by Andrew Self

In an attempt to catalogue these species, a reptile survey was carried out at the reservoir in 1995 (Atkins and Herbert). Using this information and personal observations of several of the regular birders at Brent it is possible to give a brief list of the reptiles and amphibians that have been recorded and a summary of their status.

Grass Snake   *Natrix natrix*
There are only a few records of this species, the only traceable ones being one near the Rifle Range in the 1960s (per L. Batten), and one swimming in North Marsh on September 2nd 1994.

Slow-worm   *Anguis fragilis*
Two were observed in May 1989 near the Sailing Base, and have been recorded on several other occasions since then.

Common Lizard   *Lacerta vivipara*
Previously a common and widespread species but it may now be locally extinct. The last record is of one in March 1994 on the former rubbish dump area.

Red-eared Terrapin   *Chrysemys scripta elegans*
Since the late 1980s there have been a number of illegal releases of this native American terrapin into the reservoir. It is most often seen in the summer when one or more basks in the sunshine on some piece of discarded rubbish or log in the reservoir. One was reported laying eggs in the lawn near the main hide but this record could relate to an escaped tortoise. As many as six were counted in the summer of 1997.

Common Frog   *Rana temporaria*
Occasionally adults are found in the waterside vegetation, but the most obvious signs of their presence are masses of frogspawn – and later the tadpoles – in ponds, especially the bomb crater pond on the North Bank.

Marsh Frog   *Rana ridibunda*
This alien species is known to have been released into the reservoir in the 1960s and was heard frequently in East Marsh up until 1973. The reservoir was drained in 1974 and it disappeared after this. The only record since then is of one calling daily beside the small hide in East Marsh in mid-May 1998. It, or another was later heard alongside the North Bank of the main reservoir in July.

Common Toad   *Bufo bufo*
A fairly common and widespread species. Spawn and tadpoles are regularly

seen in ponds adjacent to the main reservoir. There was some evidence of a decline from the 1950s, when spawning took place in the reservoir until the mid 1980s. Since then Toads, aided by imported spawn, have increased in the ponds created in the 1980s and early 1990s but spawn has not been noted in the reservoir itself in recent years.

Smooth Newt *Triturus vulgaris*
Although rarely observed this species is known to be fairly common around the reservoir. These appeared to form the main diet of the Purple Heron in May 1999.

References
Atkins, W. & Herbert, C. (1995) Reptile Survey of the Brent Reservoir (Welsh Harp).

Smooth Newt

Fish, *by John Colmans*

It is an extraordinary fact, but remarkably little is known by naturalists about the fish of the Brent Reservoir, in spite of their importance as a food supply (in particular for key species such as Great Crested Grebe *Podiceps cristatus* and Common Tern *Sterna hirundo*), and more generally as an indicator of the health of the reservoir's water. This lack of knowledge is primarily because angling is now forbidden at the reservoir. Towards the end of 1994 a problem with the sluice mechanism at the dam required the British Waterways Board, which owns the reservoir, to completely drain it. Part of the drainage programme involved removing all the fish from the reservoir for temporary storage elsewhere until the reservoir could be refilled. This provided a unique opportunity for assessing the species mix in the reservoir.

In all 6,770 lbs of fish were caught during this operation. Of this total, 6,440 lbs (95 per cent) were Roach *Rutilus rutilus*. The majority of the remaining 5 per cent consisted of Carp *Cyprinus carpio* and Pike *Esox lucius*. Statistically insignificant species were: Perch *Perca fluviatilis*, Stickleback *Gasterosteus aculeatus*, Tench *Tinca Tinca*, Bream *Abramis brama*, Crucian Carp *Carassius carassius* and Goldfish *Carassius auratus*. The last three species were represented by single individuals.

Two points need emphasising: one is that the catching techniques involved almost certainly meant that some small species of fish or some young fish escaped netting. The second is to note the conclusion of the author of the report of this operation, that the reservoir holds far fewer fish in proportion to its size than would have been expected. He suggests that predation by Cormorants *Phalacrocorax carbo* and low water quality may be among the factors involved. Certainly, we are used to the sight of Common Terns arriving at the reservoir during the breeding season carrying fish which have clearly been caught elsewhere. An assessment of this problem in more detail would be very welcome.

(Thanks to Mr J W Ellis, Fisheries and Environment Manager, British Waterways Board, Southern Region, for permission to quote from his report).

Damselflies and Dragonflies (Odonata), by Roy Beddard

Introduction

Conditions for insects of the order Odonata have improved substantially at the reservoir during the past 20-30 years, such that there are now 11 species regularly breeding at the site. Watching and counting dragonflies has become a regular part of the activities that people look forward to each summer and up to 10 separate species have been observed on good days in August. In the summer of 1974 the reservoir was drained and not refilled until September, and conditions appeared to be ideal for a major extension of willows and other marshland vegetation into the two marshland areas that we know today. Large-scale management work on these marshes throughout the 1980s greatly increased the variety and amount of habitat suitable for dragonflies. Many small pools, canals/ditches and lagoons were created, especially in and around the Northern Marsh. Records from the earlier years, in particular prior to 1974, are scant and at best anecdotal. In the following species accounts detailed records from 1997 are used to create a picture of the best areas and flying times for the main species in a typical year.

The systematic list of species follows the classification used in Hammond, *The Dragonflies of Great Britain and Ireland* (1985).

Azure Damselfly   *Coenagrion puella*
Widespread, common breeder, late May-late August.
Although fairly common, this insect is difficult to separate from Common Blue Damselfly. Although on occasion hundreds may be present, in most cases they cannot be attributed specifically, and hence the numbers referred to here are certainly underestimates. On those occasions when special care is taken in observation, it appears that this species usually stays close to water. If not actually over water, then it will be on pathways or vegetation close by. It is found in the vegetated margins all the way around the reservoir, but the highest numbers are to be found in the Northern and Eastern Marshes. In 1997 the earliest recorded were on June 20th, over 20 were specifically identified on July 20th and 10 seen on August 10th were the last for that year.

Common Blue Damselfly   *Enallagma cyathigerum*
Widespread, very common breeder, late May-September.
Identification difficulties were described in the previous species account, but despite this the species is usually the most numerous dragonfly to be found at the reservoir and on occasion numbers will be in the hundreds. As with Azure Damselfly, Common Blue is to be found all around the reservoir, often at quite considerable distances from the water. In these instances it will often be found flying over adjacent rank grassland, sometimes in quite large numbers. The

earliest recorded in 1997 were on June 8th; on several dates between late July and mid-August well over 100 individuals were recorded; and the last for 1997 were 20 seen on August 18th.

Large Red Damselfly *Pyrrhosoma Nymphula*
Previously very rare but becoming more common (only one record in late May), late May-early July.
Until 2000 there had only been one record of this species and the date recorded ruled out any possibility of confusion with darter species. Two males of this species were present on the small acid pond in the Field Studies Centre during June 2000. Mating pairs were observed the following year.

Blue-tailed Damselfly *Ischnura elegans*
Common breeder, late May-late August.
This species is unlikely to be confused with other damselflies and can be seen over large areas of the Eastern and Northern Marshes but never far from the water and from vegetation. It appears to be more tolerant of pollution than other species, and has been recorded near the trash-trap on the River Brent. Although fairly common it is not usually seen in large numbers at this site. The exception to this was in spring 1996, after a period when the reservoir had been completely drained for several months in the winter, when there were many hundreds if not thousands present, especially in the Eastern Marsh. In 1997 the first were seen on June 8th, the maximum of five was recorded on August 2nd and the last was seen on August 18th.

Banded Demoiselle *Calopteryx splendens*
Very rare (only three records), mid May-early September.
This beautiful insect has been recorded just three times at the reservoir: two records in June/July 1993 and one on August 28th 1999. The habitats at the reservoir are generally not suited to this species: the water is too polluted and this species is normally associated with meandering lowland streams in meadowland bordered by sunlit trees. Cornhill Meadows in the Lea Valley is a typical site with a thriving population, and this site, together with the Gade valley near Watford, are probably the closest regular breeding sites to Brent Reservoir. The first record at Brent was of a male perched on the trash-trap over the River Brent in the Eastern Marsh. It was seen in early June during a common breeding bird census. The second, also a male in the same year, was perched on the jetty of the Youth Sailing Base, possibly a little later in the summer and perhaps the same individual. The third record was of a male perched in the *typha* bed just in front of the main hide.

Southern Hawker *Aeshna cyanea*
Scarce but annual, breeds in very small numbers, June-early October.

This species is usually seen later in the season, recorded only once or twice in most years. It has most often been seen at rest on low bushes or branches of small trees and generally seen along the north bank of the main reservoir. In September 1974, when the water level had been restored after the reservoir had been drained, this dragonfly was reported in very large numbers (Leo Batten *pers. obs.*). The only record in 1997 was on a typically late date, October 6th.

Brown Hawker *Aeshna grandis*
Regular breeder in small numbers, late June-early October.
This is probably the most easily recognised large dragonfly at the reservoir, with its size, brown coloration and bronze-tinged wings making it very distinctive. It can be seen on most visits to the reservoir during June to early September. The earliest insect seen in 1997 was on July 5th and four were observed on several dates in August, the last being recorded on September 6th. It is most often observed on the wing, patrolling over water, actively chasing prey and maintaining its territory. The favoured locations at the reservoir are the two back pools in the Northern Marsh.

Migrant Hawker *Aeshna mixta*
Common and widespread breeding species, late July-October.
The Migrant Hawker is much the commoner of the larger dragonflies at the reservoir and in some years several hundred can be present during August. This species is both a common breeder and also has a migrant component to its population which may account for the widely fluctuating annual occurrence. It is the smallest of the *Aeshna* dragonflies to be found at the reservoir and initially this is perhaps the easiest clue to its identification. It is often present quite late in the season, most years bring October records and it has been recorded at the reservoir in November. 1997 was a fairly typical year; the first two were seen on July 21st, with up to 10 being seen fairly often in August, and the last record being of two on October 22nd.

Emperor Dragonfly *Anax imperator*
Widespread, regular breeder in small numbers, late May-late August.
Although records are concentrated in the two marshes this insect can be seen anywhere around the site but usually within 100 metres of the reservoir and is most often seen in flight over the water where its large size and slightly droop-ing abdomen make it easy to identify. It is territorial and readily chases off all other dragonflies. Females have often been seen ovipositing, laying eggs on floating vegetation, especially in the Northern Marsh. In 1997 the first record was of one on June 7th and a peak of four were seen on August 2nd. In most years there are few records after mid-August.

Black-tailed Skimmer   *Orthetrum cancellatun*
Recent colonist, regular breeder in small numbers, July-August.
This species is a recent addition to the reservoir's list, having been recorded for the first time in the summer of 1994. It is known to travel long distances and to readily colonise new sites and recently was recorded for the first time at Alexandra Park. Adults are often to be found on bare earth or shingle banks where they bask in the sun for extended periods.

Broad-bodied Chaser   *Libella depressa*
Regular breeder in small numbers, late May-early August.
Soon after the completion of the early-1980s management work this species was often to be found in the shallow pools where a stream emerges from beneath the scrub area on the dump. However with the colonisation of these pools by Phragmites reed and the disappearance of the open water they are now more often to be found on the large shallow pools at the rear of the Northern Marsh. They are strongly territorial, the males often standing guard on regularly used perches from where they can fly to intercept intruders. They can be seen at the Brent from late May, and in 1997 the first record was of a female on June 8th. The summer's highest count was five on August 2nd, and the last seen was on August 12th.

Ruddy Darter   *Sympetrum sanguineum*
Localised, possibly a regular breeding species, early July-October.
The Ruddy Darter is very localised in its distribution at Brent Reservoir and most records are close to water and usually from the back pool in the Northern Marsh. It is seldom recorded in the wide variety of habitats frequented by the similar Common Darter. The earliest records are usually in early August and in 1997 the first two were seen on August 2nd. It is possible that Brent records relate to immigrants. The best count was of six on the fairly late date of October 4th and the last two were recorded on October 21st.

Common Darter   *Sympetrum striolatum*
Widespread, common breeding species, late June-October.
Elsewhere in the south of England this species can be seen from mid-June onwards. However, at the Brent Reservoir the first adults don't usually appear until late July/early August. It is one of the most widespread dragonfly species at the site and can be found in a wide range of habitats. Common Darter is one of the species that can often be found at a considerable distance from water, being frequently seen in dry woodland-edge habitats on the north bank. In 1997 six were seen on August 2nd, and a week later the year's best count of 14 was on August 9th. Individuals are recorded almost as late in the year as Migrant Hawkers, and 1997 was no exception with seven seen on October 21st and the final two the next day.

Conservation for Dragonflies at Brent Reservoir

Clearly much of the work undertaken over the past 20-25 years has been of benefit to Odonata species, and future conservation activity will be focused on maintaining the habitats already created. In addition some species have very specific requirements, for example Black-tailed Skimmer needs expanses of sun-baked mud or shingle for basking and this will be provided in an appropriate location (in this case on the Eastern Marsh wader and shingle bank). Vegetation will be cleared from this island on an annual basis and areas of clear mud bank created. More generally, ditches and canals will be cleared on a rotational basis to prevent their being choked with vegetation. As appropriate, new areas of wetland will be developed to provide additional habitat for a wide range of species including dragonflies: an example will be the extension of the marshy area at the end of Neasden Recreation Ground. Where possible, work will be undertaken to improve water quality, usually in conjunction with the Environment Agency: an example might be the use of reedbeds for the filtration of in-flowing streams. Adopting the measures outlined here it is hoped that the current list of species can be maintained and their populations allowed to increase.

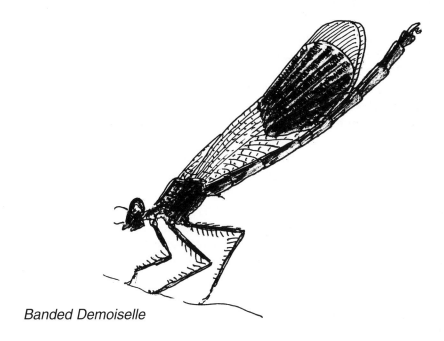

Banded Demoiselle

Butterflies, by Roy Beddard, John Colmans,
John Dobson and Andrew Verrall

Introduction

There have always been butterflies to be seen around the reservoir and a list of those seen shows that about one quarter of British butterfly species are seen every year, and over one third of the British butterflies have been seen at the site over the years. This is surprising due to the pressures on the very existence of these delicate insects. Allotment owners using powders and sprays must keep up a constant war on caterpillars which would eat the food that they are trying to grow. The same would apply to the plant nurseries. The playing fields are mown to a degree that makes them useless for the butterflies that need longer and less disturbed grassland for their breeding cycles. But a few naturally wild corners have been left undisturbed by man, and with the peaceful cemetery and nearby Nature Centre suitable for butterfly breeding as well as the mature stands of oak, many butterflies are not only surviving but are showing a welcome increase even if others are experiencing persistent decline.

Most local trends would appear to mirror the national position. Added to this the fact that some species migrate into the area from distant parts in the South, like the Painted Lady from Southern Europe and North Africa, and the locally rare Clouded Yellow which turns up in good years. Brief details of all species definitely seen in the area are given. To complete the picture, a few historical records from the distant past are included. However, a few more species that may have occurred in the area but for which there is no concrete evidence available, have been omitted. With more awareness of butterflies by more people, there is scope for further detailed studies in the future.

The records below come from several sources. Some were supplied by C. Herbert and data on the biology of the species and their distribution and status in the Butterfly Conservation Hertfordshire and Middlesex recording area is from Murray (1996) and Sawford (1987). There is also some reference to the best book available on the subject of London butterflies, by Colin W. Plant, *Butterflies of the London Area*. A few other sample records are given for the reservoir, to bring us up-to-date within the timescale of this book. Observers of butterfly rarities and historic records are also credited.

Small Skipper *Thymelicus sylvestris*
A widespread and common species in Southern Britain; generally common at the reservoir, especially in July (29 on July 9th, 1996). Larval food-plants include a variety of soft grasses, particularly *Holcus lanatus* (Yorkshire Fog).

Insects

Plate 15

A. Dark Green Fritillary, first and only record, July 1999, (Andrew Self)

B. Comma, a fairly common species in the area, (Roy Beddard)

C. Speckled Wood, a much increased and now very common butterfly, (Roy Beddard)

D. Marbled White, a very recent colonist, (Roy Beddard)

Plate 16

A. Common Blue, a common species in the area, (Roy Beddard)

B. Elephant Hawk-moth, a well established species, (Andrew Self)

C. Broad-bodied Chaser, a common dragonfly in the area, (Roy Beddard)

D. Large Red Damselfly, a recent colonist, (Roy Beddard)

Essex Skipper *Thymelicus lineola*
The first-ever records in Middlesex came from the reservoir in 1959. It may now be commoner but can be overlooked due to the difficulty in distinguishing it from the Small Skipper. A close look reveals jet black tips to the underside of the antennae. At the reservoir it is seen in June, July and August; there were 9 on July 11th, 1996. It has its national stronghold in the Home Counties, particularly around the Thames Valley and estuary. Larvae found on various grasses including *Dactylis glomerata* (Cocks-foot) and *Holcus mollis* (Creeping Soft Grass).

Essex Skipper

RB

Large Skipper *Ochiodes venata*
Fairly common and seen every year at the reservoir in June, July and August (5 on June 23rd 1996). Widespread but more local than *T. sylvestris*, particularly in agricultural and urban areas. Larvae found on *Dactylis glomerata* (Cocks-foot).

Grizzled Skipper *Pyrgus malvae*
Now never seen in the area but there is one record in recent years with some older records of this species which is still found further out of London. A record in *London Naturalist* 29, 46-84: seen at the reservoir (LRW, pers. comm.). This

butterfly has undergone a substantial national decline since this record. Although there are a few recent records for Hertfordshire and Middlesex, none were seen in 1995 (Murray 1996). A butterfly of unimproved and rough grassland, its larvae occur on a variety of plants including *Rosaceae* and *Rubus spp.*

Clouded Yellow   *Colias croceus*
Several records in recent years: July 30th 1983 (AES), September, 1993 (JC), August 3rd 1996 (LAB, AGV), August 18th 1996 (ASMS), October 17th 1998. Specimens of this butterfly turn up from time to time, usually during invasion years such as 1983. The highest counts ever were made in the latest invasion year, 2000. After the first one on June 10th, small numbers were seen regularly between August 20th and September 10th, the peak being 9 on August 21st. A migrant species, the numbers arriving in the UK vary considerably from year to year. It may breed here but rarely successfully over-winters in the UK. Larvae on a range of Leguminous plants including *Trifolium spp.* (Clovers).

Brimstone   *Gonepteryx rhamni*
Not established but in spring some fly through the area on what seems to be a spreading out in search of new breeding sites. Fairly common at the reservoir in spring 1996 with sample records of one male on May 6th 1996, and one female on April 29th, May 1st, May 16-18th and June 20th 1997. A widespread and conspicuous species, particularly early in the year with the appearance of adults from hibernation. Present in low numbers over much of suburban Middlesex (Murray 1996). Larvae on *Rhamnus catharticus* (Purging Buckthorn) and *Frangula alnus* (Alder Buckthorn).

Large White   *Pieris brassicae*
Very common and widespread, with numbers increased in some years by continental immigration. At the reservoir max 24 on July 22nd 1997. Larvae on various plants including *Reseda lutea* (Wild Mignonette) and various *Cruciferae*.

Small White   *Pieris rapae*
A very common and widespread species, with a migrant component to the UK population. At the Brent max 21 on April 9th 1997. In addition to cultivated Brassicas the larvae utilise a number of wild food-plants including *Sisymbrium officinale* (Hedge Mustard) and *Cardaria draba* (Hoary Cress).

Green-veined White   *Pieris napi*
A very common and widespread species seen every year at the reservoir. Sample record: 13 on June 20th 1997. Larvae on various plants including *Sisymbrium officinale* (Hedge Mustard) and *Armoracia rusticana* (Horse Radish).

Orange Tip *Anthocharis cardamines*
Now common from early April to late June. This species was not, however, present at the reservoir during the late 1950s (pers. comm. LAB) and it could scarcely have been overlooked. So this is a comparatively recent arrival to the area. At the reservoir 13 (10 males, three females) on April 13th 1997. Larvae on various *Cruciferae* including *Alliaria petiolata* (Garlic Mustard), *Sisymbrium officinale* (Hedge Mustard) and *Cardamine pratensis* (Lady's Smock).

Purple Hairstreak *Quercusia quercus*
Fairly common around oaks and brambles on the north bank of the main arm of the reservoir in July 1996. Nine on July 21st 1997 after an early record of one male on June 20th. This species is probably on the increase in Greater London and may potentially be found wherever there are oak trees (CWP, pers. comm.). This butterfly is under-recorded due to its habit of making short flights around the tops of oaks and of flying mainly in the evening. At the reservoir we make a point of searching for it (usually with success) on the south-facing sides of oak trees on hot days.

White-letter Hairstreak *Satyrium w-album*
Recorded just once at the reservoir: on July 20th 1995 (ASMS) around old hedgerows on the north bank of the main arm of the reservoir. A welcome addition to the fauna of the site, this butterfly is rare in London (CWP, pers. comm.). It may exist in small colonies, sometimes on a single tree. Records are sparse in Hertfordshire and Middlesex but it is probable that it is currently increasing in numbers. In recent years the species has colonised Hampstead Heath and Alexandra Park. Like the previous species this butterfly is under-recorded. Although formerly associated particularly with flowering elm, it is now known to survive on elm suckers in hedgerows and on Dutch Elm Disease resistant flowerless strains (Heath). Ova are normally deposited in south-facing sheltered situations.

Small Copper *Lycaena phlaeas*
A widespread but local species probably in overall decline. 1995 however was a particularly successful year for this butterfly in Hertfordshire and Middlesex (Murray 1996). At the Brent max 5 on October 18th. Larvae on *Rumex acetosa* (Common Sorrel) and *Rumex acetosella* (Sheep's Sorrel).

Common Blue *Polymmatus icarus*
Fairly common at the reservoir in the last few years over waste ground and grassy areas. 6 males on August 9th 1997. A double brooded species, the larvae have been recorded from a number of species of leguminous plants including *Lotus corniculatus* (Bird's-foot Trefoil).

Holly Blue *Celastrina argiolus*
Common at the Brent Reservoir in spring 1996 with 12 on April 27th. A common butterfly in urban areas, but sometimes undergoing considerable fluctuations in numbers from year to year. The spring generation feed on the flowers of *Ilex aquifolium* (Holly) while butterflies on the wing in July and August oviposit on *Hedera helix* (Ivy). A number of other food plants have been noted.

Red Admiral *Vanessa atalanta*
A common species although not often seen in numbers. A few seem to over-winter successfully although the species would probably not survive in the UK without a substantial influx of migrants, normally occurring between May and July. At the reservoir max 5 on August 15th 1996. Larvae mainly on *Urtica dioica* (Stinging Nettle).

Painted Lady *Cynthia cardui*
There was an exceptionally large and early influx of this butterfly into the UK in 1996. It was fairly common at the reservoir in June 1996 with six on the 9th. Then numbers increased steadily during the summer until a peak was reached in August with 30-40 on Buddleia on the Woodfield Park disused tennis courts on August 26th. This butterfly cannot over-winter in the UK but arrives here in variable numbers each year from Southern Europe and North Africa. It does however breed here and the larvae feed on a variety of common plants, principally *Cirsium* and *Carduus spp.* (Thistles).

Small Tortoiseshell *Aglais urticae*
A common and widespread butterfly undergoing some fluctuation in numbers depending on the survival of the over-wintering population of adults. Sometimes extremely common at the reservoir: 37 on May 5th 1996 and 36 on April 12th 1997. Larvae on *Urtica dioica* (Stinging Nettle) and *U. urens* (Small Nettle).

[**Camberwell Beauty** *Nymphalis aniopa*
On April 23rd 1940 one was seen in Hendon.]

Peacock *Inachis io*
A resident species, occasionally reinforced by migrants. Normally common throughout Hertfordshire and Middlesex, the adults overwinter in hollow trees, etc. At the reservoir 22 were seen on April 12th 1997 and again 20+ on August 2nd 1997. Single brooded, the larvae usually on tall specimens of *Urtica dioica* (Stinging Nettle).

Comma *Polygenia e-album*
Regularly seen. The evidence suggests that this attractive insect has increased in numbers in recent years. It was fairly common at the reservoir in

1996 with 8 seen on July 13th. Over-winters as an adult and may have two or occasionally three generations a year. Larvae on *Urtica spp.* (Nettles).

Dark Green Fritillary *Argynnis aglaja*
One recent record. A female was watched feeding on thistles in a sunny corner of the north bank on July 18th 1999 by six people and was also photographed. This species has become extremely rare in London especially north of the Thames.

Marsh Fritillary *Eurodryas aurinia*
Before the reservoir was built, going far back into history, this butterfly was found in the water meadow habitat in 1700, between Neasden and Hendon, the exact location of the reservoir. For this reason it takes its place on the all-time list.

Speckled Wood *Paragre aegeria*
A recent colonist; this species was not recorded from the reservoir during the 1980-86 survey for the London Butterfly Atlas (C. Herbert, pers. comm.) In this period it has also colonised many new sites in Hertfordshire and Middlesex (Murray 1996). It was not recorded at the Brent until the late 1980s, but is now common around the reservoir, for example 19 on April 13th 1997. Larvae found on grasses in shaded places, principally *Dactylis glomerata* (Cocksfoot) and *Agropyron repens* (Common Couch).

Marbled White *Melanargia galathea*
Some recent records. On a notable day for butterflies at the reservoir, one flew past near the Dark Green Fritillary on July 18th 1999 (ASMS). This species is rare in urban London but records like this are typical; for instance the first one recorded at nearby Fryent Country Park was seen on July 25th 1996 (Murray 1997). One seen on at least six dates in 2000, from June 18th to July 19th between Cool Oak Lane and West Hendon Playing Fields.

Wall Brown *Lasiommata megera*
This species is currently in serious decline in Hertfordshire and Middlesex, probably reflecting a national trend (Murray 1996). It was still common in the early 1960s but has all but died out in our area. Further records of this butterfly from Brent Reservoir would be of considerable interest. Larvae on a variety of grasses including *Dactylis glomerata* (Cocksfoot) and *Holcus lanatus* (Yorkshire Fog).

Gatekeeper *Pyronia tithonus*
Regular and becoming more so, this once scarce species showed a considerable increase in numbers during the 1990s. More or less absent from central

and suburban London just over a decade ago, this butterfly has recently colonised many sites in the city (Murray 1996). In 2000 the maximum seen on a single day was 75. Larvae on a variety of grasses.

Meadow Brown *Maniola jurtina*
Generally common in any rough grassland area of the reservoir from mid June, most noticeably in July. Common around the reservoir in 1996. 84 were counted on July 13th 1996 plus another count of 34 on June 20th 1997. Perhaps less numerous than it was. Larvae on various grasses, particularly *Poa pratensis* (Smooth-stalked Meadow Grass).

Small Heath *Coenonympha pamphilus*
A local but formerly widespread species in which the colony size may be very small in restricted habitats. This butterfly has declined significantly in Hertfordshire and Middlesex in recent years. It appears to be particularly vulnerable to long dry summers when the larvae may dessicate (Murray 1996). Once common throughout the summer, it is now only occasionally seen at the reservoir, in 1996 there was one seen on August 25th and in 1997 there was a sighting on June 1st. Larvae on a variety of fine-leafed grasses, particularly *Festuca spp.* (Fescues) and *Agrostis spp.* (Bents). There have been no further records.

References

Heath, J., Pollard, E., Thomas, J. A. *Atlas of Butterflies in Britain and Ireland*, Viking. 1984.

Murray, J. B. *Hertfordshire and Middlesex Butterfly Report for 1995*. Butterfly Conservation, Herts. and Middlesex branch 1996.

Murray, J. B. *Hertfordshire and Middlesex Butterfly Report for 1996*. Butterfly Conservation, Herts. and Middlesex branch 1997.

Sawford, B. *The Butterflies of Hertfordshire*. Castlemead Publications, Ware. 1987.

Plant, Colin W. *Butterflies of the London Area*, LNHS. 1987.

Moths, by Andrew Self

The following list of moths has been collated from various sources, mainly from a trap run by myself (denoted 'trapped') during 1998 and 1999 as well as from the LNHS publication: *Larger Moths of the London Area* (denoted 'LNHS'). There are also personal observations of moths seen during the day by several other observers. The moths were trapped (and released) in Harp Island Close which backs onto the reservoir dam.

A brief statement about the status of each moth (where known) has also been given (based on the London or Middlesex status as given by Plant (1993). The systematic list follows Skinner (1984) from where the scientific names can also be found.

Six-spot Burnet. Common around reservoir during day, eg 55 on 10.7.99
Narrow-bordered Five-spot Burnet. Common, eg 250 on North Bank on 5.7.98
December Moth. Trapped, uncommon in urban Middlesex
Small Eggar. (LNHS), now extinct in London
The Lackey. Trapped, common
Emperor Moth. Trapped, local
Figure of Eighty. Trapped, widespread in London
Oak Hook-tip. Trapped, common
Scalloped Hook-tip. Trapped, uncommon in urban Middlesex
Blair's Mocha. (LNHS), one at Kingsbury on 12.10.59, a rare migrant in London
March Moth. (LNHS), common
Blotched Emerald. Trapped, local
Common Emerald. Trapped, common
Maiden's Blush. Trapped, local
Blood-vein. Trapped, common
Mullein Wave. Trapped, local
Least Carpet. Trapped, local
Dwarf Cream Wave. Trapped, local
Small Fan-footed Wave. Trapped, common
Riband Wave. Trapped, very common
Garden Carpet. Trapped, very common
Shaded Broad-bar. Trapped, also seen during day, common
Common Carpet. Trapped, very common
Yellow Shell. Seen during the day, very common
The Spinach. Trapped, common
Red-green Carpet. Seen during the day in Eastern Marsh, scarce but recently increasing

Dark Marbled Carpet. Trapped, local
Common Marbled Carpet. Trapped, very common
Barred Yellow. Trapped, common
Blue-bordered Carpet. Trapped, local
Spruce Carpet. Trapped, very local in Middlesex
Broken-barred Carpet. Trapped, common
Winter Moth. Attracted to house lights, very common
Small Rivulet. Trapped, common
Toadflax Pug. Trapped, common
Lime-speck Pug. Trapped, very common
Wormwood Pug. Trapped, common
Currant Pug. Trapped, common
Tawny Speckled Pug. Trapped, common
Brindled Pug. Trapped, common
Double-striped Pug. Trapped, very common
Treble-bar. Trapped, also seen during the day, local
Chimney Sweeper. Seen during day on North Bank, max c20 on 14.6.92, extremely local
Yellow-barred Brindle. Trapped, local
Brimstone Moth. Trapped, also seen during the day, very common
Clouded Border. Seen in Eastern Marsh, max three on 21.6.98, common
Scorched Carpet. Trapped, local especially in urban areas
Bordered Beauty. Seen in Eastern Marsh, very local especially in urban areas
Scalloped Oak. Trapped, very common
Swallow-tailed Moth. Trapped, very common
Feathered Thorn. Trapped, common
Dotted Border. Trapped, common
Dusky Thorn. Trapped, very common
Canary-shouldered Thorn. Trapped, common
Purple Thorn. Trapped, common
Early Thorn. Trapped, common
Peppered Moth. Trapped, very common
Oak Beauty. Trapped, common
Willow Beauty. Trapped, very common
Common White Wave. Trapped, also regularly seen in Eastern Marsh, common
Common Wave. Trapped, also regularly seen in Eastern Marsh, common
Clouded Silver. Trapped, common
Light Emerald. Trapped, common
Elephant Hawk-Moth. Trapped, very common
Poplar Hawk-Moth. Trapped, also seen during day, common
Eyed Hawk-Moth. Trapped, common

Lime Hawk-Moth. Trapped, very common
Pine Hawk-Moth. Trapped on 5.7.98 and 6.7.99, a rare migrant to
    Middlesex
Buff-tip. Trapped, very common
Poplar Kitten. Trapped, local
Swallow Prominent. Trapped, common
Pale Prominent. Trapped, common
Lunar Marbled Brown. Trapped, common
The Vapourer. Trapped, common
Brown-tail. Trapped, common
White Satin Moth. Trapped, local
Common Footman. Trapped, common
Cinnabar Moth. Trapped, also regularly seen during the day, very common
Ruby Tiger. Trapped, very common
Buff Ermine. Trapped, very common
White Ermine. Trapped, very common
Muslin Moth. Seen during day in Eastern Marsh, widespread but local
Heart and Club. Trapped, local, especially in North London
Dark Sword-grass. Trapped, regular immigrant
Turnip Moth. Trapped, very common
Heart and Dart. Trapped, very common, the most numerous moth
    trapped at Brent
Shuttle-shaped Dart. Trapped, very common
Flame Shoulder. Trapped, very common
The Flame. Trapped, very common
Large Yellow Underwing. Trapped, very common
Lesser Yellow Underwing. Trapped, very common
Lesser Broad-bordered Yellow Underwing. Trapped, very common
Broad-bordered Yellow Underwing. Trapped, very common
Autumnal Rustic. Trapped, local especially in North London
Ingrailed Clay. Trapped, common
Small Square-spot. Trapped, very common
Setaceous Hebrew Character. Trapped, very common
Double Square-spot. Trapped, common
Square-spot Rustic. Trapped, very common
Six-striped Rustic. Trapped, local
The Nutmeg. Trapped, very common
The Shears. Trapped, local
Bright-line Brown-eye. Trapped, very common
Dot Moth. (LNHS), very common
Cabbage Moth. Trapped, very common
The Lychnis. Trapped, local
Small Quaker. Trapped, common

Powdered Quaker. Trapped, common
Common Quaker. Trapped, very common
Clouded Drab. Trapped, very common
Hebrew Character. Trapped, very common
The Clay. Trapped, very common
Smoky Wainscot. Trapped, very common
Common Wainscot. Trapped, very common
Shoulder-striped Wainscot. Trapped, common
The Wormwood. Trapped, very local
Black Rustic. Trapped, local but spreading
Deep-brown Dart. Trapped, local
Early Grey. Trapped, very common
Blair's Shoulder-knot. Trapped, common
Large Ranunculus. Trapped, very rare in Middlesex but increasing
The Satellite. Trapped, common
Red-line Quaker. Trapped, common
Yellow-line Quaker. Trapped, common
The Chestnut. Trapped, common
The Sallow. Trapped, common
Dusky-lemon Sallow. Trapped, very local
Centre-barred Sallow. Trapped, local
Lunar Underwing. Trapped, common
Poplar Grey. Trapped, very common
The Sycamore. Trapped, very common
Alder Moth. (LNHS), very rare in Middlesex
Grey Dagger. (Identity not confirmed by dissection), trapped, common
Knot Grass. Trapped, very common
Marbled Beauty. Trapped, very common
Bird's Wing. Trapped, local
Copper Underwing. Trapped, very common
Old Lady. Trapped, also seen during the day, very common
Angle Shades. Trapped, very common
Straw Underwing. Trapped, very common
The Olive. Trapped, very local
The Dun-bar. Trapped, very common
Dark Arches. Trapped, very common
Small Clouded Brindle. Trapped, very local
Double Lobed. Trapped, local
Tawny Marbled Minor. (Identity not confirmed by dissection), trapped,
     very common
Marbled Minor. (Identity not confirmed by dissection), trapped, very common
Middle-barred Minor. Trapped, very common
Cloaked Minor. Trapped, very common

Common Rustic/Lesser Common Rustic. (Specific identity not known), trapped

Flounced Rustic. Trapped, very common

The Crescent. Trapped, very local especially in urban London

Bulrush Wainscot. Trapped, local especially in urban London

Webb's Wainscot. Trapped, very local in London, first record for Middlesex on Aug 1st 1999

Small Mottled Willow. (LNHS), a rare immigrant, recorded in Kingsbury in 1962

Pale Mottled Willow. Trapped, very common

The Uncertain. Trapped, very common

Vine's Rustic. Trapped, very common

The Rustic. Trapped, local

Burnet Companion. Regularly seen during the day, max 17 on 19.6.99, local

Burnished Brass. Trapped, very common

Golden Plusia. Trapped, local

Silver Y. Trapped, abundant immigrant and partial resident

Beautiful Golden Y. Seen during the day, common

The Spectacle. Trapped, very common

The Herald. Trapped, very common

Red Underwing. Trapped, also seen resting during the day, very common

The Snout. Trapped, regularly seen in Eastern Marsh, very common

Small Fan-foot. Trapped, common

Common Hawthorn Ermel. Trapped

Yellow Satin Grass-veneer. Trapped

Common Grass-veneer. Trapped

European Corn-Borer. Trapped, uncommon immigrant

Endotricha flammealis. Trapped

Brown China-mark. Trapped

Small China-mark. Trapped

Garden Pebble. Trapped

Rush Veneer. Trapped, uncommon immigrant

Mother of Pearl. Trapped, also regularly seen during the day in Eastern Marsh

Small Magpie. Trapped, also regularly seen during the day in Eastern Marsh

Eurrhypara coronata. Trapped

Hedya nubiferana. Trapped

Chequered Fruit-tree Tortrix. Trapped

Large Fruit-tree Tortrix. Trapped

Green Oak Tortrix. Trapped

Currant Twist. Trapped

Degeer's Longhorn. Regularly seen during the day, max 43 on 15.6.96

Common Plume Moth. Trapped, also seen during the day
White-shouldered House Moth. Trapped
Brown House Moth. Trapped

References

Plant, C. 1993. *Larger Moths of the London Area.* LNHS.
Skinner, B. 1984. *Colour Identification Guide to Moths of the British Isles.* Viking.

Six-spot Burnet

Chapter 6
Access to Brent Reservoir

John Colmans

Access to the reservoir is unrestricted, except across the dam at the Wembley Stadium end. Entry may be obtained from several places but those unfamiliar with the site, whatever mode of transport they are using, are best advised to approach from Cool Oak Lane, NW9 (turn off the Edgware Road, the A5, at the sign of 'The Harp' public house). Just before the bridge at the foot of Cool Oak Lane there are two gates on the left-hand side giving access to a footpath which leads around the car park towards the Eastern Marsh and the two hides. At the end of the bridge a footpath on the left-hand side which forms part of the Capital Ring leads along the north bank of the reservoir towards the dam. A footpath on the right-hand side (cross over the road) leads alongside the allotments, past newly installed picnic tables, towards the dump and the Northern Marsh. The alternative approach to the western (dam) end of the reservoir is via Birchen Grove, NW9, a turning off Blackbird Hill, NW9. Access to the hides is by key only, obtainable from Roy Beddard of the Welsh Harp Conservation Group on 020 8447-1810.

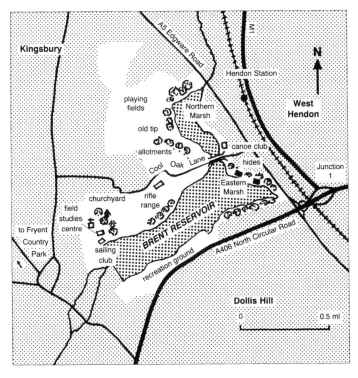

Please ensure when leaving the hides that all shutters are secured and that the door is locked: these hides are very prone to vandalism.

By car
A new car park containing spaces for around 30 cars has now opened on the south side of Cool Oak Lane. Those approaching via Cool Oak Lane and unable to park there are advised to park in Woolmead Avenue or one of the adjacent roads. Under no circumstances should you park in the Youth Sailing Base car park, which is for users of the Sailing Base only. There is very limited parking further along Cool Oak Lane in Woodfield Park, by the playing fields. Those approaching down Birchen Grove can park along the road and also in the sailing club car park. Alternatively, there is car parking space in the car park close to the Northern Marsh by the Hendon Bowls Club, access to which can be gained via Goldsmith Avenue off the Edgware Road. Finally, there is also car parking space at Neasden Recreation Ground on the south bank of the reservoir adjacent to the North Circular Road.

By bus
Routes 32, 83, 142, and 183 run along the Edgware Road. The nearest stops are no more than five minutes' walk from the reservoir. Route 112 runs along the North Circular Road, which forms the southern boundary of the reservoir, and from which access may also be obtained. Routes 182, 245, 297 and 302 run along Blackbird Hill; it is approximately eight minutes' walk along Birchen Grove to reach the reservoir.

By train
Hendon Station (on the London–Bedford Thameslink Line) is only five to seven minutes walk away. On leaving the station turn right along Station Road then left when you reach the Edgware Road (at this point called West Hendon Broadway). Cool Oak Lane is about a hundred metres away on the other side of the road. Trains are usually every twenty to thirty minutes and consultation of a timetable is advised. The nearest underground station is Hendon Central (Northern Line). Bus number 83 can be caught from this station. Buses 83, 182 and 297 can be caught from Wembley Park (Jubilee and Metropolitan Lines), alight at Blackbird Hill. Alternatively, bus 142 can be caught from Brent Cross Shopping Centre, not far from Brent Cross (Northern Line).

Wheelchairs and footwear
The path that leads to the first hide is wide enough for wheelchair access and there is a ramp allowing access to the hide from the path. The second hide is not accessible to wheelchairs. Although the paths are much less muddy than they used to be, wellingtons or thick boots remain advisable after heavy rain.